END OF AN ERA

END OF AN ERA

THE RISE AND FALL OF INDIRA GANDHI

by C. S. PANDIT

ALLIED PUBLISHERS PVT. LTD.

ALLIED PUBLISHERS PRIVATE LIMITED
15 Graham Road Ballard Estate Bombay 400038
5th Main Road Gandhinagar Bangalore 560009
13/14 Asaf Ali Road New Delhi 110002
17 Chittaranjan Avenue Calcutta 700072
150-B/6 Mount Road Madras 600002

First Published June 1977
Reprinted June 1977
Reprinted July 1977
Reprinted July 1977

© Allied Publishers

Printed & Published by R.N. Sachdev at Allied Publishers
Pvt.Ltd. 4 Najafgarh Road, New Delhi 110015

To My Parents

CONTENTS

PREFACE ix

I — BEGINNING OF THE END
(June 1975 to March 1977) 1

II — REIGN, NOT RULE
(January 1966 to February 1967).............. 18

III — STRUGGLE FOR POWER
(March 1967 to January 1969) 29

IV — SPLIT IN THE CONGRESS
(February 1969 to December 1970) 49

V — UNDISPUTED LEADER
(December 1970 to October 1971) 70

VI — HER FINEST HOUR
(March 1971 to December 1971) 86

VII — THE DECLINE SETS IN
(December 1971 to January 1973) 105

VIII DISENCHANTMENT GROWS
(February 1973 to January 1974).............. 122

IX — A PEOPLE'S MOVEMENT
(February 1974 to June 1975)................ 142

X — INTERNATIONAL RAMIFICATIONS
(1971 to 1977)   162

XI — END OF AN ERA
(June 1975 to March 1977) 180

PREFACE

THIS book has been written more in sorrow than in anger, for it traces step by step the downfall of one who had the makings of one of India's great Prime Ministers. It is the story of Indira Gandhi as the third Prime Minister of India, of her achievements, of her difficulties and of her failures. It is also the story of one for whom the generation I belong to had a special affinity having been inspired by her father's *Letters to His Daughter*, his *Glimpses of World History*, his own *Autobiography* and, not the least, his *Discovery of India*. When Indira was elected leader of the Congress Parliamentary Party and as a consequence the leader of this country in January 1966, nobody, not even her worst enemies, talked of the perpetuation of the Nehru dynasty. Indira had earned her leadership in her own right. But when she tried to foist her over-ambitious son through undemocratic means on an unwilling nation, she forfeited her own right to remain as the leader of this great country. She apparently lost her judgement and discrimination about what behoves a democratic leader, and whether moral and political challenges should ever be met by ruthless administrative action.

As a newspaperman during the eleven years of Indira's Prime Ministership, I had occasion to watch, report and interpret the march of events from close quarters. What has been narrated in this book is based on facts as I have known and the way I have understood them. Certain events, about which I could not have direct knowledge, have been interpreted for me by people who were placed in positions of power and authority in those days. I have also interviewed a large number of people in politics and administration for information which a reporter cannot possibly have first hand.

A lot of information, not yet substantiated, has been coming out since the defeat of Indira Gandhi at the hustings. Much of it concerns corrupt and unethical practices indulged in by people close to Indira Gandhi during the 19 months of the National Emergency. In some cases even her personal collusion is alleged. I have preferred to ignore such information, except where I had no reason to doubt the facts at my command, pending full enquiries which are being ordered by the successor Government of the Janata Party. But I have not overlooked the fact of deterioration in the style of functioning of Indira Gandhi herself in the last two years of her regime, her dependence for advice on people whose image in public was not above board, and her apparent condoning of acts which were not in keeping with either the basic tenets of the party she headed, or the highest norms of democracy, which the country expected of Nehru's daughter. One cannot just explain away this precipitate moral and political decline by saying that she was a prisoner in the hands of a coterie of ruthless individuals, and that she was told only what they wanted her to know. More so because her own son was the leader of this coterie and he could not have done anything without her knowledge and approval. If he did, and if she was not able to control him, she had not only become an indulgent mother but an incompetent Prime Minister, which was worse.

What she could not see herself or would not admit, the electorate showed to her by not only rejecting her in her own home constituency, but also rejecting Sanjay and every single Congress candidate in the northern nine states. Could there be a greater and more direct indictment of a leader who, only six years ago, had got a fantastic mandate from the people against the combined might of the entire Opposition, the Press and the business community in the country?

What happened during these six years to discredit her so thoroughly? It is commentary enough that in today's politics of India there is no Nehru in the forefront. Indira will have to ponder for a long time to really understand that it was not just Sanjay, who was the cause of all this. She herself ignored that broad vision of world history her father had tried to instil in her and failed to impart it to her son and prepare him for the role he was so keen to perform. She had failed as Nehru's daughter, as the country's chosen leader, and also as a mother.

The one redeeming feature in the whole story is the fact that even after having got Parliament to extend the life of the last Lok Sabha by another year, Indira felt it necessary or was forced to seek a fresh mandate from the people in March 1977 — a time when she need not have held elections. What compelled her to take this decision? Apart from the wrong assessment of the Intelligence Services and the party workers about her own popularity and the party's standing with the people, it is now being said that she got scared when a Sarvodaya worker reportedly sacrificed himself through self-immolation in Wardha as a protest against the imposition of Emergency, against the mass arrest of Opposition leaders, including Jayaprakash Narayan, and against the extension of the life of the Lok Sabha. The incident was never reported because of the strict censorship in those days, but it is believed to have shocked not only the inmates of the Paunar Ashram, but also Indira in New Delhi. She knew time had come for her to face the people if she wanted to prevent such gruesome incidents. How far this one unreported incident led to the holding of elections is not easy to gauge now; what is important, however, is to realize that if she had not ordered elections when she did, the country would have passed through a real bloodbath. Preparations were being made all over the country to launch a kind of satyagraha, in which self-immolation might have figured prominently. The more the tortures in Indian jails, the more determined was the spirit of the people who had gone underground to continue the fight. The arrest of George Fernandes was a setback, but not for long, for others were still at large and ready to carry on the fight.

Ordinarily, Indira was not the type who got scared easily. She had matched her wits against leaders of Super Powers during her heyday in 1971 and had held her own on the question of Bangladesh. It does not lie in the mouth of discredited President of the United States, Richard Nixon, to take credit for something which never happened and to blame India and her leader of something which was never contemplated. In a television interview on May 12, 1977, Nixon told his interviewer, David Frost, that India planned to invade West Pakistan in 1971, inviting a potential clash with China. And it was pressure from the U.S.A. and the Soviet Union that prevented Indira Gandhi to carry out the invasion. His 'totally reliable' source for this information needs to be disclosed in order to show how misinformed the White House was all along in those critical days. The Chief of the Political Section in the American Embassy was a diplomat named Lee Stull. His reports were based on the gossip collected from newspaper correspondents in New Delhi about what went on in the Union Cabinet meetings. One correspondent fed him the dope that the Cabinet had discussed the possibility of finishing the Pakistani Military machine now that they had an opportunity to do so, and it had been generally approved that Indian troops should be ordered to go to Islamabad as soon as Dacca fell. To make his story more authentic the correspondent quoted the then Defence Minister, Jagjivan Ram, as his source. Jagjivan Ram has already denied the allegation as 'poppycock', but it is interesting to note that Lee Stull and his boys rushed the story to Washington as most reliable and authentic. By the time the letter that Nixon claims to have written to Indira Gandhi could even have landed in New Delhi, decision had already been taken to have only holding operations in the western sector.

The day Dacca fell, this very diplomat, who was present in the diplomat's gallery in Parliament to hear Prime Minister's statement, was, therefore, taken completely by surprise that she had decided within an hour in consultation with her entire council of Ministers to call a unilateral ceasefire. The question of invading Pakistan had never arisen, but Lee Stull, perhaps to justify his earlier despatch, might have informed Washington that Indira had been forced to call the ceasefire under pressure from Nixon and Brezhnev. For once it was not Indira but Nixon who had been misled. I have described this incident in detail here because Nixon's TV statement came after the book had been written. The chapter dealing with the Indo-Pakistan war refers to the diplomat being surprised at the ceasefire decision. But after Nixon's interview, it has become necessary not only to set the record straight but also to name the diplomat concerned.

Now to perform the most pleasant task of acknowledging my debt to those without whose help and encouragement I could not have undertaken the writing of this book. The list of those who have helped me with information and interpretation is so long that it would be impossible to mention everyone of them. Still I owe special debt to the present Chairman of the Janata Party, Chandra Shekhar, and the former Principal Secretary to the Prime Minister, P. N. Haksar, whose valuable suggestions prevented me from going wrong on many points of fact. My thanks are also due to all those who agreed to be interview by me at short notice. I shall also remain indebted to my brother, Dr. Lalit K. Pandit, for his suggestions and final revision of the draft. In spite of all this, if any mistakes have gone unnoticed, the fault is entirely mine.

Finally, this book could not have been written but for the loving care and encouragement of my wife and sons.

Bombay
May 15, 1977

C. S. PANDIT

CHAPTER I

BEGINNING OF THE END
(June 1975 to March 1977)

It WAS a bright spring morning of late March in New Delhi with its gardens in full bloom. But there was no bloom at No. 1 Safdarjung Road, the official residence of India's third Prime Minister, which presented a depressing and dismal appearance. It was exactly a week after the ignominious defeat of Indira Gandhi in her constituency in the Rae Bareli District of Uttar Pradesh in the sixth Lok Sabha elections. The cars on the opposite pavement were far less than their earlier customary number. The ring of security men around the complex, too, was much reduced and lacked the spit and polish of only a week ago. There was the lonely sign of the Reception Office, but anyone could just walk in after a cursory security inspection by tired men who knew that power had flown elsewhere. Even so there appeared a continuous stream of visitors. Most of them were defeated Congressmen, still staggering under the impact of the Janata 'hurricane'. Many did not seem to know what had hit them. Many refused to believe that they had lost even their security deposits in a constituency they had represented for three terms. Some of them were convinced that the elections had been rigged by disgruntled local officials in favour of the Opposition. For them Indira had been invincible for over a decade, and they still had hopes that she would somehow rise again to rescue them and the party from this total rout, the like of which Congressmen had never experienced right from 1937 when they had fought elections for the first time.

There were others who had come merely to see the defeated face of absolute power. They seemed to gloat over the turn of events, feeling self-righteous as they, too, had contributed their vote towards the downfall of the once charismatic Prime Minister. There were also some who had a sense of remorse now for having thrown out a leader, whom they might not have loved as they had her father, but whom they had always respected and feared. They were the type who longed for a sense of security and stability, which they did not have any more with the change of the establishment. Many a man and woman walked out with tears. Some even murmured that the nation had not been fair to Jawaharlal's daughter who, in her own right, had been a great Prime Minister and builder of modern India. It was often said by some perceptive political observers in the past that at the rate she was developing into a world statesman, she might even outshine her great father. Jawaharlal Nehru, they conceded, was a loved leader who could do no wrong. She, in contrast, had come through a very harsh test. For nobody, not even those in the party who were instrumental in bringing her to power after Lal Bahadur Shastri's death in January 1966, accepted her starting credentials merely because she was Jawaharlal's daughter. They rather thought that she would only be a dumb Prime Minister who would reign, while they would actually rule. This was the common talk in New Delhi in those days. That, it turned out, was the first mistake the party bosses made, for which they had to pay dearly two years later. It resulted in the great split which led to the squeezing out of the party of almost all of them. And the party has now paid a still bigger price with its complete rout in the northern Hindi belt, where the Indian National Congress had dug its roots deepest ever since it was born ninety years ago. The party, which had brought independence to the country 30 years ago under the leadership of Mahatma Gandhi, lies in shambles today — a house divided against itself. It might take some years and the emergence of a new leader to build up a new edifice upon these foundations, appropriate to the changing times.

Meanwhile, the country has seen the end of the Nehrus at the forefront of India's polity. The question that will long be debated is: How did this come about and who was primarily responsible for it? In the last days of her totally authoritarian rule, Indira Gandhi appeared completely isolated even from her own party men, except for a handful of sycophants who had surrounded her professing total personal loyalty. Also snapped were her direct links with the people. Thus, a Prime Minister, who had distinguished herself by her uncanny sense of political timing, was found blundering every now and then. By way of feedback she got only what the people around her wanted her to hear and not what was the actuality. This must be surmised, otherwise one can never explain her decision to rush into an election at the most inappropriate time when the people's wrath against her had reached its peak because of the inhuman actions of the administration at the behest of some important power-mad persons surrounding her. It is now said that her ambitious son, Sanjay Gandhi, with the help of Defence Minister, Bansi Lal, her political private secretaries, Yashpal Kapoor and R. K. Dhavan, had made her a virtual prisoner and she was willy nilly forced to endorse all actions initiated by this gang. Facts, however, point to the contrary. She was as much a party to all the decisions emanating from the Prime Minister's house as any other individual.

The rising tide of mass resentment against growing corruption in high places, encouraged through a system of selective political patronage and coupled with acute economic distress in the countryside in the wake of two years of drought and galloping inflation, created a certain scare in the ruling coterie that unless they reacted strongly, their days were numbered. The emergenne of Jayaprakash Narayan, affectionately known as JP all over the country, as the focal point of that mass resentment further added to their fears. Perhaps, Indira Gandhi was the most scared of the lot, because she had by then not only isolated herself from the people of India, but also from her senior colleagues in the Cabinet and the party, who had provided her the necessary moral and political support in the past in taking challenging decisions. But her style of functioning over the years had undergone a sea change. She seemed to suffer from a strange sense of insecurity even when she was most secure for all practical purpose and as a consequence never allowed any of her close advisers to continue in that position too long lest they assume undue power and importance. She would often reduce persons holding important offices to utter impotence.

Indira Gandhi's distrust of her political colleagues dates back to the time when she first assumed office only to find herself surrounded by political bosses who would not let her do anything they did not approve of. Subsequently, it became an established part of her strategy that no one well up in the party hierarchy was to be allowed too long to enjoy her confidence and proximity. Probably another reason for her isolation from her senior colleagues was her being a woman — of course, she would never admit it herself — and therefore feeling a reluctance to talking to them directly. Invariably her dialogues with important leaders would be carried on through emissaries who sometimes misunderstood what was expected of them and more often projected their own ideas and interests only to complicate matters.

As the movement, starting 1973 onwards, launched by the Opposition under the guidance of Jayaprakash Narayan, gathered momentum, Indira Gandhi found herself more and more cut off from her senior colleagues. Her Cabinet became a group of people endorsing all that she wanted done, even if they had any reservation. Among themselves, too, they had no communication for fear of being spied upon and accused of conspiring against her. Even when they had identical views on an issue, those views seldom found expression in the Cabinet meetings lest the one expressing them was singled out for reprisal subsequently. Rumours about impending Cabinet changes were floated every now and then to keep up tension and a sense of insecurity among her Council of Ministers and their supporters in the party. Fear stalked the corridors of power in New Delhi. The Parliamentary party, too, became the handmaiden of some ruthless manipulators acting in the name of the Prime Minister. Any other centre of power was sought to be immediately subdued or destroyed. The Party President had no entity or authority of his own any more. The Congress Working Committee seldom met during this period and the Parliamentary Board had almost ceased to exist except on paper. When the Working Committee did meet, as on the eve of the Gauhati Session of the A.I.C.C. in late 1976, it unanimously endorsed programmes prepared at the Prime Minister's house without much discussion.

A logical corollary of all this was a greater reliance on administrative action to meet political and moral challenges. This was very much in evidence during the time JP's movement took a definite shape. In this period Opposition leaders in Parliament often found themselves frustrated, because all their attempts to raise controversial issues reflecting on the integrity of important individuals, connected with the Government or near the seat of power, were papered over by administrative action, whether it was in regard to the allotment of land to Sanjay Gandhi for his Maruti Project, or it was in regard to the Nagarwala case, or even in the case of the Pondicherry import licence scandal in which the late Lalit Narayan Mishra, as Foreign Trade Minister, was allegedly involved. The greater and greater dependence on the administration for survival of those who were thus under political attack led to some trusted but unscrupulous officers and bureaucrats assuming unlimited powers. They knew full well that the people they were called upon to defend, through not strictly legal action, were strong enough politically not only to be able to save them in case of excesses, but might also be willing to pay a sufficiently high price for it. In fact, in the last few years this gave rise to a kind of highly sophisticated system to blackmail the very people in positions of political authority who had initiated the setting up of the so-called committed officialdom.

While the political challenge to Indira Gandhi grew with JP blessing the 'Nav Nirman' movement of the Gujarat students and starting his own on the same lines in Bihar, the Prime Minister took recourse to three diversionary tactics to discredit both these movements.

The first was to link JP's movement with the difficulties she was having in normalizing relations with the United States. Indo-U.S. relations had touched rock bottom in the wake of the Bangladesh developments and India's explosion of a nuclear device in May 1974. Off and on she publicly warned the nation of possible subversive involvement of, and continuing threat from, foreign intelligence agencies. There might have been some basis for it. But public pronouncement about such threat of subversion was mainly to discredit important individuals who were known to have political links abroad in some western countries and who were in total sympathy with JP's movement.

The second was to discredit militant trade unionists like George Fernandes, who were also the real activists behind JP, for getting foreign funds. At the same time all trade union movements were sought to be crushed with a heavy hand. The climax was reached in the ruthless suppression of the Railway strike in May 1974 against which even the then President V. V. Giri had raised his voice. That was the end of Giri who wanted a second term as President but never got it. Soon after the fear of political authority spread to almost all walks of life. Lalit Narayan Mishra was at that time the Railway Minister. He had by then been identified in the public mind as the symbol of all corrupt politics based on money power. The suppression of the Railway strike earned him the stigma of a ruthless Minister who had used the Defence of India rules and other Draconian laws to subdue railwaymen. It is, however, a matter of conjecture whether Mishra was really responsible for all that he was accused of, or he was being made a tool in the hands of more unscrupulous individuals around the Prime Minister. To be more precise, some important people in the Congress hierarchy always felt that Lalit Narayan Mishra was the evil genius who had really evolved the strategy of meeting moral and political challenges through administrative action involving even the intelligence services of the country. It was carried to a fine art in the hands of his protege and friend, Bansi Lal. Some others, who, too, have been closely associated with the powers that were, feel that somehow Mishra, who had very many likable qualities, got caught in the grip of people like Yashpal Kapoor, R. K. Dhavan and Sanjay Gandhi. He was made to perform certain acts under the threat of his own political eclipse. When he found it more and more difficult to perform those functions in the face of increasing attack on him from the Opposition as the perpetrator of all that was corrupt in the Government and the Congress, he knew that his days were numbered.

Just a few weeks before Mishra went to Samastipur to meet his destiny, I had occasion to meet him at his Akbar Road residence in New Delhi. He was a terribly worried man, wearing all sorts of beads, emulets, charms and jewels to ward off the evil eye. He had also been on many a pilgrimage to various shrines all over the country to propitiate gods. He told me at that time that he was terribly afraid he would not survive for long. 'I have too many enemies.' It was not clear whether he had a hunch of his impending end, or he was merely hinting at a possible political demise. It was also in the air at that time that he would soon be dropped from the Union Cabinet.

The third diversionary step taken by Prime Minister Indira Gandhi to meet the mounting political challenge from the Opposition was to launch a high pressure propaganda against the infiltration of the armed forces and security services by volunteers of the discredited Rashtriya Swayam Sewak Sangh who also provided the Jana Sangh with its militant cadre. She, furthermore, sought to link the growth of certain clandestine religious organizations with possible connections with the Opposition, like the Ananda Marg, with the alleged increased activity in the country of foreign intelligence agencies like the Central Intelligence Agency of the U.S.A.

Perhaps there was some basis for the second surmise because the Ananda Marg appeared to have a lot of money at its disposal and a highly organized propaganda machine with its headquarters in the Philippines. But even till today no definite link has yet been established between the Ananda Marg and the murder of Lalit Narayan Mishra as was alleged in the first investigation reports. The Indian Intelligence Services, most of which were under the direct charge of the Prime Minister herself, were put on the alert to get all possible evidence of involvement in any sphere of activity of foreign intelligence agencies, like the CIA, the West German and the South Korean intelligence agencies, which were supposed to be very active in India. Steps were also taken to stop foreign assistance or hospitality being accepted by people in sensitive professions like politics, education, scientific research and journalism. Administrators were also prevented from accepting any such hospitality without prior clearance from the Government.

Simultaneously, a high-powered committee of the heads of important para-military organizations like the Central Reserve Police and the Border Security Police and the intelligence agencies like the Intelligence Bureau and the Central Bureau of Investigation were asked to review the possible repercussions in the country in case Jayaprakash Narayan was arrested. This exercise was undertaken about six months prior to the actual arrest and imposition of the National Emergency. At that time, Abdul Ghafoor was the Chief Minister of Bihar and he had asked the Centre's permission to arrest JP.

The consensus in this high-powered committee of Central Police and Intelligence chiefs was that it would lead to widespread unrest and violence in the country. However, it was at a meeting of this committee that the chiefs of the Intelligence Bureau and the Central Bureau of Investigation at that time suggested that all that reaction could be prevented through a clamp down of full emergency powers all over the country. They singled out the press and the mass media for total control. It is therefore wrong to say that imposition of the Emergency was a sudden decision, and that it was Sanjay Gandhi's idea as has often been made out in public by some authoritative persons. In fact, the chiefs of the IB and the CBI were then asked to prepare contingency plans in case it was felt necessary to put their suggestion into operation at short notice. The Head of the Home Ministry was kept blissfully ignorant of all these preparations which were meant to crush JP's 'total revolution' at an appropriate time.

At that time, however, no one took the election petition against Indira Gandhi in the Allahabad High Court too seriously. Raj Narain was known to have specialized in filing election petitions after defeats in elections and since the petition in question had gone on for about three and a half years, it was felt that suitable administrative action and a certain amount of pressurization of the Judiciary would result in a favourable verdict. The only person, who disagreed with this complacent attitude and warned the Prime Minister as early as December 1974 that the petition was taking an alarming turn and the case should be taken more seriously, was the late Lalit Narayan Mishra.

The warning apparently went unheeded because Yashpal Kapoor, who was the main cause of this petition as the Prime Minister's chief election agent in 1971, continued to assure her that there was nothing serious in the petition and she would win ultimately. The verdict of the Allahabad High Court on June 12, 1975, therefore came as a rude shock to No. 1 Safdarjung Road. Coinciding with the increasing tempo of JP's movement against corruption in high places, the verdict eroded whatever little moral authority the Prime Minister still enjoyed over the people. Even so, the public at large gave her the benefit of doubt. Important luminaries in the legal community, including Palkhivala, went on record that the adverse judgment was on merely technical grounds and could not stand in the Supreme Court if an appeal against it was properly handled. Jayaprakash Narayan naturally cashed in on this fresh assault on Indira Gandhi's fast-eroding political and moral authority by calling upon her to step down from Prime Ministership. This was despite the limited stay granted by the High Court and the conditional stay granted by the Supreme Court vacation judge a fortnight later.

The day Indira Gandhi decided to meet this challenge to her authority by clamping internal Emergency and arresting all important Opposition leaders in the country in a predawn swoop, her fate was sealed. This was the blackest act of her regime which can never be washed away by any earlier acts of statesmanship which had brought international glory to this country. Anyone who opposed the clamping of the Emergency and the arrests of the Opposition leaders or who even remotely counselled her stepping down had to pay for it in some way or the other. The stories current at that time that her first reaction was to step down and then fight in the Supreme Court seem to have no basis. There may be some truth in the report, however, that Sanjay Gandhi, Bansi Lal, Yashpal Kapoor and her personal private secretary R. K. Dhavan might have prevailed upon her at this point of time not only not to resign, but also to put into operation the contingency plan prepared by the chiefs of the Intelligence Bureau and the Central Bureau of Investigation at her behest about six months earlier.

It is, of course, a fact that within ten minutes of the receipt in New Delhi of the first reports of the adverse judgment by the Allahabad High Court all Cabinet Ministers rushed to her residence to assure her of their total support and loyalty. Viewed against the background of the widespread fear and uncertainty among the Council of her

Ministers at that time, this act of spontaneous support by her Cabinet colleagues, including Jagjivan Ram who was one of the first to reach her residence, was conveyed to the outside world with great fanfare as the main reason for her decision to stay on and fight it out. Between June 12 and June 25, the day the vacation judge of the Supreme Court gave his conditional stay, it was conveyed to the public through controlled mass media channels, which had by then become almost perfect, that Indira Gandhi may after all step down. Even names of some individuals such as the then Defence Minister, Sardar Swaran Singh, the Chief Minister of West Bengal, Siddhartha Shankar Ray, and the Railway Minister, Kamalapati Tripathi, were floated as possible interim Prime Minister, until she cleared herself through an appeal in the Supreme Court. This was done mainly to gauge the reaction among party members. It was then that Jagjivan Ram went to her and told her in no uncertain terms that so long as she was the Prime Minister, she had his full support; but if she decided to step down, he would insist on the party electing the new leader. He did not relish the idea of her nominating an interim Prime Minister.

It is also true that during the last talk JP had with Indira Gandhi in an effort to find some compromise on the advice and persuasion of common friends, she had associated Jagjivan Ram with the talks on her side. It was subsequently put out that while a settlement seemed imminent on the basis of keeping the Bihar Assembly in suspended animation, Jagjivan Ram had led to the breakdown of the talks by insisting on greater clarity on the issue of whether the suspended Assembly would have to be dissolved finally or it could be revived. JP obviously wanted the first course to be followed and had agreed to suspended animation for the time being as a face-saving for the Government. He was quite clear about his objective that the Assembly would have to go and fresh elections held. He was willing to allow the Government to decide the appropriate time for this operation. In no case would he countenance revival of the same Assembly. That was not the Government's understanding and Jagjivan Ram was the one to point out that constitutionally the suspended Assembly could be revived once normalcy was restored. Such a manner of shifting the blame for any failures had led to considerable misunderstanding and lack of faith between the Prime Minister and her seniormost colleague over a period of time. Other colleagues also felt the same way but preferred to keep quiet. They were summarily called at six in the morning on June 26, 1975, to be confronted with National Emergency and all that it implied as a *fait accompli*. President Fakhruddin Ali Ahmed had been made to sign the order the previous night and the round-up of all important Opposition leaders including JP and Morarji Desai had already been effected. The press, too, had been brought under total censorship and directed not to publish the names of those arrested. In Delhi power supply to most newspapers was discontinued for twenty-four hours lest anyone of them tried to defy the Government. Faced with this drastic action, the entire Cabinet was stunned, but none had the courage to express his true feelings. Only the then Defence Minister, Sardar Swaran Singh, registered his mild disapproval and subsequently paid the price when he was unceremoniously dropped from the Cabinet. Till then a minister without portfolio, Bansi Lal, whose main qualification was his hold on Sanjay Gandhi, was given this highly sensitive and important portfolio. By the time he left, following his crushing defeat in the elections, he had already annoyed all the Services Chiefs by his crude and unorthodox way of functioning.

The subsequent twenty-one months were a nightmare for the people of the whole country, particularly for the people of Delhi, where trusted officers were brought on the recommendation of Sanjay Gandhi and Bansi Lal to let loose a reign of terror, the like of which had not been seen even during the British rule. Senior Cabinet Ministers found that decisions about their Ministries were made above their heads and they had no choice but to concur. The two sensitive Ministries, Home and Information and Broadcasting, were completely overhauled. The then Home Secretary N. K. Mukerjee was shunted off to Civil Aviation and Tourism for expressing his disagreement with the need for clamping Emergency. His next man was shunted off to his home State of Madhya Pradesh as a senior member of the Board of Revenue. Instead, officers about to retire and willing to do the bidding of these people were brought as replacements. The Home Minister apparently had no say in all this, for the then Minister of State for Home, Om Mehta, enjoyed the confidence of the Prime Minister or persons around her and was the main executioner of the policies decided by them.

In the Information and Broadcasting Ministry the sophisticated and perhaps the most successful Minister, Inder Gujral, had to make room for an ambitious and ruthless politician, Vidya Charan Shukla, because the former would not pay court to either Sanjay Gandhi or Bansi Lal. One of his faults was that he would not allow his subordinates in the news room of All India Radio to take orders from outsiders even if they happened to be closely related to the Prime Minister herself. This cost him his own ministership. But he was more perturbed about his Director of News, who was summarily asked to go on leave for not taking orders on phone from Sanjay Gandhi in keeping with the best norms of journalism and instructions of his Minister. This incensed the Prime Minister's power-mad son so much that he even threatened the News Director and Minister Gujral with immediate dismissal. Gujral was shifted to the Planning Commission until Indira Gandhi found him suitable enough to represent the country as its Ambassador to Moscow. Shukla, who took his place was of the new breed of hatchet men. He had two senior police officers to help him in his Ministry to bring under control the mass media including the press and the film industry.

Having thus taken the plunge to meet the challenge to her moral authority through ruthless administrative measures, Indira Gandhi was left with no alternative but to connive at and condone more and more authoritarian action by the new ruling coterie around her. Initiative apparently slipped out of her hands and went into the hands of an over-ambitious and ruthless young man who displayed hardly any sense of moral values in exploiting his close relationship to the Prime Minister to persuade, pursue and pressurize important people from all walks of life to bend them to his will. There were industrialists, intellectuals, businessmen, film people, journalists and bureaucrats who were persuaded, some times even by the mother herself, to pay court to the emerging leader. He had plans not only to dethrone all those who had exercised or shared power with his mother in some measure, but to virtually execute a coup in the ruling party itself.

It is no accident that the Youth Congress suddenly acquired undue importance and power under his patronage, and that his indulgent mother, instead of giving the lead to the All India Congress Committee at its last Gauhati Session, publicly proclaimed that "the Youth Congress had taken the thunder out of the parent body's session". At the earlier Chandigarh Session, Sanjay had hovered in the background, sizing up individuals who might side with him in a confrontation. His main agent all along was Bansi Lal. At Gauhati, Sanjay came out openly and the next few months saw his ascendance to absolute power which he exercised in the name of his mother. The few Congressmen who had watched with apprehension his emergence on the political plane were naturally the ones to be arrested the moment Emergency was clamped. Among them were Chandra Shekhar, an elected member of the Congress Working Committee and the one individual whom Indira Gandhi had feared most, Mohan Dharia, a former Minister of State in her Council of Ministers, and the Secretary of the Congress Parliamentary Party, Ram Dhan, who was a protege of Chandra Shekhar. Ostensibly they were arrested and suspended from the party along with some other rebel Congressmen to strike terror in the hearts of other party men who might have harboured ideas of organizing any resistance against such authoritarian trend in the party and the Government.

The next to be dealt with were the so-called 'progressives' in the party who had links not only with the Communist Party of India but also with the Soviet Union. The CPI had already come in for some serious denunciation by Sanjay and Indira Gandhi herself. It was as much a notice to the CPI as to the progressives in the Congress that the honeymoon between the two parties was over. The economic policies of the Government also started reflecting at this time a certain pragmatism which was most welcome to the business and industrial community. Representatives of some big business houses in the country made a bee-line to cultivate the new youth leader, who, they thought, could be persuaded to end the domination of the leftists in the party. K. K. Birla, an important scion of the famous house of the Birlas, became a close adviser and fund-raiser for the Prime Minister and her son to the utter dismay of the entire leftist lobby in the country and the party. Many of the so-called progressives saw the writing on the wall and themselves started denouncing the CPI.

Having thus made sure of total subservience in the party and even outside in some sensitive spheres, the ruling coterie in the Prime Minister's house then decided to seek the advice of the Intelligence Services on the party's prospects in case of a snap poll. The officers in these agencies had, however, learnt by experience in the last few years that it was futile to tell the truth if it did not suit those in power as it only earned their wrath. To give an example of the highhandedness of the coterie, we have the story of an able and senior police officer on deputation from Uttar Pradesh to Delhi who had to seek the intervention of an influential member of Parliament like Chandra Shekhar to get post-haste transfer back to his State on concocted grounds because he found it impossible to carry out the orders from the Prime Minister's house. He was asked to arrest the contractor constructing the Safdarjung overbridge in New Delhi for the collapse of one of the piles when the overbridge was halfway through. When the officer pointed out that the collapse of the pile could not be taken as a criminal offence by the contractor, and that there was no legal provision for arresting the contractor, he was peremptorily told from the other side in the name of the Prime Minister herself that he would have to find a way or else regret his action.

It is well known that the contractor had earned Sanjay Gandhi's displeasure when a wall constructed by him on a design insisted upon by Sanjay against the advice of the contractor's engineer at his factory in Gurgaon had collapsed killing some persons. The loss involved amounted to some lakhs of rupees, which the contractor refused to make good. It was to teach the contractor a lesson that he would remember that, it is further alleged, some workers at the overbridge site were bribed to see that one of the piles was not according to specifications. Fortunately, the pile collapsed much before the overbridge was ready. It was hoped that the noise that would follow in Parliament would help the powers that were to get the contractor arrested. What happened in that case is neither important nor material now. But the police officer managed to escape to his State before he was forced to take, according to his understanding, a purely illegal action on orders conveyed orally by a person in the name of the Prime Minister. The Chief Minister of U.P. at that time was Kamalapati Tripathi and K. C. Pant was the Union Minister of State for Home. Otherwise this transfer could not have taken place.

This kind of pressurization was experienced by almost all the police officers working in the various para-military and intelligence agencies under the Central Government. It is therefore no surprise that their report to the Prime Minister on her party's poll prospects conveyed that this (early 1977) was the most appropriate time to hold elections and the Congress was certain to get a minimum of 320 seats in a House of 542. Justifying this conclusion, the report pointed out that the economic conditions in the country were just right to favour the ruling party. The granaries were full, and there was no guarantee that the monsoon would be good for the third year running. At the same time it was pointed out that shortages had started developing in some essential commodities like edible oils; prices, too, had registered an alarming increase of about twelve per cent in the past ten months after remaining steady for about a year. If the crops were not as good in the coming season, there was every possibility of inflation again raising its ugly head. In that case the ruling party might find it difficult to face the electorate. Taking all these factors into consideration, the intelligence agencies had recommended that this was the most appropriate time for holding a snap election. It was also argued that as most of the Opposition leaders were in jail and would have very little time to organize even if they were released immediately (this report was made sometime in the latter half of December 1976), the ruling party would definitely have a clear advantage.

Sanjay, who, it seemed, was working out the strategy of having snap elections for the Lok Sabha, had also similar reports from the Youth Congress workers from various states. The only question that worried him was that of a growing opposition to his emergence as a power in States like West Bengal, where he had failed to displace the Chief Minister, and in Bombay, where the B.P.C.C. President, Rajni Patel, wielded considerable influence and power even after his denunciation by the youth leader publicly. Sanjay was mainly interested, however, in reducing the influence of Jagjivan Ram in the party. According to Sanjay's calculations Jagjivan Ram, who was virtually number two in the Cabinet, was the only leader capable of having a solid group of loyal supporters of about seventy to eighty in the Congress Parliamentary Party. He also had a considerable national following. If Indira Gandhi was to be the supreme leader after a snap poll, she needed a solid group of about 150 loyal supporters in the party all the time. If that could be ensured, Sanjay was confident, the rest of the party members, who usually sat on the fence watching the power game, would automatically move over to his mother's side. To achieve that end he proposed to force nearly two hundred of his chosen Youth Congress members on the Congress as the party candidates, ignoring the claims of party men of much longer standing. He was confident that if seats for his candidates were chosen carefully, at least a hundred and fifty of them would be definitely returned.

These arguments were, perhaps, for only public consumption. For, behind this strategy seemed to be a much more diabolical design to carry out a virtual coup in the Congress organization as well as the Congress Parliamentary Party so that his own ascendence as the undisputed leader was politically sanctified by the party itself. The only miscalculation in this strategy was due to a complete lack of any information either from the intelligence sources or from his own Youth Congress workers about impending revolt by Jagjivan Ram the moment elections were announced and Emergency relaxed for that purpose. Even the bugging devices placed in each minister's bungalow did not pay for once.

About this time a high-level strategy planning session was held in which Sanjay, Bansi Lal, Om Mehta and V. C. Shukla participated apart from Yashpal Kapoor and R. K. Dhavan. It was decided at this meeting that as soon as elections were announced, the Emergency should be relaxed for that period only; it should not be lifted. Similarly, press censorship was to be relaxed without disbanding the censorship set up either at the Centre or in the States. Mohamed Yunus, Special Envoy of the Prime Minister, who was also a participant, suggested that rumours about the impending elections which had already spread should be effectively scotched so that when the Prime Minister made the actual announcement, she should be able to reap the advantage of a surprise move. The then Defence Minister Bansi Lal and the Minister of State for Home Om Mehta undertook to go on record publicly that there was no question of holding elections at that time. This they did with consummate skill at public meetings very far apart from each other. But the announcement about holding elections in March, made by Indira Gandhi herself on January 18, failed to produce the dramatic impact that it was expected to do for the simple reason that following the gradual release of the Opposition leaders earlier no one had taken the statements of Bansi Lal and Om Mehta very seriously. On the contrary, the released leaders had some hunch that elections might come much sooner than expected and had therefore initiated moves to merge into one party.

This was obvious from the way they were able to decide not only on a name, a flag and an election symbol without much recrimination, but also the number of seats to be contested by each constituent of the Janata Party, that came into being as a consequence, and Jagjivan Ram's Congress for Democracy which he formed after resigning from the Congress. If any side had surprise in store for it, it was the ruling caucus, no member of which expected the Opposition to organize itself so fast. Besides, the dramatically timed resignations from the Congress of the Food and Agriculture Minister Jagjivan Ram along with the former Chief Ministers of U.P. and Orissa, H. N. Bahuguna and Nandini Satpathy, with their followers from the Congress, took them completely unawares. It was this development more than anything else which removed the fear of the ruling caucus from the public mind. The initiative passed out of the hands of Indira Gandhi and her advisers, who till then had hoped to browbeat the electorate through a controlled mass media, particularly in the rural areas, to vote for Indira Gandhi. They had been blissfully unaware of the strong popular resentment, particularly in the States above the Vindhyas, against the ruthless implementation of Sanjay's sterilization programme. Despite Shukla's efforts to make the newspapers to black out Opposition news and to press them to publish Government handouts on the so-called gains of Emergency, harrowing tales of suppression, repression and torture started finding their way into the newspapers. The tide had turned, for Indira Gandhi and her advisers, as so often happens in authoritarian regimes, had become the victims of their own propaganda. People were not deceived by twenty-one months of scrupulous control of all the written and spoken words. This realization must have come as a shock to all of them, but they had not given up yet.

Aware of the style of functioning of the Government in the past three years, Jayaprakash Narayan had impressed upon the leaders of the Opposition the absolute necessity of maintaining a very mild and low profile even under provocation. For, he feared that once the realization dawned on the power-drunk coterie around the Prime Minister, they would do anything to give themselves a justification to call off the elections, even if it meant imposing martial law. He heaved a sigh of relief when Jagjivan Ram came out. Even then he was not very wrong, because there is a persistent belief that an attempt was made to get the then President Fakhruddin Ali Ahmed to sign something which he declined to do. What greater proof could there be of the kind of bossism verging on virtual dictatorship that prevailed in those critical days that Indira Gandhi was able to force a gentle and loyal President, who had stood by her through all the crises in the past, to violate the Constitution by signing the order proclaiming National Emergency a day before it was announced to the Cabinet. The question of the Cabinet's approval obviously did not arise, for by the time they were informed the arrests had already been made all over the country. It is this incident which has given substance to the belief that the President was once again approached on The 11th of February at about two in the morning and asked to sign another document. The President who had returned to Delhi only the previous day, cutting short his State visit to Malaysia for reasons of health, for once refused to oblige.

No one knows for certain, except perhaps a handful of individuals, what was in that document. But Jagjivan Ram who was close to

Fakhruddin Ali Ahmed did allude to a possibility of the Government trying to clamp martial law in case the ruling coterie felt that the calling of elections had been a mistake and the wind was definitely against them. The President refused to be a mere rubber stamp this time. Even a reported threat that he had been made the President not for his own sake but to serve their ends, and that he would regret having asserted his right to do only what he considered strictly constitutional did not work. All the same, it is widely suspected that the total heart attack that he suffered later in the morning was probably the result of this latest confrontation he had with someone he had given his total friendship and loyalty all these years. The real story might come out some day. Some allusions to what seemed to have happened on that fateful morning have already been made public by the Imam of Juma Masjid of Delhi. The only fact known is that the President's sister in a hysterical mood after his death openly accused them 'of killing her brother'. At one stage, it is said, she became so insistent in denouncing the powers that were that a doctor had to be asked to give her a sedative. Ever since a curtain of silence has been rung over the whole episode.

History will not excuse Indira Gandhi for the last two years of her ruthless authoritarian rule during which she not only destroyed some of the cherished democratic values, but also herself and her party. No doubt there were achievements during her rule of eleven years which might have classed her as one of the great Prime Ministers of India, had she not succumbed to the temptation of perpetuating a dynastic rule by projecting her son as the new leader of the country through means that were far from democratic. A question that will ever remain unanswered and a puzzle is whether Indira Gandhi's call for elections in March 1977, when she had already got a captive Parliament to extend the life of the Lok Sabha by another year, was a fatal miscalculation or a deliberate gamble. For once she had completely failed in her political judgement and timing.

CHAPTER II

REIGN, NOT RULE
(January 1966 to February 1967)

SHOCKING news stunned Delhi on the morning of January 12, 1966. The morning editions of all newspapers were delayed, for just at the time of going to press, news had landed from Tashkent of the death of the then Prime Minister, Lal Bahadur Shastri. Only the previous evening he had been hailed as the apostle of peace, having signed the historic Tashkent Declaration with President Ayub Khan of Pakistan, thus ending the state of hostility between the two countries following the 1965 conflict. The President, Dr. Radhakrishnan and the seniormost Cabinet Minister, Gulzarilal Nanda, were the first to be informed of the sad news on telephone. And before the newspapers had hit the stands, there was an unending stream of mourners moving towards No. 10 Jana Path, the official residence of India's second Prime Minister.

A short, soft-spoken man, Lal Bahadur Shastri had been chosen by the party bosses in preference to the more rigid and assertive Morarji Desai, through a scheme of consensus, perhaps under a misconception that he would be pliable. But within months this quiet little man from the banks of the Ganga in Varanasi proved that he was nobody's stooge, and had nerves of steel. In the beginning his short stature and soft manners excited laughter in public, but soon he displayed a compelling personality. And Pakistan's uncalled for aggression in 1965 provided him an opportunity, of course at a tremendous cost, to prove that he was as strong and able a leader as one could hope for at that critical moment. His sudden death after signing the Tashkent Declaration let loose a whole lot of rumours at that time. He had been a heart patient earlier and the strain of negotiating under tremendous pressure from the leaders of the Soviet Union proved too much. The moment the agreement was signed he got in touch with his family in New Delhi. Soon after he was found gasping for breath by his personal physician. He might have come under attack for having bartered away Haji Pir in Kashmir, but his death muted all criticism of the Tashkent Declaration, which, in any case, remained a non-starter once Pakistan got back what she had lost.

It was a cold January morning in Delhi when a chartered plane landed at Palam airport bringing the 'king-maker' and leader of the so-called 'Syndicate' of the Congress bosses. He was away in Madras, when news reached him of the death of Lal Bahadur Shastri. An industrialist and a close friend of long standing immediately chartered the plane for the Congress President K. Kamaraj to be in Delhi in time for the State funeral. The friend was no other than Ram Nath Goenka, owner of the *Express* newspaper empire. Perhaps he had hoped to influence the choice of the next Prime Minister of the country. Not many of his ilk had liked the choice of Lal Bahadur Shastri, after Jawaharlal, in preference to Morarji Desai. But the leader from Tamil Nadu remained firm and uncommunicative. He dismissed the crowd of journalists gathered at the airport without saying a word and drove away to his residence. No one had any inkling of what he had in mind, except, perhaps, that he would again prevent Morarji from getting the Prime ministership.

Even before the ashes had cooled on the pyre of Lal Bahadur, followers of Morarji had staked his claim for the throne. Some activity was also initiated on behalf of Gulzarilal Nanda who had been sworn in as the acting Prime Minister. But there was no activity or excitement at No. 1 Safdarjung Road, at that time an ordinary ministerial bungalow facing the prestigious Gymkhana Club, and the residence of Nehru's daughter Indira. She had been persuaded by Lal Bahadur Shastri to join his Cabinet as Minister for Information and Broadcasting on her father's death.

Despite having acted as her father's confidant, housekeeper and hostess throughout his tenure as India's Prime Minister, Indira remained shy, retiring and soft-spoken. She felt most at home among a highly cultured and sophisticated crowd of New Delhi. Of all who flocked around her at that time, most dropped out on their own or were dropped one by one. Only Dr. Karan Singh remained steadfast and loyal. The Ministry given to her required a sensitive mind, and she is still remembered by professionals in that Ministry, who came in contact with her, as the best Minister they ever had.

Behind Indira's mild exterior was a determined mind. The country already knew about it from the time she had been the Congress President. Her father was then the Prime Minister. And true to his democratic faith, he resisted all pressure to throw out E. M. S. Namboodiripad's Marxist Ministry in Kerala, since it had been duly elected and had a clear majority. It was only Indira Gandhi, as Congress President, who could persuade him to visit the State and witness for himself the popular agitation, of course, encouraged by the Congress itself, against the Ministry.

In personal life, Indira is a most charming individual capable of winning the admiration and loyalty of anyone who comes in contact with her. No one imagined that one day she would turn out to be the most authoritarian Prime Minister of this country. There was hardly any talk of her becoming the next Prime Minister till then except in pure good humour. But fate had ordained otherwise. At the residence of the Congress President, a consensus was gradually emerging in favour of Indira among the party bosses, who felt slighted at the gradual assertion of his authority by the late Lal Bahadur Shastri whom they claimed to have made the Prime Minister. They now schemed of having a reigning queen while they would actually rule from behind the scenes. 'The Syndicate', as they were known, comprised Atulya Ghosh of West Bengal, S. K. Patil of Bombay, S. Nijalingappa of Karnataka and N. Sanjiva Reddy of Andhra Pradesh. The Congress President K. Kamaraj, who had acquired national prominence in the wake of the notorious Kamaraj Plan of Nehru, was their presiding deity.

Kamaraj, a bachelor, kept an open house. Anyone could walk in at any time except during the sacred hours of the afternoon when he had his daily siesta. This was one luxury he liked to indulge in and would never miss even if there was pressing business awaiting him. His evening chats with newspapermen attracted the world press, for once again the dark, tall man with flashing eyes from the South had been cast in the role of the 'king-maker' and the obviously enjoyed every moment of it. His infectious laughter was his best weapon to fend off inconvenient questions with. He did not have a command over English or Hindi; yet he could be very precise on any matter he wanted to comment upon.

Rumours had already started floating that his choice had fallen on Nehru's daughter, but he would not confirm it himself. He called a meeting of the Congress Parliamentary Party on January 19 to elect the new leader. Having been once deprived through the consensus method, Morarji was determined to give a fight. Election could not be prevented, and it had become Kamaraj's responsibility to ensure that Indira won with an overwhelming majority.

Many admirers of Kamaraj could not understand at that time why he did not stand for the Prime ministership himself, giving thereby a lie to the belief in non-Hindi circles that India's Prime Minister would always be from the Northern Hindi heartland, particularly Uttar Pradesh. Whenever this question was posed to him, Kamaraj's gesticulating reply used to be: 'No English. No Hindi. How?' He used to be vehement in his refusal to even consider the possibility if someone pointed out that he was most suitable as he had been a very successful Chief Minister of Tamil Nadu, and that he could always appoint a trusted lieutenant, as he had done in Madras, to act as his spokesman in Parliament and outside. Besides, the system of simultaneous translation was due to be installed in Parliament. His objection, therefore, arose out of very different reasons. Many did not credit him with the breadth of vision necessary to hold the high office. He also seemed to suffer from an innate lack of self-confidence. But anyone who met him was struck by his grasp of complicated international problems and his knack of summing up his reactions in the simplest of words. What he could not explain in English, he would say in Tamil to be translated by his Secretary.

The prosaic record of the meeting of the Congress Parliamentary Party on January 19, 1966 says: 'The party elected Indira Gandhi to succeed Lal Bahadur Shastri as the leader of the party. Of the total membership of 551, the number of members present was 526. Indira Gandhi won with 355 votes against 169 secured by the other candidate, Morarji Desai. The meeting was conducted by the Congress President K. Kamaraj.' But behind the bald announcement is the fascinating story of political horse-trading in the Tamany Hall style, since all those involved in the changeover were playing for very high stakes. Little did those, who had plumped for Indira, realize that the soft-spoken sophisticated scion of the Nehru family had an iron will and the arrogance of the Nehrus, which brooked no interference. And one day, soon to dawn, she would not only squeeze them out of the party which they thought they controlled, but would also turn those left behind into mere stooges to be extolled or destroyed at her sweet will. In fact, this style of functioning grew to such an extent that in due course it corroded her sense of fair play and moral judgement, and led to her ignoring all that was noble in the democratic tradition left behind by her father. Perhaps, it was her ambitious and uncontrollable son that became her blind spot.

Kamaraj, after having secured the concurrence of his cronies to the selection of Indira Gandhi as the next Prime Minister, went about the task of getting her elected with a big majority in a most deliberate and meticulous manner. Morarji Desai, who nursed a grievance against him for preferring Lal Bahadur earlier, was also in no mood to compromise. Apart from the support he enjoyed in his home State of Gujarat he had also secured the support of Chandra Bhanu Gupta, the influential leader of Uttar Pradesh, which returned the largest number of Parliament members. Morarji also had support in two important caste groups in Bihar, the Rajputs and Bhoomihars, who had, for long, dominated the Congress politics in that State. The challenge to Indira Gandhi therefore was a formidable one. The only way to meet it was to mobilize the entire resources of the State bosses, so that members from their areas stood solidly behind them in the crucial election. But that alone was not enough. Much more was required to be done to get that support mobilized and converted into votes on the fateful day.

Once Indira Gandhi's name had been proposed by the powerful men in the party, she, too, plunged into the fray with her characteristic cold calculation. That was also the beginning of her system of choosing one or two close and trusted political advisers. The first such adviser on the scene was the shrewd Chief Minister of Madhya Pradesh, Dwarka' Prasad Mishra. He had come into political limelight, after remaining in the wilderness for over a decade, merely because he had dared criticize Nehru when he was Home Minister of his State. Nehru, in his own way, kept dissenters and assertive bosses at arm's length. In his view D. P. Mishra was a close associate of Sardar Patel and therefore needed to be kept away. Indira Gandhi, however, brought about a *rapprochement* between the two and that rehabilitated Mishra as the Chief Minister of Madhya Pradesh.

Once back in power, Mishra very soon shot up as the strong man of Madhya Pradesh and a shrewd political operator on the national plane. On the eve of the election, he organized a meeting of almost all the Congress Chief Ministers in New Delhi to pledge open support for Indira Gandhi. The only dissenter, perhaps, was the U.P. leader, C. B. Gupta, though he knew that on the name of Indira the majority of Congress members of Parliament from his State would surely line up behind her.

The other possible dissenters from important States, like Mohanlal Sukhadia of Rajasthan and Brahmananda Reddy of Andhra Pradesh, were tamed by Atulya Ghosh and Kamaraj. In the Parliamentary Party the main pillars of Indira's strength were Y. B. Chavan, C. Subramaniam, Asoka Mehta and Dinesh Singh, the last acting as the main link between the party and the new leader. Subsequently, Dinesh Singh annoyed almost everyone including Kamaraj by his cocky airs and politics of manipulation in the name of the Prime Minister. Another Chief Minister who played a very crucial role at the time and earned for himself a direct rapport with Indira Gandhi, without Y. B. Chavan's good offices, was V. P. Naik of Maharashtra. That he survived much longer in office in his State than any other Chief Ministers of those days was, perhaps, due to this direct relationship. This relationship got spoilt only in the last few years, when he came into conflict with the Prime Minister's hand-picked boss of Bombay, Rajni Patel. But that was in keeping with the scheme of things as they developed. Even Rajni Patel lost his importance soon, a few weeks before the Congress suffered its debacle at the hustings in March 1977.

At the meeting in the Central Hall of Parliament on January 19, 1966, Morarji Desai was trounced, as was expected, by more than double the number of votes he got. Was it some kind of premonition of the shape of things to come or was it the method adopted by the party bosses that prompted Morarji Desai even at that time to strike a note of warning in his speech congratulating Indira Gandhi? He hoped that in future, at any rate, 'an atmosphere of fearlessness would be cultivated in the party and the country'. How prophetic were his words, although at that time they seemed to be rather uncharitable and directed against those who had got Indira elected! A day earlier his attack was more forthright. In his appeal to M.P.s, he had said: 'Those who, by virtue of their positions had a special responsibility to be above personal prejudices and animus, seem to have decided that the search for unanimity should mean the elimination of all those whom they do not like.'

Morarji Desai further stated: 'I have been greatly distressed to see how all kinds of unhealthy precedents are being set up to claim unanimous support for the choice of a few people who are in positions of authority.'

Kamaraj declined to comment on this direct attack on his methods. Atulya Ghosh, the boss of West Bengal, and D. P. Mishra, the main political adviser of Indira Gandhi at that time, described Morarji's statement as an 'insult' to Members of Parliament. They said it was a 'reflection on them' to suggest that they were being pressurized by those in the organization or by the Chief Ministers. But that was exactly what had happened. Indira Gandhi's assumption of power had been inauspicious. It is an irony of fate that the people, whom Morarji denounced on that occasion, were the ones with whom he was forced to make common cause not too long after in their combined fight against Indira Gandhi's steady consolidation of power and authority in herself, both in the Government as well as in the party.

Within hours of her election as the new leader of the Congress Parliamentary Party, Indira realized that she was not her own master. She had hardly any say in the formation of her Cabinet and the distribution of important portfolios. They had already been decided for her by the party bosses who had engineered her election. They, however, allowed her to take into her Cabinet Jagjivan Ram, who had remained out of power for nearly three years under the Kamaraj Plan. She also invited Fakhruddin Ali Ahmed, at that time Finance Minister of Assam, to join the Central Cabinet. The portfolios given to them were hardly commensurate with their standing in the party. But they came, for she needed loyal friends, surrounded as she was by those who were not of her choice but of those who wanted to dominate her.

Asoka Mehta was another confidant, mainly on economic policy, and was given the Planning portfolio. Dinesh Singh moved into the limelight at that point. The Prime Minister took the oath of office along with her Cabinet colleagues on January 24. Three days later a Presidential order said that the Prime Minister, who also held charge of External Affairs, would 'assign such functions as she may' to the Minister of State for External Affairs, who was none other than Dinesh Singh.

These last two appointments did not find favour with the party leaders, who felt that there was, behind these appointments, an element of defiance in Indira Gandhi. For the time being they slept over it, waiting for the right opportunity to strike back. It came within a few months. Asoka Mehta, as Deputy Chairman of the Planning Commission in Lal Bahadur Shastri's Government, had a note prepared strongly advocating drastic devaluation of the rupee in keeping with the persistent advice of the World Bank to the Government of India. He had the support of C. Subramaniam. He wanted it to be considered by Lal Bahadur Shastri soon after the then

Finance Minister T. T. Krishnamachari had left his Cabinet. The vacancy was filled by an unknown entity called Sachin Chowdhary on the recommendation of Atulya Ghosh. But Shastri was on the point of leaving for Tashkent and suggested that he would consider the whole issue on his return. Unfortunately, he died and the succession battle diverted attention to the more immediate political problems.

By June the Government of Indira Gandhi seemed to have settled down. Asoka Mehta, now a full member of the Cabinet, put forward his proposal. Indira had hardly any grounding on economic matters and, therefore, consulted some of the ministers in her Cabinet holding economic portfolios. The only Minister who vehemently opposed the move for rupee devaluation was the then Commerce Minister Mahubhai Shah. It was a total victory for the western lobby in the Government when, on June 5, the Government announced devaluation of the rupee by 36.5 per cent. This was done without any prior consultation with either Kamaraj or any other party leader.

Kamaraj was so incensed that he came out publicly against the Government's decision. Thus a gulf was created between Kamaraj and Indira. Till then they were supposed to be working in close concert. Although Indira realized within a few months that the devaluation was a very unpopular decision and perhaps a mistake, she never excused Kamaraj for publicly denouncing her Government's decision.

Meanwhile, Opposition was building up a tempo of political agitation — a common practice in the last year before a general election. Late in October an anti-cow slaughter demonstration outside Parliament House turned violent. Some of the processionists tried to set fire to some vehicles and buildings on and around Parliament Street. Attempts were also made to set fire to Kamaraj's house on Jantar Mantar Road. He barely escaped from the angry crowd by the skin of his teeth. The police had to use considerable force to bring the situation under control and the docile Home Minister Gulzarilal Nanda took the entire blame on himself and resigned from the Cabinet on November 9, to be succeeded by Y. B. Chavan. Simultaneously, the Education Minister M. C. Chagla was shifted to External Affairs which had been under the Prime Minister's direct charge. And in this reshuffle Fakhruddin Ali Ahmed was shifted to the Education Ministry. These changes, too, were not to the liking of the political bosses, who were seething with rage and waiting for an opportunity to hit back.

As the general elections, due in February 1967, approached, Indira Gandhi realized her major weakness. The party purse strings were in the hands of people who had no love lost for her. On the contrary, they had ganged up to ensure that she did not have a solid group of her own in the new party. But they had no intention of throwing her out at that moment, because she alone could have kept Morarji away from power. Each one of the State bosses was known to have collected huge amounts for the elections, but the coffers of the party were empty. Indira also realized that even though she headed the Government, businessmen and industrialists went to people like S. K. Patil, C. B. Gupta, Atulya Ghosh and their proteges in her Cabinet to make policy deals in exchange for election funds. She was still too new to the game. It was to make it difficult for these people to openly collect funds, the way they had been doing so far, that she pressed for a ban on company donations to political parties. The proposal was first placed before the Congress Working Committee. Apart from further annoying the party bosses, nothing much could be achieved at that time.

In the selection of party candidates also she found herself being outmanoeuvred. The party bosses had a clear majority in the Central Election Committee of the Congress. Moreover, they also dominated their respective State Election Committees. Thus, even the recommendations from below were hardly in her favour. No one at that moment either took the Opposition challenge seriously or considered it necessary to go to the people. The mood of the party managers was one of supreme confidence and complacency. They never expected that almost all of them would be defeated in the Parliamentary elections and, for the first time, the party would come with just a bare majority at the Centre and lose almost half the States to Opposition coalitions. All of them had lost the mass appeal they might have enjoyed once. S. K. Patil, who was known for long as the uncrowned king of Bombay, was trounced in South Bombay constituency by a young and budding trade unionist, George Fernandes. This giant-killer was later to become the main target of Indira Gandhi's wrath against all those who opposed her during her last few years in power.

At that time, however, she alone of all the Congress leaders was able to attract crowds, to influence them and to get votes for the Congress. Being Nehru's daughter proved an advantage. On top of it she had the necessary stamina to undertake a hurricane tour of the whole country for electioneering. Of course, she bypassed the constituencies of most of the senior leaders. But in the eyes of the people at large she had arisen as a charismatic leader on the Indian scene. She had carried the party to a marginal victory in Parliament singlehanded against heavy odds.

The defeats suffered by almost all the older leaders was indictment enough of their way of functioning. The greatest surprise came from Tamil Nadu where Kamaraj, the national Goliath, was humbled by a mere college student. Also humbled were his cronies like S. K. Patil and Atulya Ghosh. N. Sanjiva Reddy was the only one among the old bosses to return to Parliament. The 'Syndicate' had lost much of their prestige in the party. But they still occupied important positions in the organization. The party itself had been badly mauled in most States. If it retained a working majority at the Centre, it was mainly due to Indira Gandhi's personal appeal for the people. In a House of 521, the Congress strength had been reduced to a mere 281.

The only other leader who had returned with his prestige intact was her arch rival, Morarji Desai. Once again, he staked his claim for the leadership of the party.

Though defeated at the hustings, the party bosses had not lost their effectiveness to manipulate party affairs. They had had a foretaste of Indira's efforts to be free from their domination in the one year she had been the Prime Minister. While Kamaraj still preferred her to Morarji, and in a confrontation was determined to see that she won, a new conspiracy was hatched at S. K. Patil's initiative to clip Indira's wings by inducting Morarji as an alternative centre of power in the Central Cabinet. A deal was struck with him, through the good offices of the U.P. leader C. B. Gupta that Morarji would be the Deputy Prime Minister in charge of Finance to checkmate any attempts by Indira to project a radical or popular image of herself.

Thus began a strange association between Morarji Desai and those who comprised the 'Syndicate'. Till then he had been totally opposed to what he often described as the politics of manipulation of those party bosses. Kamaraj could never really reconcile himself to associating so closely with him. But he had no choice, for all the others in the 'Syndicate' were in favour of such co-operation in order to keep Indira Gandhi under restraint. Indira also was too helpless to oppose this new link-up between Morarji Desai and the party bosses.

At this juncture she secured the services of Parmeshwar Nath Haksar as the Principal Secretary to the Prime Minister. A direct recruit to the Foreign Service at the dawn of independence, Parmeshwar Nath had a leftist background from his early days at Allahabad where he had first come in contact with Nehru. Nehru persuaded this bright young intellectual to join the newly constituted Foreign Service. During the next three decades he held some very important diplomatic and administrative posts and discharged his duties with distinction.

When Indira became Prime Minister, Haksar was our Acting High Commissioner in London. Her choice for the head of the Prime Minister's secretariat fell on this brilliant direct recruit to the Foreign Service to the chagrin of most senior civil servants in the Central Secretariat. There was tremendous hostility to Haksar's appointment in the beginning. But within a few months he had established his authority and earned the respect of his colleagues in other Ministries. In due course, he became one of the most able and powerful civil servants who also exercised considerable political authority indirectly.

It was his advice — perhaps the first on a political issue — to the Prime Minister to convert her fight with the party bosses into an ideological one. He apparently convinced her that she was no match to them in the politics of manipulation, but that she could definitely exploit their defeat at the hustings to her advantage by giving a radical orientation to her Government's economic programme.

Kamaraj himself preferred a radical programme of socio-economic change. But he gave precedence to his personal loyalty to his friends and colleagues, most of whom were not very enamoured of socialist slogans. They hoped to use a rigid and at that time apparently conservative Morarji to thwart any attempts by Indira to shift towards greater State control in economic planning — an anethema to their friends and financiers in the industrial world. Indira's first test was over and she had come out of it with flying colours only to face a stiffer challenge in the years to come.

CHAPTER III

STRUGGLE FOR POWER
(March 1967 to January 1969)

SOON after the fourth general elections an intense power struggle began within the Congress Party between Indira Gandhi and a young band of radicals who had returned to the Lok Sabha on the one side, and the defeated party bosses who knew that their survival depended on somehow retaining positions of influence in the party on the other. These bosses had come to be derisively described, particularly in some of the leftist journals in the country, as the 'Syndicate'. Despite their resentment, this name stuck to them until they were squeezed out in an open split in the party two years later. It is interesting to know, in the words of some of the 'Syndicate' members themselves, how and when this combination came into being and what were its objectives. Writing an introduction in 1970 to a booklet by Atulya Ghosh on the split in the party, S. Nijalingappa, the then Congress President, vehemently asserted that 'the members of the so-called "Syndicate" never worked to get themselves into positions of power; they never wished to become Ministers at the Centre or elsewhere'.

Describing how and when the 'Syndicate' came into being, he wrote:

'If the beginning of the "Syndicate" is to be reckoned from the meeting at Tirupati Hill in 1963, those who had gathered there wanted to decide who should be the next President of the Congress. We decided at that time that Shri Kamaraj should be the next Congress President. One of the members who took this decision was Shrinivas Maliah who was at that time a close associate of Nehru and was the General Secretary of the Congress during Panditji's (as Nehru was referred to in those days) presidentship. At that time and in that meeting we considered it desirable that as Nehru was getting old, Lal Bahadur Shastri should succeed him as the Prime Minister. Our opinions regarding Kamaraj as A.I.C.C. President and Lal Bahadur Shastri as the Prime Minister of India were later accepted without much opposition. Even after Shastri's death the very same people were mainly responsible for having Shrimati Gandhi accepted as Prime Minister.'

This extract from the writing of an authoritative member of the 'Syndicate' is proof enough of the coming into being at the time of Nehru's last few days of a powerful caucus in the organization which wanted to determine and dominate the future power pattern in India. Its members, according to Atulya Ghosh, were S. Nijalingappa of Karnataka, N. Sanjiva Reddy of Andhra Pradesh, the late U. S. Maliah, a member of the Congress Parliamentary Party from Mysore, S. K. Patil from Bombay, Atulya Ghosh himself from West Bengal and Kamaraj from Tamil Nadu. It was no accident that there was no representation from the Hindi-speaking states. It is also true that there were some ideological differences among those people, because some of them, like Atulya Ghosh and Kamaraj, had welcomed radical moves like ending of privy purses and privileges of princes and nationalization of banks much before Indira used them as effective instruments in her power struggle with these very party bosses. Others, like S. K. Patil and Nijalingappa, were totally opposed to such moves. What was common among the 'Syndicate' members was their loyalty to each other which transcended ideological differences, for each of them had come to control the party machine in his respective state through identical process of elimination of all dissent and now they had combined to control power at the Centre knowing that the towering personality of Jawaharlal was shortly to leave them for ever.

As Atulya Ghosh very rightly points out in his booklet, Morarji was never a part of this 'Syndicate'. But he was a strong leader in his own right, rigid, conservative, inflexible and far from the so-called radicals. He had his own associates like Chandra Bhanu Gupta of Uttar Pradesh. Unlike the 'Syndicate' leaders, he never compromised on what he considered right and moral. This kind of rigidity was anethema to the 'Syndicate'. But they shrewdly decided, at the initiative of S. K. Patil and through the good offices of C. B. Gupta, to enlist Morarji's services as Deputy Prime Minister and Finance Minister after the 1967 elections to checkmate Indira's radical posture which, they felt, was assumed only to denigrate them in the public eye. It suited Morarji admirably. He seldom raised his little finger to help either side in its personal power struggle, unless it helped him to project his own image of impartiality, judging all issues on merits. In the Government he often obstructed radical policy decisions which he felt were meant only for dramatic impact. He was thus able to resist successfully all attempts to implement the ten-point economic programme adopted at the Delhi Session of the All India Congress Committee in May 1967.

There was an insistent demand from the Prime Minister's side in the Working Committee on the eve of this session for adoption of nationalization of banks and general insurance as the main plank of the economic programme. But Morarji was able to prevent it with the help of S. K. Patil and others of the 'Syndicate'. Instead, he offered a compromise that they should first try, for at least two years, 'social control of banking institutions to achieve the socio-economic ends that were supposed to be achieved through nationalization. Since he was able to prevent a decision on bank nationalization, he gave in on nationalization of general insurance as soon as feasible. The economic programme also called upon the Government to undertake State trading in exports and imports.

On the face of it the programme appeared quite radical. But everyone knew that on the main issue of bank nationalization the Prime Minister had had to give in. This was also reflected in the speeches in the open session of the A.I.C.C., most of which were very critical of the Working Committee's decision. Even Indira had occasion to remark about the obstructive tactics of the old leadership. This session was, however, transformed at the fag end into a great victory for the radicals who had lined up behind Indira Gandhi when Mohan Dharia, a young socialist from Maharashtra, flung a resolution on the tired and half-sleepy audience committing the Congress to abolition of privy purses and privileges of princes. The party leaders, only half of whom were present at the meeting at that moment, were taken completely by surprise. The resolution was carried by a majority and one had a public exposure of those in the leadership who had been opposing such radical measures. For once, senior leaders like Morarji Desai, S. K. Patil and others were forced to vote on the losing side. Y. B. Chavan, who was sitting among the delegates and could have prevented such a show-down, remained neutral.

Although both Kamaraj and Atulya Ghosh had long been votaries of this proposal, the whole 'Syndicate' was furious at the way they had been made a laughing stock in public so soon after they were forced to accept Dr. Zakir Hussain as the Congress candidate for the presidentship of India as against a second term for Dr. Radhakrishnan, to whom Kamaraj was apparently committed. Morarji Desai and his group, too, were far from happy at the turn of events both in the open session and in the Party's Parliamentary Board where Indira had precipitated a division on Dr. Zakir Hussain's candidature. There was a division on the latter issue in the Syndicate itself — Atulya Ghosh, on his own admission, voting with Indira Gandhi, Y. B. Chavan, Jagjivan Ram and Fakhruddin Ali Ahmed in favour of Dr. Zakir Hussain, while Kamaraj, S. K. Patil and Morarji Desai favouring a second term for Dr. Radhakrishnan. It was made out in public, however, as a major tactical victory for Indira over the party bosses. This kind of propaganda warfare, at which she soon became a past master, annoyed the 'Syndicate' much more than the selection of Dr. Zakir Hussain. They felt, perhaps rightly, that the whole operation was intended to humiliate them publicly. The 'Syndicate' also felt let down by Y. B. Chavan, a member of the Working Committee, who had remained quiet and neutral when his protege from Maharashtra, Mohan Dharia, sprung the resolution on abolition of privy purses on a tired A.I.C.C.

It has often been argued that Y. B. Chavan himself wanted to project a radical image of his own. As Home Minister he would have had to implement the A.I.C.C. decision. If it went through, he hoped to earn the credit. If it failed, the responsibility could always be shifted on to the Prime Minister. But Indira Gandhi proved a far superior tactician, taking all the credit for both the moves during which the 'Syndicate' had found itself on the wrong foot. The radical group headed by Indira projected these successes as victories for secularism and socialism. The implication was that the 'Syndicate' was reactionary and non-secular. The tacticians on the Prime Minister's side knew that, in a political fight, what really mattered was what the people believed, not what had actually transpired. And it was pretty clear after the Delhi Session of the A.I.C.C. that the people were convinced by and large that Indira did want to bring about certain socio-economic changes. But she was being prevented by the older party bosses determined to perpetuate their own influence and power in the organization. This had become all the more necessary to them for their survival after their defeat in the elections.

An important factor that helped Indira Gandhi to project herself as a dynamic leader with a following of her own was that a large number of young socialists, who had come into the Congress both from the Communist Party of India and the now defunct Praja Socialist Party, had, from 1962 onwards, collected around her in the party. After the elections the P.S.P. group, comprising Chandra Shekhar, Mohan Dharia, Krishna Kant and some others who had come into the Congress along with Asoka Mehta, was the more active both in the Parliamentary Party as well as in the A.I.C.C. Indira's first confrontation with the 'Syndicate' after her re-election as the leader of the Parliamentary Party was at the Delhi Session of A.I.C.C., where this group was the most active in her support. But another group of leftists, with past Communist connections, was gradually organizing itself along with some avowedly pro-Soviet members in the Congress Party itself to ultimately assume the role of the main champions of Indira Gandhi. For the time being, all the leftists, who had all come into the Congress almost at the same time, had come together under Indira's leadership to act as a pressure group for accelerated socio-economic change in the country. She was accepted as their leader in their fight against the reactionaries in the Congress, which included the then Deputy Prime Minister Morarji Desai and the members of the Syndicate. Inside Parliament, the attack was mainly directed against Morarji. He retaliated by capturing a majority in the Executive of the Parliamentary Party. It became the main forum of attack on the Prime Minister and her policies. Despite that the leftists, though small in number, appeared more active in the party. Whenever there was an attack on the Prime Minister and her policies in the executive, some kind of a counter-attack was organized by the leftists either through a signature campaign or by the mere issuing of statements.

It is also interesting to note that about this time, certain individuals assumed importance far beyond their years in the party. The most prominent among such individuals was Dinesh Singh who soon shot up from the position of a Minister of State to that of a Minister of full Cabinet rank heading the Ministry of Foreign Trade. It was not the ministry that was important, but his proximity to the Prime Minister and his role as the political fixer and the main hatchet-man for her. His rise to power had been so spectacular and sudden that he became the target of many a slanderous attack, which did not reflect too well on the Prime Minister either. Dinesh Singh was no leftist. In fact, when the question of the abolition of privy purses came up in the party for implementation as a directive from the A.I.C.C., he organized, with the help of his friend and follower Bhanupratap Singh of Narsingarh an opposition within the ruling party against such a move. This gave the leftists in the party an opportunity to start a campaign against Dinesh himself as a reactionary and the leader of a group of privileged people who had wormed their way into the confidence of the Prime Minister. Although Dinesh continued to be important and wielded considerable power in the party for some more time as the youngest Minister for External Affairs, from all accounts this was also the beginning of the end of Dinesh Singh as the main adviser and the head of what was known in those days as the 'Kitchen Cabinet' of Indira Gandhi. He had become too ambitious.

Parameshwar Nath Haksar, Principal Secretary to the Prime Minister, who had also come almost at this time as an important adviser of the Prime Minister among all the officials, was the first one to realize that Dinesh did not have the qualities for the type of political responsibility that had been thrust upon him because of his proximity to Indira. Others, who had started as the main pillars of her strength like Y. B. Chavan, Asoka Mehta, C. Subramaniam along with Dinesh Singh, were gradually pushed to the background partly because of her reluctance to take anyone except Dinesh into confidence and partly because the latter himself started sowing seeds of suspicion about these people in her mind so as to gain her total confidence. All this was possible because she preferred not have direct dialogue with her colleagues. Instead, she depended on Dinesh Singh at this time to be her emissary to her senior colleagues. This was resented particularly by those who had been her greatest supporters at the time of her fight with Morarji in 1966, and who expected her to repose confidence in their loyalty to her. Dinesh saw to it that no such equation should develop for them.

Lack of direct communication also affected her relations with the so-called radicals in the party who had lined up behind her but had hardly any direct access to her. Inder Gujral, who had organized these young radicals into what had come to be known as 'Back Benchers' Club and who had now become a Deputy Minister and an important camp follower of Dinesh, was utilized to keep the radicals in line. But Gujral's proximity to Dinesh was also affecting his own standing with other leaders. Another factor that was gradually dividing the ranks of the radicals in Parliament as well as in the organization, was the suspicion that had grown between those who had originally belonged to the Socialist Party and those who, at one time or the other, had been either cardholding communists or fellow-travellers. This mutual suspicion remained below the surface for some time. It came into the open when rumours were set afloat that the former socialists among the radicals owed allegiance to Y. B. Chavan rather than to Indira Gandhi.

Moreover, the so-called former communists found in the Prime Minister's Principal Secretary a kindred spirit and rallied round him to get near the seat of power. A cleavage, along sharp ideological lines, thus developed between the young radicals having different backgrounds. It became wider in about a year's time when the Back Benchers' Club became part of the Socialist Forum. The Forum was originally started by the former Home Minister Gulzarilal Nanda with the help of his confidant and Deputy, Lalit Narayan Mishra, to bolster Indira Gandhi's image as a radical leader. Soon the radicals made common cause with Lalit Narayan and managed to isolate all those among them who either owed loyalty to some other leader or had had a Congress Socialist past.

Dinesh, never very happy with the methods adopted by the former Communists and Haksar's growing influence among them, thus came closer to radicals like Chandra Shekhar. Y. B. Chavan, too, extended his patronage to people like Mohan Dharia. These were strong links which prevented the so-called former communists in the Socialist Forum from completely squeezing out the former Socialists who themselves were no mean organizers. They soon made their presence felt when Chandra Shekhar got elected as General Secretary of the Parliamentary Party and their group secured sizable representation in the Party Executive. Indira Gandhi's well-known prejudice against this group had its beginning from this time although they, too, were to play a very significant role in her fight with the 'Syndicate' on the eve of the split in 1969.

All these developments in a way helped her to give her fight with the party bosses a further radical aura. The Jabalpur Session of the All India Congress Committee was fast approaching and she was advised to make an issue of bank nationalization on the policy plane and also insist on the replacement of Kamaraj as Congress President on the principle that anyone defeated in an election should not hold this high party post. Whoever were her advisers at this time — Haksar and Dwarka Prasad Mishra topped the list — knew that the rank and file were in tune with her way of thinking and would go all out to support her in any radical stance she took against the bosses. The speeches at the A.I.C.C. Session more than proved it. But the party bosses were in no mood to surrender on either score. On the question of bank nationalization they lined up behind Morarji Desai who got his scheme of social control of banks accepted, even if it was only on a trial basis for a period of two years. The majority in the Working Committee agreed with him and therefore Indira Gandhi had to relent on this issue.

On the question of having a new President at the next Congress Session, there could be no dispute on the principle, already accepted, that a leader defeated in the polls should not hold this exalted party office. It also ruled out leaders like S. K. Patil and Atulya Ghosh who, too, had lost their seats in Parliament in the last general election. The party bosses therefore saw to it that there was no consensus on any other name to succeed Kamaraj. The idea seemed to be to ultimately force a *status quo*. Policy-wise the session was a clear victory for Morarji although the general run of speeches in the open session was in favour of bank nationalization. On the question of party presidentship, Indira had a partial victory insofar as she was able to make the party bosses commit themselves to a principle. But she and her advisers knew that the 'Syndicate' would try their level best to thwart any attempt to install a Congress President who did not have their confidence and approval. The question was left undecided at Jabalpur and the next two and a half months witnessed a terrific power struggle in which no holds were barred and which, in retrospect, appears as a dress rehearsal of the great fight that was to follow leading to the historic split in the party and emergence of Indira as the unquestioned leader of the Congress from 1969 onwards.

Morarji's social control of banking institutions remained a phrase on paper. No one could clearly understand what was meant by it and how it was to be implemented. But the possibility of an early nationalization of banks had been nullified. There was some disappointment in the rank and file and the circles close to the Prime Minister felt thwarted and disheartened. They also perceived for the first time very clearly that although Morarji was not a part of the 'Syndicate', he was at the head of a group of another set of party stalwarts who were totally opposed to radical experimentation with the economy because they feared it would inevitably lead to increasing Soviet influence in the country. It also became clear that in an open showdown, this group and the 'Syndicate' would come together, despite Kamaraj's personal antipathy to Morarji. Even so, Indira was determined to see that Kamaraj, who had had a term of nearly four years, stepped down from the party post. It was an irony of fate that the very man, who had made her, had now himself become her main target.

As soon as the leaders returned from Jabalpur, search began for the next Congress President. The name of the former Home Minister Gulzarilal Nanda was floated from the Prime Minister's side. The other side matched it with the name of the strong and dynamic Chief Minister of Rajasthan, Mohanlal Sukhadia. He had managed to bring the Congress back to power in his state after a spell of political instability. Other states were also suffering from similar instability. Short-lived coalitions of desperate groups pulling against one another was the order of the day as the Congress had been reduced to a minority in the last elections. Even in states like Madhya Pradesh and Haryana, where the Congress had a marginal majority, its governments were soon toppled through indisciplined floor-crossings. In some states the same individuals changed sides more than once for purely personal gains in terms of money or temporary power which gave them an opportunity to amass wealth. Corruption became so rampant even among the Opposition groups that the people felt disgusted with continuing instability and politics of opportunism. This was not the alternative to the Congress they had voted for. The moment floor-crossings started in Madhya Pradesh, the shrewd Chief Minister of that state, D. P. Mishra, convinced the Centre that the only way to stop such indisciplined defections was to dissolve the Assembly, put the state under a short spell of President's rule and then hold fresh elections. There was a big controversy on at that time as to whether a Chief Minister, who found his party being reduced to a minority, had a right to recommend to the Governor that the Assembly should be dissolved and fresh elections held without first testing his strength on the floor of the House. The Opposition maintained that a Chief Minister, who had lost his majority, had no right to make such a recommendation and even if he did so, the Governor was not bound by his advice. The Congress, however, maintained that a Chief Minister who had a majority and who found this majority being converted into a minority through indisciplined defections, had the right to demand a fresh opportunity to seek the mandate of the people without facing the Assembly whose character had already been changed by floor-crossings. This was the basis on which D. P. Mishra was allowed to recommend dissolution of the

Madhya Pradesh Assembly and a short spell of President's rule to be followed by fresh elections.

The Central leaders decided against Sukhadia's nomination as the next party chief, because the Congress did not have a very comfortable majority in the Rajasthan Assembly and it was only his astuteness that had kept the party government going. His removal from Rajasthan, it was feared, might have led to the fall of that government. There was no other name on which a consensus seemed possible. The Syndicate leaders hoped that ultimately Indira might relent in favour of Kamaraj, who had been a very successful Party President. It was also argued that since all other important posts had gone to the north, it was but fair that the party post should remain with somebody from the south. Even if Kamaraj had to go, they wanted somebody from the south to take his place. This suggestion was perhaps made in the hope that the 'Syndicate' would then be able to sponsor S. Nijalingappa, Chief Minister of Karnataka. Nijalingappa himself was not very keen to give up the Chief Ministership for the party post and rejected all such overtures of his friends.

By late November, Indira and her advisers realized that she would not be able to have the next Congress President of her choice. It was therefore decided to adopt Nijalingappa as her candidate in a gesture of magnanimity. The strategy was worked out with great precision and secrecy lest Kamaraj got to know of it earlier than they had planned. Nijalingappa, who was in New Delhi at that time, was dining one evening with the British High Commissioner, when a frantic message reached him that the Prime Minister would like to talk to him as soon as he could reach her residence. The Mysore Chief Minister reached the Prime Minister's house about eleven at night and was with her for about 45 minutes, during which she almost persuaded him to take over the party presidentship. According to Nijalingappa's statement later while he agreed to her request, he wanted a formal announcement to be withheld until he had had discussions with Kamaraj next morning. Instead both he and Kamaraj were surprised to see screaming headlines in the morning newspapers indicating that Indira had persuaded Nijalingappa to give up the Chief Ministership of Mysore to take over the presidentship of the Congress. The news dispatches gave the general impression that Kamaraj was not very keen on the change, and it was Indira who had in fact broken the impasse by selecting somebody who was known to be a member of the 'Syndicate'. The fact of the matter was that S. K. Patil had persuaded

Kamaraj and Indira to accept Nijalingappa in case agreement on any other name was found difficult. The way the Prime Minister's camp tried to take credit for something, which could not possibly be described as a victory for them, annoyed not only the 'Syndicate' but made Nijalingappa hostile to Indira even before he had taken over the party post. Although he was elected President of the Congress unanimously on December 7, 1967, the Prime Minister's camp had serious misgivings which were proved right not very long after at the Congress Session at Hyderabad on January 8, 1968.

In his very first address as the party chief, Nijalingappa talked of "the lack of clarity about our objectives" and called for some reforms in administrative and economic fields. He came out openly against gigantic industries, particularly in the state sector, and urged greater attention to be paid to seeking a break-through in agriculture through more irrigation. He also advocated a reorientation of the Government's economic policies in order to shift the emphasis to agro-industries. This had been the line long advocated by institutions like the World Bank and certain American economic experts who did not approve of India's policy of 'the commanding heights of the economy remaining in the hands of the state'. The tone of Nijalingappa's address was taken as the first shot in the power struggle that was to develop later in the year between Indira Gandhi at the head of the radicals in the party and the party bosses who were totally opposed to any radicalization of Indian politics.

More than policies it was personal power of certain individuals in the party that was really at stake. This was also the time when India was moving closer to the Soviet Union. India's dependence for her military hardware on that country was well known. The two had become major trading partners and often had identical stance on international political issues. The leaders of the Soviet Union had taken increasing interest in the emergence of Nehru's daughter as the new leader of this country and hoped to continue the same kind of cordial relations which existed between the two countries during Nehru's time. They had no doubt that so long as Indira relied on radical economic policies inside the country and maintained a strictly non-aligned stance in her international relations, she would always be of help to the Russians in their polemics with the Chinese who had been continuing a long dialogue with the Americans for ultimate recognition and normalization of relations. The Soviet Union's increasing cultivation of India and the efforts of the Americans and the Chinese to move towards normalization of their mutual relations which had been in deep freeze for almost two decades went on almost simultaneously and on parallel lines. Some of the party bosses, including Morarji Desai and Nijalingappa, were far from being happy with these developments. They somehow wanted to put a stop to the radicalization of politics internally and to India's further drift towards the Soviet Union externally. They feared otherwise an inevitable march towards totalitarianism.

The Hyderabad Session of the Congress thus marked the beginning of the ideological conflict that developed into a fierce fight in the subsequent months. The elections to the Working Committee at this session proved that the party bosses, in combination with Morarji Desai, had a complete hold on the A.I.C.C. Indira found her own nominees for the Working Committee, including Gulzarilal Nanda and D. Sanjivayya, being dropped in preference to nominees of the 'Syndicate'. She was thus reduced to a minority in the highest executive of the party.

In April, Nijalingappa struck the second blow when he made a statement at a luncheon meeting at the Press Club of India in New Delhi that 'if it became necessary in the interests of the country, the Congress would enter into a coalition with like-minded democratic parties at the Centre'. It was something uncalled for particularly from the head of the organization. Nijalingappa was known to have had talks with leaders of the Jana Sangh and the Swantantra Party about this time, presumably, on the possibility of such a coalition at the Centre. But the statement itself was most embarrassing to the Government enjoying a clear majority in Parliament. Nijalingappa had also threatened at that meeting that 'Congressmen who did not respect the ideals of the party would be removed from it'. It was widely interpreted as a warning to Indira herself. Both she and Deputy Prime Minister Morarji Desai, who was not with the 'Syndicate' on these issues, rejected the idea of a coalition government at the Centre. Indira retaliated by accusing Nijalingappa of encouraging defections and toppling of state governments by such statements. Describing it as 'the phase of degenerate politics', she disclosed how it had led to the fall of 14 governments, both Congress and non-Congress, within one year. Uttar Pradesh, Haryana and Madhya Pradesh had to be put under President's rule. It was after the mid-term election in Haryana in May 1968, that Bansi Lal, a young protege of Gulzarilal Nanda and Lalit Narayan Mishra from their Bharat Sevak Samaj days, was selected to be the Chief Minister.

By this time Lalit Narayan Mishra had gained the confidence of Indira Gandhi. He was a member of her Council of Ministers and when a search started for a dynamic and young candidate for Haryana's Chief Ministership, Lalit suggested the name of the forty-year old Bansi Lal, at that time a rather unknown member of the Rajya Sabha. The Prime Minister accepted the suggestion immediately. That launched the most successful but ruthless leader of Haryana into one of the most prosperous states of India. He had got things done, such as electrification of all villages in the state, within record time. No respector of human dignity, he abused, threatened and changed civil servants over the telephone, if what he wanted was not done immediately. He outdid even the famous builder of Punjab, Pratap Singh Kairon. And Bansi Lal did show results, but at what a cost! A mild soft-spoken member of Parliament had turned into a ruthless, authoritarian Chief Minister who believed in all dissenters being forced to conform. He seemed to have developed a strong allergy to newspapers and gave an indication of what he could do to them during his conflict with *The Tribune*. He cut off all its Government advertising and ordered a ban on its circulation among officials of his state. As the originator of the idea of clamping total emergency during the last two years of Indira Gandhi's rule, it was he who worked out the plans to control the mass media, perhaps based on his experience in dealing with newspapers as the Chief Minister. Vidya Charan Shukla was only the hatchet-man who implemented that policy with the assistance of two police officers of the Intelligence Bureau, appointed to senior civil service posts in the Ministry of Information and Broadcasting. When Bansi Lal took over as the Chief Minister of Haryana, he pledged total loyalty to Indira personally and was ever ready to perform any function, however unpleasant, on her behalf. At that time he was just one more Chief Minister of her choice, whom she had placed in that position despite stiff opposition of some senior leaders in the party including her Deputy Prime Minister Morarji Desai.

The relations between the Prime Minister and the organization leaders continued to deteriorate during the subsequent months. Within the Cabinet, too, suspicions grew between Indira Gandhi, on the one side, and Morarji Desai, on the other. Other senior Ministers, like Y. B. Chavan, also were not happy, but always came forward to support any progressive or radical policy measures suggested by the

Prime Minister. Chagla had already left the Cabinet and younger persons, like Dinesh Singh, Lalit Narayan Mishra and even Bali Ram Bhagat, had acquired importance and confidence of the Prime Minister. Dinesh was already a full Cabinet Minister. The other two were being groomed for more important positions.

Meanwhile, Kamaraj had gone back to Tamil Nadu to reorganize the Congress which had been so badly mauled during the 1967 elections. He was touring the state from village to village and had revived the spirits of the defeated party men. He was the only leader, apart from Indira Gandhi, who had maintained direct contact with the people in his state. He was also the only other leader in the Congress with a mass appeal all over the country, although it had been tarnished a little by his defeat in the 1967 elections. He was now rebuilding his base to re-emerge as an important national leader through a by-election to the Lok Sabha from Nagarcoil seat, which had recently fallen vacant. He won that seat, as was expected, with a big margin. Kamaraj had returned as the unquestioned leader of the Congress in Tamil Nadu and a force to contend with in the party at the national level.

The year 1968 was coming to an end. The tension in the party had increased. The Prime Minister succeeded in giving ideological overtones to her fight with the party bosses. Within her Cabinet it was reflected in the growth of two different centres of power, one around Indira and the other around Morarji, as had been planned by the 'Syndicate' leaders after the last election. She found herself obstructed at every step she took to implement the party's ten-point programme. Morarji Desai's plan of social control of banking institutions had remained on paper. There had been no progress whatsoever towards expediting land reforms. Even the ceiling laws on the statute books in many states had remained unimplemented. The executive of the Congress Parliamentary Party, dominated by Morarji's followers, became a forum of constant attack on the radicals in the party and on the radical policies of the Government. Often conflicts in the executive were exaggerated to attract screaming headlines in newspapers against the Prime Minister. The official spokesman's denials were immediately contradicted openly by important members of the executive, who did not see eye to eye with him or with the leader of the party. Discipline had become lax, and any action contemplated against any member assumed factional overtones.

Almost about this time a serious controversy developed in

Parliament and outside on the respective powers of Parliament and the Judiciary, and on whether Parliament was supreme or not. The controversy began some years earlier when, by a majority judgment, the Supreme Court held that Parliament had no right to amend any of the Fundamental Rights enshrined in the Constitution. This was done in the famous Golaknath case which involved the property rights of an individual. The judgment excited extreme reaction in Parliament and the late Nath Pai of the Praja Socialist Party brought forward a nonofficial Bill to restore Parliament's right to amend any part of the Constitution. It was ultimately adopted by the Government as an official Bill and passed in Parliament. Some in the Judiciary considered it as a serious encroachment on its right to interpret the law of the land. They did not agree that, in the process, the Judiciary might sometimes perform a legislative function, which was the right of Parliament alone. This conflict got further accentuated when the former Chief Justice of the Supreme Court, Subba Row, resigned to fight for the Presidentship of the country against Dr. Zakir Hussain. Many Opposition parties, particularly the Jana Sangh and the Swatantra Party, adopted him as their candidate.

The radicals in the Congress raised a hue and cry against the Judiciary for obstructing all socio-economic measures. They demanded that judges should be appointed, not by seniority alone but for their awareness of the socio-economic needs of the people. This was the time when the phrase 'committed judiciary' got wide currency, more as a weapon in the hands of the Opposition to browbeat the Government. Within the party, too, there was a section totally opposed to any move that might undermine the independence of the Judiciary in any way. So far nothing had been done by the Government to control and curb the Judiciary, but there was strong resentment in powerful circles at, what was described by someone close to the Prime Minister at that time as, the politicization of the Judiciary. It was considered very wrong on the part of some politicians to use the Judiciary for their political fight against the Government. Some in the Congress, too, had been influenced by this kind of propaganda. There was, however, no specific plan till then to interfere with the established norms of appointing judges to the Supreme Court and even to the High Courts. That came much later when one after the other some important radical measures like the bank nationalization and abolition of privy purses of former princes were struck down by the Supreme Court. It was then that the norm of the seniormost judge automatically succeeding the refiring Chief Justice was given up for other considerations. In a way, the very people who had raised their voice against having a committed Judiciary, when there was nothing like it, hastened in effect the process of wholesale curbing of the powers and independence of the Judiciary through comprehensive changes in the Constitution.

It was perhaps the result of a new philosophy which had developed in the ruling circle that people were more important than any institution and so if an institution stood in the way of the rapid socio-economic changes, necessary for the advancement of the people, then it should be restructured. Gradually — this argument was to cover even the Constitution as well. Who was the originator of this philosophy is immaterial, but it had the solid support of the radicals who derived their inspiration from the Soviet Union. It was a dangerous philosophy, for it provided a justification to Indira Gandhi and the ruling coterie around her when they started tinkering around with the very foundations of democracy for perpetuating their personal power. None realized that the difference between genuine indignation at being prevented from implementing socially just policies and the haughtiness of absolute power was subtle and could destroy all discrimination between right and wrong.

Another tendency about this time, which undermined the civil service on the one side and the political executive on the other, was to play favourites at the highest echelons of administration. Having been in power for long, some of the Congress Ministers had developed personal intimacy with certain officers to the detriment of the accepted norms of merit and seniority for qualifying for a particular job. Such officers usually shifted along with their Ministers, whether they were senior or qualified enough to hold the new jobs. Still more insidious was the practice to float rumours at the start and end of each session of Parliament of impending changes in the Cabinet. This kept everyone in the Government and in the party on tenter-hooks. It created sense of insecurity among the members of the Council of Ministers and encouraged a tendency among some of the more ambitious members in the party, wanting ministerial posts, to act as spies for people supposed to be enjoying the confidence of the Prime Minister. Over the years the practice became so sinister that even close friends avoided talking frankly to each other on political matters. A handful of young operators like Lalit Narayan Mishra and Yashpal Kapoor were fast acquiring undue importance in the power structure and were mainly responsible for this reprehensible development in the party. Mishra's influence in the Intelligence Services, too, had remained intact from his days as Deputy Home Minister under Gulzarilal Nanda and he had developed a close liaison with many a senior service officers in his capacity as Minister of State for Defence Production. He had his favourites among the civil service officers also and used them with consummate skill to keep himself informed about what went on in almost all the important Ministries.

Dinesh Singh was another who had cultivated a nucleus among the civil servants owing personal loyalty to him. He was the most important Cabinet Minister, for he had the total confidence of the Prime Minister or, at least, that was the impression he conveyed outside. In Parliament, too, he started organizing a group of his own, but he could not get over his caste and community affiliation and therefore failed miserably in his efforts. Besides, his sudden prominence and proximity to the seat of power also annoyed senior leaders like D. P. Mishra and Uma Shankar Dikshit who, too, enjoyed the confidence of Indira Gandhi. The resentment against Dinesh remained muted for the time being lest it was misunderstood as mere jealousy. But these leaders were determined to see that he did not stay long in that position. Another person who was not very enamoured of Dinesh was the Prime Minister's Principal Secretary. It was nothing personal. Only that P. N. Haksar was of the view, as stated already, that Dinesh lacked the calibre required to fulfil the responsibilities that flowed from the Prime Minister's confidence he enjoyed at that time. In spite of all this no one could prevent Dinesh's promotion in February 1969, to the prestigious External Affairs Ministry. He was India's youngest Foreign Minister ever, and, perhaps, that was also the reason why he failed to hold on to that exalted position for very long. The world arena in those days was far too complicated for him to be able to play an effective role. At home he had already annoyed almost all the senior colleagues by his accelerated promotions. It was therefore no surprise that many, who were totally loyal to the Prime Minister, ganged up to see the end of Dinesh Singh, which came in due course.

While Dinesh was at the height of his glory, his opponents combined to promote Lalit Narayan as a foil to him. Lalit's style was in total contrast to that of Dinesh, and he seldom showed any trace of arrogance that comes with power. On the contrary, he had a very pleasant way of worming his way into the hearts of people from all strata of society. One could find the lowest of the lowly and the mightiest of the mighty from the political or the industrial world flocking to his house to pay court. Each one of them received a courteous welcome and a precious minute with the Minister. Lalit's many good friends included newspapermen whom he cultivated assiduously. Such were some of the qualities that endeared this much-misunderstood personality on the Indian political scene of those days. Not many, perhaps, know the important role he played in bolstering a solid support for Indira Gandhi in the Parliamentary Party and the organization when she was openly challenged by the party bosses with expulsion from the primary membership of the Congress. But that is anticipating events which will be narrated in their proper sequence. A third individual who got all the opportunities at this time to be close to the Prime Minister, but failed to capitalize on them, was Bali Ram Bhagat. He worked as Minister of State for Foreign Affairs directly under the Prime Minister for some time before getting independent charge of the Ministry of Foreign Trade.

It is necessary to digress a little here. Every political party has needs for funds to run its organization and finance its candidates during election times. Ever since the Congress started fighting elections there had always been some individuals whose importance in the party was in direct proportion to their ability to collect funds. These collections, even when company donations were legal, were mostly unaccounted. The words of the individual collecting the funds sufficed in the olden days, when Sardar Patel or Rafi Ahmed Kidwai performed this essential function. In fact, soon after Sardar Patel's death, his daughter Maniben Patel handed over a comparatively huge sum to Nehru as party funds which were lying in Sardar Patel's safe. Nobody ever doubted the integrity of those stalwarts of independence struggle. When Kidwai died, his family hardly had anything to live on. Subsequently small bosses mushroomed all over the country and started collecting funds on their own. The most important among these were the Chief Ministers. Next in the line were influential Pradesh Congress Chiefs. For quite some time the owner of the *Express* empire, Ram Nath Goenka was the financier and collector of funds for the Congress until he broke away from Indira. Two important fund collectors of the sixties were S. K. Patil of Bombay and Chandra Bhanu Gupta of Uttar Pradesh. Since there was a proliferation of fund collectors in the party, accounting at one central point became almost impossible. Besides, some of these leaders had established direct rapport with important industrialists and could get any amount as *quid pro quo* for policy modifications affecting their business.

When Indira Gandhi's fight with the 'Syndicate' became serious, she found herself handicapped because of paucity of funds. Her friends among the big business got scared of her radical postures and her susceptibility to political pressure from the Soviet Union. Most of the industrialists, therefore, made common cause with the 'Syndicate' and Morarji to control and contain Indira, if they could not throw her out. It was at this time that Dinesh was made Foreign Trade Minister. But he lacked the necessary cunning to use his office to raise funds. He preferred to play the hatchet-man. The next to get this Ministry was Bali Ram Bhagat. But his performance, too, did not come up to the mark. If the position could be utilized to raise funds for Indira's politics, nobody would have bothered whether the individual concerned had also lined his own purse. But Bhagat failed and rumours started that he had done much better for himself than for the Prime Minister. Soon after he found himself out of the Government.

It was then that the name of Lalit Narayan Mishra was suggested to Indira. Among his godfathers at that time were D. P. Mishra and Uma Shankar Dikshit, both of whom exercised considerable influence at the Prime Minister's residence. So was set in motion what came to be known as the 'politics of big money' at which Lalit became a past master. His total involvement in this kind of politics of manipulation through money power led to his ultimate downfall and death. While he remained completely loyal to Indira Gandhi till the last, many of his detractors accused him of leading her to more and more dependence on the administrative machine to meet political challenges. Even a bureaucrat like P. N. Haksar warned her a number of times against such over-dependence on the civil service and the police. But, by then, Lalit had already got the support of a gang of three comprising Bansi Lal who was Chief Minister of Haryana, Yashpal Kapoor who had since been made a member of the Rajya Sabha from U.P., and R. K. Dhavan who had slipped into Kapoor's shoes as personal private secretary to the Prime Minister. These three were to wield unlimited powers during the Emergency along with Sanjay Gandhi. Lalit, too, had started cultivating Sanjay and helped him to raise the finances for his Maruti project. In fact, it was Lalit Narayan Mishra, who brought Sanjay and Bansi Lal together, when Sanjay was looking for land for his factory. Ever since Bansi Lal had exercised considerable influence on the Prime Minister's ambitious son.

It was about this time that Kamaraj returned to the Lok Sabha in a by-election. Despite his close association with the 'Syndicate', he never reconciled himself to policies that he thought were rightist and against the common people. He never wanted the fight with Indira to be fought on the ideological plane, for he believed the people would go with a charismatic leader like her who had also to offer a radical programme. D. P. Mishra, who was close enough to the Prime Minister at that time to give her advice on political matters, suggested to her that Kamaraj should be inducted into her Cabinet to neutralize Morarji and the 'Syndicate'. Indira agreed with this and made an offer to Kamaraj in February 1969, to join her Cabinet. This was the time she had elevated Dinesh Singh to the External Affairs Ministry and Lalit Narayan to Defence Production in a drastic reshuffle. Kamaraj wanted more time to consider her proposal; meanwhile he suggested to her to go ahead with her proposed reshuffle of the Cabinet. That, however, turned out to be the last of the proposal intended to create a cleavage among the members of the 'Syndicate'. The coming months saw one of the fiercest fight for survival in the Congress, and Indira Gandhi came out of it successfully as the most powerful and unquestioned leader of the organization.

CHAPTER IV

SPLIT IN THE CONGRESS
(February 1969 to December 1970)

FARIDABAD was the venue of the All India Congress Committee Session in April 1969. The dynamic Chief Minister of Haryana Bansi Lal had made elaborate arrangements for the comfort of the nearly 800 delegates. No effort was spared to entertain the large number of other visitors who commuted daily from Delhi to witness the beginning of the fight for supremacy between Indira Gandhi as the Prime Minister, on the one side, and almost all the senior party leaders, on the other. The first salvo was fired by the Congress President S. Nijalingappa. He openly attacked the economic and foreign policies of his own party's Government. It was an undisguised indictment of Indira Gandhi as an autocratic leader. She was accused of ignoring her colleagues in the Cabinet and the organization. The presidential address, unexpected as it was, electrified the customary placid atmosphere of an A.I.C.C. Session. Most of the delegates were incensed at this direct attack on their leader. Speeches after speeches accused the party bosses of perpetuating their own hold on the organization to the detriment of its popularity among the people.

All these speeches of the delegates had no impact on the impassive 'Syndicate' leaders, who sat unconcerned, until Indira herself came out with a scathing attack on the way the party bosses were functioning. While defending strongly her Government's policies, she expressed resentment at the implied suggestion that they were tilted in favour of the socialist countries, particularly the Soviet Union. Internally she had been accused of moving towards the communists. The session was dominated by this open conflict between the leader of the Government and the leader of the organization. While normally Kamaraj and Atulya Ghosh had always tried to identify themselves with her radical policies, for once they kept mum when Nijalingappa came up with a scathing attack on her radicalism.

But for a sudden fire, that broke out near the rostrum in the huge pandal owing to a short-circuit, the session would have ended on a still more bitter note. Some delegates felt that the fire had been intentionally started by someone to end this bitter controversy in public. The imputation seemed far-fetched at that time. But, in retrospect, it seems quite possible for a Chief Minister of Bansi Lal's style. If a twenty-four hours power cut to newspaper offices in Delhi could be ordered on his advice on June 26, 1975, the day Emergency was clamped down, so that they could not publish the names of the arrested leaders in defiance of the press censorship, it would seem quite possible for him to have engineered a serious enough short-circuit to cause a fire, as happened at this fateful Session at Faridabad. Perhaps, it was meant merely to scare the party bosses who had come out openly against the Prime Minister.

The opportunity to take the fight a step further came within a month, when the President Dr. Zakir Hussain died suddenly on May 3, 1969, after a heart-attack. It was a big blow to Indira personally, for, apart from losing a very sage and dignified friend in the Rashtrapati Bhavan, she realized that the party bosses would not allow her to have her way a second time in the selection of his successor. Even in the selection of Dr. Zakir Hussain, too, two years earlier, she had faced considerable opposition and had to force the issue to a vote in the Parliamentary Board of the party. This time she might not have the majority she had managed on the previous occasion.

For the 'Syndicate' leaders, the unexpected vacancy at the Rashtrapati Bhavan provided a god-sent opportunity to attempt encircling the Prime Minister by putting their own men, or men who thought like them, in all the other key posts around that seat of primary authority. Morarji, as the Deputy Prime Minister, had admirably fulfilled their expectations as an alternative centre of power in the Central Cabinet. Nijalingappa himself, as the party chief, could create enough irritations for Indira. Now the party bosses hoped to put up their own candidate for the office of the President of India. Constitutionally, the President might not have any executive authority, but all actions of the Government have to be taken in his name and under his signatures. A President, not in tune with the thinking of the Prime Minister, could create complications by refusing to endorse everything suggested by the Prime Minister. The idea was to harass the Prime Minister, both from the Rashtrapati Bhavan as well as from the Congress House, to such an extent that she was either

SPLIT IN THE CONGRESS

forced to quit on her own in sheer frustration or tripped into violating party discipline so that she could be asked to step down. Morarji could, then, easily slip into her shoes. Except for Kamaraj, all other members of the 'Syndicate' had shed their prejudice against the leader from Gujarat. To carry out his plan, they felt in Neelam Sanjiva Reddy, who was one of them since the Tirupati meeting of 1963, the ideal choice for the next President of India. Once their mind was made up, they went about getting as wide an acceptance for his candidature as possible. They knew full well that Indira would never accept him, and might force a division in the party on this issue, as, in fact, she did ultimately. Nijalingappa therefore established contacts with leaders of the Jana Sangh and the Swatantra Party for their support of Sanjiva Reddy's candidature. He had already talked publicly about the possibility of the Congress entering into a coalition with like-minded parties at the Centre. The Congress enjoyed only a marginal majority in the Lok Sabha after the 1967 general election. He, perhaps, argued that in case Indira was forced out of the party with her radical followers, it would not be difficult for their party to enter into a coalition government with the Jana Sangh and the Swatantra Party which, together, had a combined strength of 78. Obviously, the 'Syndicate' did not expect Indira to take with her more than this number from the Congress Parliamentary Party in case a split took place.

Thus, a calculated plan was put into operation by getting the leaders of these two parties to commit their support for Sanjiva Reddy's candidature. They also secured the approval of the Deputy Prime Minister Morarji Desai. With Morarji on their side, the party bosses were evenly matched with the supposed supporters of the Prime Minister in the party's Parliamentary Board, which had to make the final choice of the party candidate. They now required one more vote to ensure the selection of Sanjiva Reddy, in case the Prime Minister opposed his candidature. To avoid an open confrontation the 'Syndicate' sent some Working Committee members to Indira Gandhi on a probing mission. The 'Syndicate' did not want V. V. Giri the acting President, for various reasons, one of them being his advanced age. Indira did not commit herself, nor did she mention any other name, not even that of Jagjivan Ram, whom she suddenly proposed at the fateful meeting of the Parliamentary Board at Bangalore. But, it was quite clear she was not happy with Sanjiva Reddy's choice. Lobbying for the 'Syndicate' candidate, as he became known, continued openly until it was time for the Congress leaders to proceed to the historic Bangalore Session of the A.I.C.C. on July 10.

Indira was aware, that a show-down had been planned by the 'Syndicate' leaders in combination with the group headed by Morarji Desai, not only on the selection of the Congress candidate for the office of the President of India, but also on economic policy. A resolution had been drafted considerably watering down the radical programmes of the party. P. N. Haksar, who was one of the closest advisers of the Prime Minister at this time, suggested that she should not allow the fight to get focussed on the selection of the party candidate. Instead, she should forestall any such move from the other side by shifting the emphasis on to policy differences. Thus, an economic policy note was hurriedly prepared and sent to Bangalore with Fakhruddin Ali Ahmed. The Prime Minister delayed her own departure for Bangalore by a day. Thus, she was not present at the Working Committee meeting when this note was suddenly placed before it, while the draft resolution on economic policy was being considered.

Fakhruddin Ali Ahmed reached the meeting late. Other supporters of the Prime Minister in the Working Committee such as Subramaniam, Jagjivan Ram and Uma Shankar Dikshit, too, were not aware of the existence of the note and were also taken by surprise when it was placed before the meeting. While all members of the 'Syndicate' felt incensed at this manoeuvre to shift the limelight to policy differences, Atulya Ghosh and Kamaraj immediately changed their tactics by suggesting a total acceptance of the note, although the accompanying letter had described it as 'mere stray thought jotted down in a hurry'. Writing about this incident in his booklet on the split, Atulya Ghosh said: 'Even Nehru, during his long stewardship of the Congress, never treated the Working Committee in this fashion. After the split, it normally occurred in the minds of several of our friends that the Prime Minister's note had been presented in that abrupt manner to slight the Working Committee.'

On the second day of the Working Committee meeting the Prime Minister was present and without much discussion the note was accepted unanimously. This tactical withdrawal of the 'Syndicate' was meant to nullify the propaganda, already current among the A.I.C.C. delegates, that some members of the Working Committee were trying to block Indira's efforts to radicalize the Congress. The note specifically called for nationalization of financial institutions, as opposed to their social control, which had been accepted at Morarji's insistence at a previous occasion, ceiling on unproductive expenditure and conspicuous consumption, appointment of a monopolies commission, and imposition of heavy penalties on those who indulged in restrictive trade practices — all these items were meant to expose the allegedly reactionary attitude of the party bosses. It also urged speedy implementation of land reforms. The Working Committee persuaded Morarji himself to move the new resolution, incorporating the Prime Minister's note in the A.I.C.C. It was adopted unanimously, as if there were no reservations on its content in any of the leaders' minds or those of their followers. The fact of the matter was that everyone, who wanted to confront Indira in the Parliamentary Board on Sanjiva Reddy's candidature for the office of the President of India, felt that policy issues should not be allowed to intrude into a purely personal power struggle. Besides, the party bosses had always been able to effectively water down, at the implementation level, all the radical resolution of the party from Avadi Session onwards. The adoption of this note did not bother them too much, for they hoped to either control or squeeze the Prime Minister out from her position in the not-too-distant future.

On the last day of the session a meeting of the Parliamentary Board was held for the selection of the party's candidate for the office of the President of India. Although she had not let anybody know her mind on this question, Indira had apparently come prepared from Delhi with an alternative name, hoping that her Cabinet colleagues, barring Morarji, would stand by her in the Parliamentary Board meeting. Perhaps, she had some fore-knowledge of V. V. Giri's decision to stand as an independent in case he was not adopted as the party candidate. She created quite a consternation in the Board meeting by suddenly proposing the name of her senior colleague, Jagjivan Ram, when Sanjiva Reddy's name was proposed from the other side. The issue was then pressed to a vote. Sanjiva Reddy secured five votes against three. Here was a surprise that annoyed her most. Home Minister Y. B. Chavan had voted for Sanjiva Reddy against her proposal and contrary to her expectations. She wished the announcement of the result to be withheld for some time, but the other leaders thought otherwise and announced the decision immediately.

Within minutes of the announcement, an angry Indira Gandhi told a hurriedly assembled press conference at Raj Bhavan, where she was staying, that those who had tried to humiliate her will have to face the consequences. She maintained that, as Prime Minister, her concurrence to a candidate for the high office of the President was absolutely necessary, because, the two had to function in concert. If they enjoyed on rapport, the functioning of the Government would be greatly hindered. Her anger against her colleague, the then Home Minister Y. B. Chavan, was obvious. A newspaperman rushed to Chavan, staying in a nearby suite in the Raj Bhavan itself, to inform him that 'the wounded tigress had roared and she will have her pound of flesh soon'. The implication was clear. Everyone had concluded at that press conference that no sooner did she return to Delhi than she would ask for the Home Minister's resignation. Chavan himself felt so, since he did not comment on the interpretation given to him of her angry remarks. The same day Giri resigned as the Acting President to contest for the presidentship as an independent candidate.

Indira left for New Delhi by a special plane. Present with her in the plane was the former Chief Minister of Madhya Pradesh D. P. Mishra, who had in the meantime become a close adviser on political matters, particularly on her confrontation with the party bosses. It was his suggestion that she should ignore the Maharashtra leader, for on policy matters he had always been with her. If she were to hit him now, it would only be interpreted as an act of personal pique and vendetta. In any case, Chavan posed no threat to her position. Rather, she had now an opportunity to strike at her main rival and opponent in the party, Morarji Desai, who had been foisted on her as the Deputy Prime Minister against her wishes. This advice also found approval of her Principal Secretary, P. N. Haksar, who was the other adviser she trusted most. By the time she reached Delhi, she had regained her composure and there was not the least trace of the indignation she had displayed only hours earlier at Bangalore.

For the next three days there was a complete lull in Delhi, perhaps, in anticipation of the storm that was to break out on July 16, resulting from a brief announcement from the Rashtrapati Bhavan that the Deputy Prime Minister Morarji Desai was being relieved of his Finance portfolio. The Prime Minister herself assumed charge of that Ministry. Within a few hours of this announcement Morarji submitted his resignation from the Cabinet. The interpretation of this dramatic development among the party bosses was that it was a retaliation for her being ignored by the Congress Parliamentary Board at Bangalore on the selection of Sanjiva Reddy as the presidential candidate. Indira's supporters were equally vehement that she had taken this dramatic decision, to relieve Morarji of the Finance portfolio, in order to implement the economic resolution passed by the A.I.C.C. They asserted that although the party bosses had adopted the programme and Morarji had been persuaded to move it for adoption in the A.I.C.C., he was known to be opposed to some of its main features, such as nationalization of all financial institutions. He had scuttled this proposal earlier by urging social control of banking institutions on an experimental basis for two years, but had actually done nothing in that direction.

A bitter Morarji told reporters that he had heard something about his being relieved of Finance already on July 14 from some persons indirectly. He said: 'She wants to have her own way. I do not know, it might be a kind of retaliation. But I have done nothing to deserve it.' He also disclosed that Indira had earlier told C. B. Gupta, the then U.P. Chief Minister, that some Congress leaders had been conspiring against her. Even though she had subsequently denied having directed her remarks against Morarji, he insisted that Gupta had confirmed that her reference was really to him and no one else. Gupta had always been close to Morarji and had never liked Indira.

In his statement in Parliament five days later, explaining why he had resigned from the Cabinet, Morarji said that the 'summary' manner in which he was relieved of the Finance portfolio would have made his continuance in the Central Cabinet 'dishonourable'. He also said: 'I could have continued in the Government only at the cost of my self-respect and as a silent spectator of methods that may endanger the basic principles of democracy.' At that time these remarks were considered uncharitable.

Had not the Government nationalized 14 commercial banks within an hour of the exit of Morarji from the Union Cabinet, Indira could not have regained initiative on the ideological question which the statements of the various leaders including Morarji had tried to cloud by emphasizing the element of personal vendetta involved in the whole episode. Described as a 'momentous decision' in circles close to the Prime Minister, bank nationalization evoked mixed reaction in political circles and pushed to the background the party polemics arising out of Morarji's virtual dismissal from the Cabinet. Among the Syndicate leaders, Kamaraj and Atulya Ghosh welcomed the decision in spite of their differences with Indira over the manner in which she had eased out Morarji. But, she had succeeded in shifting the limelight to ideological differences from the intense power struggle that was raging in the organization.

The reactions of the people outside were still more divergent. The doyen of Indian Industry, J. R. D. Tata, described it as a 'tragic mistake'. Jayaprakash Narayan, speaking at a public meeting at Rajkot on July 27, characterized the nationalization of banks as 'wrong and unwarranted'. He said, it would only enhance the powers of the present rulers and not solve economic ills. Meanwhile, on a writ petition, the Supreme Court issued an order staying the nationalization of banks. The Government countered it by taking over the managements of these banks by an executive order pending the decision of the Supreme Court on the appeal against bank nationalization.

A new technique of displaying popular support to the Prime Minister was evolved at this time which, in due course, developed into a highly specialized method to show to the world and to the Prime Minister herself that she was very popular with the poor, which, of course, was given the lie in the latest elections held in March 1977. The day after the nationalization of banks was announced, Congress workers in Delhi, getting the cue from somebody in the Prime Minister's house, brought to her residence boards of taxi drivers, scooter-rickshaw drivers, class four employees of the Government and even slum dwellers in separate groups, shouting slogans in favour of Indira Gandhi as their chosen radical leader, so as to display their total support to her. In the first few days it was quite a novelty in New Delhi and, naturally, newspapers gave these popular demonstrations a big build-up. But, as they became too frequent, doubts began to arise about their spontaniety. It was soon obvious, that these demonstrations had been organized in a very careful manner in order to demoralize the party bosses who had already been thrown on the defensive. The banks, whose managements had been taken over, were asked to be specially generous in granting loans to taxi-drivers and scooter-rickshaw drivers, and soon new taxis, displaying the generosity of one or the other of the nationalized banks, became a common sight in Delhi. Every day newspaper offices were flooded with Government hand-outs on credits extended to such small people. This, too, began to be looked upon as a joke within a few months. But, the sycophants, who had proliferated around the seat of power, thought it to be an easy and effective way of pleasing Indira Gandhi and winning her favour. In due course, these demonstrations, which had continued till the last days of Indira in power, only succeeded in giving her a completely distorted picture of her standing with the people.

At the time of bank nationalization, however, Indira was apparently riding on the crest of a popularity wave, which had swept the country in the wake of reports that she was being obstructed in her efforts to bring about rapid socio-economic changes by the older party bosses. Her popularity with the people at large went up in the same proportion as the resentment against her among the party leaders, including Morarji Desai, who had finally made common cause with the 'Syndicate' against her.

Within the Parliamentary Party there grew a distinct feeling of an impending crisis in the Party Executive, dominated as it was with Morarji's men, who were assuming an increasingly hostile posture towards the leader. It was reminiscent of the days when a disillusioned Nehru, after the Chinese attack of 1962, was pressurized by the Party Executive to drop the then Defence Minister Krishna Menon and then, in quick succession, another trusted colleague K. D. Malaviya. But, Indira was neither a disillusioned nor a tired leader. In fact, she was growing in popularity and the whole country seemed to be with her in her fight with those leaders who appeared to be backed only by the vested interests, which had been directly affected by her radical policies like bank nationalization. With one stroke she had got rid of her main rival and opponent in her Cabinet and forced the party bosses on the defensive in a matter of ideology.

It gave Indira only a temporary reprieve, because an attack was soon to be mounted against her on two fronts. The petition against the bank nationalization in the Supreme Court was an issue on which almost all conservatives in the country stood united. The second front was to form in August, when the election of the new President of the country was due. Although Indira had expressed at Bangalore a strong resentment at the selection of Sanjiva Reddy as the party's candidate, as leader of the Parliamentary Party, she was virtually forced to propose his name. At that point of time no clear-cut strategy had been worked out in her camp to meet this challenge. She had to assess her own strength in the Parliamentary Party and the A.I.C.C. before taking any precipitate step. V. V. Giri, who had resigned as the Acting President to fight as an independent candidate, had been adopted by all the leftist parties like the two Communist parties, the Socialists and even the D.M.K. Lined up behind the 'Syndicate' candidate were all the rightists including the Jana Sangh and the

Swatantra Party. The division was clear-cut on ideological lines and in this some of the younger leftists in the Congress did a remarkable job in bringing about a similar polarization inside the Congress itself.

As the time for the election on August 20 approached, emissaries were despatched secretly to all states to find out how many leaders in the Giri's side. These emissaries were also asked to make a clear assessment of the chances of Giri's victory in that eventuality. The electoral college for the presidential election consists of members of Parliament and members of all the State Assemblies. The number of votes assigned to an M.P. is higher than that assigned to an M.L.A. After a scrupulous estimate made on the spot, it was felt that, with just a little luck, Giri could win with a small margin. Meanwhile, pressure was mounting on Indira to openly appeal for support for the Congress candidate, N. Sanjiva Reddy, who had already resigned from the Speakership of the Lok Sabha. She resisted these pressures and even declined to issue a whip to party members, as desired by the Congress President Nijalingappa, but refrained from coming out openly herself in favour of Giri.

A little stroke of luck, that was required to see Giri win, came from U.P., where Charan Singh promised him the support of Bharatiya Kranti Dal in the U.P. Assembly. Even then it was not possible to assess how many Congress M.L.A.s, afraid as they were of the state boss, C. B. Gupta, would come out openly against the party candidate unless Indira herself gave them a call to do so. About four days before the actual polling, Kamalapati Tripathi, who was number two in the State Cabinet, rang up the Prime Minister's residence in Delhi to say that there would be a landslide for Giri in U.P., if she came out openly and made an appeal in support of him. This was the signal for her to persuade the party bosses to allow Congress members for freedom of vote in this election. The die was cast and, as is well known, she carried the day with V. V. Giri winning with 42,0077 votes against 40,5427 secured by Sanjiva Reddy. As expected, it was a near thing, but the final result was a public slap on the face to the party bosses and a new feather in Indira's cap. Never had an election so far excited so much interest and suspense in the country as this one and never had an election been as crucial in shaping Indira Gandhi into one of the most powerful Prime Ministers.

The election left the Congress party deeply divided. Jagjivan Ram and Fakhruddin Ali Ahmed, two of her senior colleagues in the Cabinet, stood solidly by her in this crisis. So did state leaders like

Kamalapati Tripathi and D. P. Mishra. In fact, Jagjivan Ram and Fakhruddin Ali Ahmed played a crucial role at this time by accusing Nijalingappa of having entered into a secret pact with parties like the Jana Sangh and the Swatantra to overthrow Indira's Government. It was this public accusation made in a letter, which paved the way for Indira's repudiation of the party's candidate. As a consequence there was 40 per cent cross-voting in the Congress at the Centre and 20 per cent in the State Assemblies. But Y. B. Chavan, who had voted in favour of Sanjiva Reddy's candidature at Bangalore, stood by his commitment and carried most of the Maharashtra Congress members of Parliament and the State Assembly with him. It was the landslide in Uttar Pradesh and Bihar, managed by Kamalapati Tripathi and the late Lalit Narayan Mishra, that tilted the balance in favour of Giri. He was hailed as the candidate of the common people.

Exactly nine days before the polling for the presidential election, Indira started a relentless war of letters against the party bosses, which completely unnerved them because of the calculated timing and forced the Party President to commit one error after another. The first letter was fired off late in the night on August 11 by Jagjivan Ram and Fakhruddin Ali Ahmed accusing Nijalingappa of collusion with the Swatantra Party and the Jana Sangh 'to topple the Central Government'. They, as stated in the letter, foresaw 'grave repercussion of this move on the presidential election'. Nijalingappa, naturally, repudiated the charge, but by the time his reply landed in newspaper offices, it was already too late for the morning editions while his opponents' letter had already snatched prominent headlines.

On August 15 Indira Gandhi herself wrote to Nijalingappa saying that while she desired unity in the party, the Congress could not merely serve as a machine for securing election of a candidate (Sanjiva Reddy) 'chosen by a small group', specially by making alliances, divorced from policies, with the Swatantra Party and the Jana Sangh. Earlier she had encouraged the demand for the right of free vote from the Congress President. Nijalingappa had tried to crush the move by suspending from the party an important member of Parliament and a labour leader, Arjun Arora, for asking for that right. That right had also been demanded by Jagjivan Ram and Fakhruddin Ali Ahmed in their letter. A day later Indira had turned down a request to issue a whip to the party saying that she 'could not be a party to winning elections by clouding principles'.

It must be stated, in fairness to both sides, that this war of attrition was first started by the 'Syndicate' leaders, who thought they could browbeat Indira into submission. But, when they found she was all set to defy them on the selection of the presidential candidate and might carry a large number of party members with her, they made the wrong tactical move of asking the Party President himself to make a direct contact with leaders of the two rightist parties. That gave Indira and her supporters an upper hand.

By August 15, with only five days left for the presidential poll, it was clear to the 'Syndicate' leaders that they had lost the fight. Atulya Ghosh told some newspapermen in his typically precise manner: 'These old fogies have developed cold feet and have lost the battle.' As a last resort Nijalingappa asked Jagjivan Ram and Fakhruddin Ali Ahmed, who had sent the first letter, to explain why action should not be taken against them for anti-party activities that might lead to 'disastrous consequences'. Addressing a meeting of about a hundred Congress members of the Parliament the same day, Indira Gandhi thundered that she had had to swallow many an insult to maintain party unity. That was the signal to her followers not to vote for Sanjiva Reddy. She had truly beaten the 'Syndicate' and Morarji combine at their own game.

The wounded tigress, as a journalist had described her at Bangalore, had finally exacted her pound of flesh and she was willing to carry on the fight to its logical end if the organization leaders so desired. Though left licking their wounds, they, too, had not given up. For the first time Morarji and his group started taking an active part in an all-out effort to purge the party of what they described as extraneous elements which had infiltrated the Congress and undermined its 'discipline and moral sense'. They tried to give moral overtones to this power struggle by accusing Indira of encouraging 'conscience vote' against the party candidate, after she had herself filed his nomination. At a meeting of the Congress Working Committee on August 25, they forced a decision to ask for her explanation. A sort of compromise was brought about through Y. B. Chavan's mediation. It proved to be short-lived, for the party bosses had not excused her for inflicting a humiliating defeat on their chosen candidate.

Matters rested there until October 9 when the conflict again flared up in the open. Indira and four of her senior colleagues in the Cabinet, who were also members of the Working Committee, accused the Party President of making 'arbitrary moves' to remove Subramaniam from the Working Committee. The four colleagues were Jagjivan Ram, Fakhruddin Ali Ahmed, Uma Shankar Dikshit and Subramaniam himself. Nijalingappa, too, was determined to throw him out along with two other supporters of the Prime Minister, Kamalapati Tripathi of Uttar Pradesh and the President of the Andhra Pradesh Congress Committee, on the plea that they were only ex officio members and, hence, ceased to be such as soon as they had lost the presidentship of their respective Pradesh Congress Committees. Indira warned if they (party bosses) tried to throw out certain people, it would create a serious situation for the party. She accused them publicly of being bent upon causing a split in the party by such methods.

The party's fate was sealed on October 31 by Nijalingappa's letter to Indira containing a severe indictment for anti-party activities by her and her supporters. The Prime Minister and her supporters, therefore, boycotted the Working Committee meeting called for the next day. Nijalingappa retaliated by dropping Fakhruddin Ali Ahmed and Subramaniam from the Working Committee on the ground that they had decided to call a parallel A.I.C.C. Session on November 22 — a move he termed unconstitutional. He also accused Indira of 'intrigue and disruption' in a letter dated November 3, in which he specifically charged her that 'you seem to have made personal loyalty to you the test of loyalty to the Congress and the country'. Prophetic words, indeed, but which seemed most inappropriate in those days.

The next day he issued a 'show cause notice' to her, demanding why action should not be taken against her for anti-party activities. In reply she refuted the charge that she was going communist and also rejected the idea that she should seek a vote of confidence from the party. But no one expected that Nijalingappa would precipitate the split in the party a reality on November 12 by expelling Indira Gandhi from the primary membership of the Congress, simply on the authority of only half of the Working Committee, following the boycott of the Committee by Indira's supporters. He directed the Congress Parliamentary Party to elect a new leader.

For about 24 hours there was a turbulent flux in the political situation, no one knowing what would happen. The Prime Minister immediately called a meeting of her Cabinet, in which seven of her seniormost colleagues gave her solid support; some, like Dr. Ram Subhag Singh, were asked to submit their resignation; others, like Jaisukhlal Hathi, left on their own. The next morning she faced the Parliamentary Party, with about 250 members present. In an impassioned speech, with tears rolling down her cheeks, she challenged those who dared expel her from the Congress. She claimed to have a far greater right to be the member of that great organization than 'some of those who were a party to this decision'. They had miscalculated that, for once, the party, and not a caucus, would decide who should stay in and lead the party.

There had been hectic lobbying throughout the night from both sides to secure support among the Congress members. The 250, who had come to the meeting, had adopted a resolution reaffirming their confidence in Indira Gandhi as their leader. Even then the position was not clear for another two days. On November 16, it was finally established that the overwhelming majority in the party had stayed with Indira, while only 65 of the 284 members of the Lok Sabha and 46 of the 150 Rajya Sabha members met to elect Morarji Desai as the Chairman of what now came to be known as the Organization Congress Party in Parliament. The New Congress of Indira Gandhi was left with 210 members out of a total strength of 523 in the Lok Sabha, thus reducing it to a minority. But there was no immediate threat to its Government, for the Communist Party with 24 members, the Marxist Communists with 19, the DMK with 25 and a number of independents had immediately pledged their support to it.

The split in the party was now complete; only the formalities remained to be gone through. What was particularly interesting during those hectic days was the rallying of the young radicals around the Prime Minister and their pressure on Y. B. Chavan to give his unreserved support to her. But, before that pressure succeeded, Kamaraj, too, tried to get the Maharashtra leader on the side of the old bosses. The temptation dangled before him was the Prime Ministership itself if they succeeded in removing Indira Gandhi. Kamaraj never wanted Morarji as the leader, but knew that if Indira was forced out, they would not be able to prevent Morarji from becoming the Prime Minister. While some members of the 'Syndicate', like Nijalingappa, S. K. Patil and even Sanjiva Reddy, had no objection to Morarji being the leader, Atulya Ghosh and Kamaraj, who professed to be the radicals, wanted somebody more acceptable and with a progressive image. In their search they hit upon Chavan, who had voted with them at Bangalore, as the only one who could be put up to prevent Morarji from coming to power. They argued that if Morarji became the Prime Minister, then all this power struggle by the

'Syndicate' would have been for nothing. They would be merely exchanging one assertive leader for another.

In Chavan's camp, too, there was a lot of heart searching. There were some diehards, like Anna Saheb Shinde, whose hearts were with the 'Syndicate'. But they did not want the unity of Maharashtra members to be destroyed. They preferred to argue and convince their leader Chavan. There were also persistent radicals among them who wanted Chavan to develop an even more radical an image than that of the Prime Minister. He himself remained quiet, listening to everyone, until the tentative offer of the 'Syndicate' came to him through an intermediary. His characteristic reply was to enquire whether they had consulted Morarji. He wanted a prior commitment from Morarji. He did not want to be a mere pawn of the power-hungry party bosses, whose conspiratorial functioning in the previous two years had disillusioned him considerably. Besides, he felt more at home ideologically with Indira than, for instance, with Morarji and S. K. Patil. When no commitment from Morarji was forthcoming, he forgot the offer and plunged wholeheartedly into the reorganization of the New Congress. But his vacillation for about forty-eight hours did considerable damage to his image in the country, apart from providing more arguments to those who had been sowing seeds of suspicion against him in Indira's mind.

On November 22 the requisitioned A.I.C.C. meeting was held in Delhi under Indira's leadership. Subramaniam was appointed interim President of the Party until the annual session, which was called at Bombay on December 26 to formally launch the New Congress. As a formality this meeting also expelled Nijalingappa from the Congress. It was claimed by this and the other side, too, that they were the real Congress. They, too, called their annual session at Gandhinagar in Gujarat on December 21. Both sessions attracted a large number of delegates, many of whom attended both. While the Gandhinagar Session was used primarily to denounce Indira Gandhi for causing the split, the Bombay Session concentrated on giving a further radical look to the new party. Although leaders of both parties wranged for a long time over their claims of representing the real Congress, in due course, it was clear that none of them represented the old united Congress. Both sections ultimately accepted different election symbols and gradually evolved different policy stances. Jagjivan Ram, who was elected President of the New Congress, summed up the situation beautifully in his address to the open session: He said: 'What we witness today is not a mere clash of personalities, and certainly not a fight for power. It is also not as simple as a conflict between the parliamentary and organizational wings. It is a conflict between two outlooks and attitudes in regard to the objectives of the Congress and the method in which the Congress itself should function.' Only eight years later the same Jagjivan Ram himself felt called upon to revolt against Indira Gandhi for what he was to describe as 'the stifling of internal party democracy'!

The main theme of Nijalingappa's address at Gandhinagar was that Indira Gandhi had subordinated some of India's policies to the Soviet Union in order to gain for herself the support of the communists. 'In fact Indira has taken some of their (communist) methods for her own use. Her professed radicalism is not meant for a thrust but to hide her inadequacies and incompetence. We are today witnessing as it were the preaching of blasphemy from the pulpit of the Cathedral itself', he declared. Utter lack of political morality in her functioning was the recurring theme of the speeches of other leaders like Morarji at Gandhinagar.

While the Organization Congress gave the impression of a party of old and frustrated leaders who had been completely outmanoeuvred, the New Congress at Bombay acquired a youthful look, full of dynamism. Chandra Shekhar, the volatile leftist leader, formerly of the Socialist Party, became an elected member of the Working Committee, while Chandrajit Yadav, another young leftist from Uttar Pradesh and a former communist, got a nominated seat. It was for the first time one noticed an attempt on the part of Indira Gandhi to balance the former socialists against the former communists, now in the New Congress. There was a definite bias in favour of the ex-communists and that led to the beginning of some friction among the so-called radicals in the Congress, who had so far worked unitedly for Indira against the party bosses through the medium of the Socialist Forum. Perhaps the rift was created intentionally by her if one is to judge on the basis of the style of functioning of Indira Gandhi that became apparent in subsequent years, for she never allowed herself to be beholden to any one set of persons or group. The New Congress Working Committee also had a sizable representation of age and experience. Among the more prominent of its senior leaders were Chavan, D. P. Mishra, who was also appointed Treasurer of the Party, Fakhruddin Ali Ahmed, Uma Shankar Dikshit and C. Subramaniam. Surprisingly, Dinesh Singh, who had been so close to

Indira during the past two years, found no place in the Working Committee despite his best efforts. It was rightly interpreted as the beginning of his downfall.

Within a month after the Bombay Session of the New Congress, the 14 commercial banks were nationalized by an ordinance. Their management had been taken over by an order of the President in July 1969, after the Supreme Court had struck down the earlier Act nationalizing these banks. Under the Ordinance issued on February 14, 1970, the banking companies were to receive enhanced compensation — Rs. 87.4 crores instead of Rs. 75 crores as proposed under the original Act — since the earlier Act had been struck down on the question of compensation. It was to be paid to the banking companies and not to their shareholders, contrary to the earlier proposal. The banking companies were also given the option of collecting the compensation in three annual instalments, or in ten-year or thirty-year securities carrying $4\frac{1}{2}$ per cent and $5\frac{1}{2}$ per cent interests, respectively. The Supreme Court had once again irked the Government for obstructing what it thought was an essential part of its programme of socio-economic change. There was a strong demand in the party, either to delete the right to property from the Fundamental Rights, or to amend the clause relating to compensation. However, neither was possible, because the ruling Congress had been reduced to a minority in the Lok Sabha after the split and was dependent for its Government's survival on the support of the two Communist parties and the DMK.

About this time, two members of Parliament, who had voted against Giri, filed a petition in the Supreme Court challenging his election. This also became a historic case, since the Head of the State decided to appear in the court himself, instead of being examined in commission. His election was ultimately upheld on May 11. But it had set a bad precedent for the future, although it had vindicated the Prime Minister.

Another event that boosted Indira's prestige at this time was the four-month visit to India — from October 1969, to February 8, 1970 — of Khan Abdul Gaffar Khan, lovingly referred to as the Frontier Gandhi or Badshah Khan, on an invitation from her. He had been living in Kabul for several years because of his differences with the military rulers of Pakistan. This was his first visit to India after Independence. He had felt very hurt and let down by the national leadership of the Congress at the time of Independence. He had disliked the idea of partition and had kept fighting the new Government of Pakistan for civil liberties and autonomy for its various provinces. Perhaps, he is one of the few leaders of our national struggle who has spent more years in jail after independence of his country than before it. His visit was a sentimental journey, and he gave full marks to the Indian leaders, particularly to Indira, for living up to the ideals of equality and democracy he had dreamt along with Mahatma Gandhi and her father during the hectic days of freedom struggle. He also chided the bigoted among the Indians for discrimination against a minority because of its religion. Once, again, the voice of secularism resounded throughout the length and breadth of the country and the cherished principle became a main plank of Indira's future policies.

While outwardly Indira's relations with her senior colleagues in the Cabinet appeared cordial, she continued to harbour a grievance against Chavan for his role at Bangalore and his indecision for about 48 hours at the time of the spilt. She wanted to shift him from the Home Ministry, but did not know how to go about it. Till then she had not acquired the imperious disdain for her colleagues in the Government that was to characterize the last two years of her authoritarian rule. She turned for advice to D. P. Mishra, who had earlier suggested to her to control the intelligence services herself. Ever since Morarji's exit from the Cabinet she had been holding charge of Finance Ministry. She now decided to take away Revenue Intelligence and Directorate of Enforcement from Finance to Cabinet Secretariat under her direct charge as suggested by Mishra. He had also advised her to try taking away the intelligence services from the Home Ministry too. If Chavan objected and made a public issue of it, then she was to desist from doing anything further. But if he acquiesced, as he, in fact, later did, she could conclude that it would be easy to shift him from Home to any other Ministry.

That is exactly what she did. She first separated the wing dealing with foreign intelligence in the Intelligence Bureau and put it under the charge of an able and trusted police officer in the Cabinet Secretariat. It later grew into a big organization known as Research and Analysis Wing, or R.A.W. for short. She also made the Chiefs of Intelligence Bureau and the Central Bureau of Investigation of full Secretary rank directly responsible to her. Having done that without much resistance from any quarters, she then undertook a major reshuffle of her Cabinet, rewarding two of her senior colleagues, Jagjivan Ram and

Swaran Singh, with the prestigious portfolios of Defence and External Affairs, respectively. Lalit Narayan Mishra, who had been a pillar of strength to her during the split days, was given independant charge of Foreign Trade, the Ministry which has been the main source of raising political funds for the party. As planned, Y. B. Chavan was shifted from Home to Finance, she herself assuming temporary charge of Home with K. C. Pant to help her as Minister of State.

In an obvious move to demote Dinesh Singh, she shifted him from the External Affairs Ministry. At first she wanted to give him an insignificant portfolio. But after considerable persuasion, she agreed to shift him to Industrial Developments and Company Affairs, which was attached to Law Ministry. This was a great humiliation for one who had exercised considerable power in her name for over two years. Dinesh had fallen from grace and did not last long in the Cabinet.

Three other younger people, who found important berths in the Council of Ministers as Ministers of State, were Vidya Charan Shukla, the later infamous Minister for Information and Broadcasting during the Emergency, Prakash Chand Sethi, who, later on, was Treasurer of the Congress during the last fateful year of Indira's rule, and Om Mehta, who was to become the main hatchet-man during the Emergency as the Minister of State for Home. At that reshuffle of the Cabinet, Sethi succeeded Mishra as Minister for Defence Production, Shukla was placed in Finance with Chavan and Om Mehta made his debut as Minister of State for Parliamentary Affairs.

In spite of all this changing and chopping of her Ministry, Indira did not have a smooth sailing in Parliament, heading as she was a minority Government. The Communists continued to press her for more and more radical reforms as a price for their continuing support to her Government. Within the party the pro-communist radicals acquired considerable prestige and became a powerful pressure group with P. N. Haksar as their main patron and adviser. This group was not very happy with the influence with the Prime Minister that leaders like D. P. Mishra, Uma Shankar Dikshit and Subramaniam enjoyed and sought Lalit's help to counteract it. However, Haksar was not very enamoured of Lalit either. In fact, he had advised the Prime Minister against the way some of the people in the party had started manipulating politics divorced from ideological principles. Among such people he marked D. P. Mishra, Uma Shankar Dikshit, who was the Treasurer of the Party at that time and was later to become the

Home Minister, Lalit Narayan Mishra, who had already acquired a notoriety for unscrupulous collection of funds and manipulation of politics through money power, and Yashpal Kapoor who, as Officer on Special Duty in the Prime Minister's Secretariat at that time, undertook political assignments not strictly above board.

Haksar's advice became known to these powerful individuals. They started a campaign against him, and, in due course, he was convinced that he should take his retirement when it fell due in September next year. He made his wish known to the Prime Minister and she raised no objection to his wanting to go away. However, there was still a year to go and he continued to do his best to keep Indira's actions ideologically oriented so that she was not accused of exercising power for its own sake or for personal gain. She gradually became the most powerful leader of the country although she was heading a minority government. The Organization Congress, now the main Opposition in Parliament, fully exploited this weakness to try to establish their charge that she was being manipulated by the Communists. While her problems internally were mounting, externally too hostile noises were being made by Pakistan against India, perhaps to divert attention from their own internal troubles caused by the growth under Mujibur Rehman of Bangla nationalism in East Pakistan.

It was a depressing time for Indira Gandhi. She needed some popular policy decision to bolster her own and the people's sagging morale in the face of mounting tensions. On September 3, 1970, therefore she got the Lok Sabha to pass a constitutional amendment abolishing privy purses of the former princes once again, thereby galvanizing the people on a popular issue. The Government was confident of getting it through the Rajya Sabha as well on September 5. But, terrific lobbying against the Bill by powerful princes, who apparently spent a lot of money in the process, succeeded in getting the Bill rejected by the Upper House for lack of just a fraction of a vote short of a two-thirds majority required for a constitutional amendment. As a counter-measure, the Government derecognized the princes by a Presidential order issued on September 7. Immediately, the princes filed a writ petition challenging the validity of this order, and the Supreme Court admitted it. On December 15, 1970, with the winter session of Parliament due to end three days later, the Supreme Court struck down the derecognition order causing considerable resentment in the Government circles.

One of the main reasons for Indira Gandhi's decision at that time to dissolve Parliament and order fresh elections for the Lok Sabha a year ahead of schedule, delinking them from the State Assembly elections, was the step by step obstruction placed in the way of implementation of all progressive measures through the help of the Supreme Court. A feeling also grew in the ruling circles that the Judiciary was not in tune with the socio-economic needs of the country, and if it continued to obstruct change, it would have to be tamed. This kind of thinking originated from the radicals and led to disastrous results in subsequent years. But before anything could be done on that score, Indira had to get a fresh and clear mandate from the people.

While rumours of a possible mid-term poll were already afloat, the Government was keen to test the reaction to such a move in Parliament before taking a firm decision. So a story was planted in the *Indian Express*, a paper which had consistently opposed Indira, that Parliament would be dissolved as soon as it rose at the end of the winter session and a mid-term poll would be ordered. The story appeared with screaming headlines on the last day of Parliament on December 18. Contrary to expectations, the Opposition reaction was rather mild. That made up the Government's mind and the dissolution of Parliament was announced on December 27. The official communique said: 'The Government had decided to seek a fresh mandate from the people to effectively implement its socialist and secular programmes and policies.' And what a mandate it turned out to be!

CHAPTER V

UNDISPUTED LEADER
(December 1970 to October 1971)

INDIRA GANDHI had been toying with the idea of holding a midterm election for the Lok Sabha, delinked from the State Assembly elections for quite some time. Although the formal decision dissolving Parliament and calling for the Lok Sabha elections a year ahead of schedule was announced only on December 27, 1970, ten days after the winter session of the Fourth Parliament had ended, preparations for the elections had begun on the Prime Minister's side much earlier. The new Foreign Trade Minister Lalit Narayan Mishra had stepped up collection of funds from the business community to such an extent that it could not be kept a secret. Often representatives of trade and industry were called up by him to Delhi and asked to produce specified amounts. Those who declined were threatened with possible raids by people of Revenue Intelligence and Enforcement Directorate, which were now operating under the Cabinet Secretariat. In Bombay financial circles stories started circulating of the amounts secured by the Foreign Trade Minister under such threats.

Others, who came forward willingly with whatever was asked for, received concessions, beyond their imagination, to expand their business and amass further resources. A number of new stars were born on the industrial firmament of India during this time. This was also the time when Sanjay's ambition to become India's Ford was encouraged by securing for him big financial assistance through the good offices of Lalit Narayan Mishra and of the then Chief Minister of Haryana Bansi Lal. The letter also allotted Government land for Sanjay's Maruti factory at Gurgaon at concessional rates. By the time elections were called, this new combine of Lalit Narayan, Bansi Lal and Sanjay Gandhi had been firmly established, with Yashpal Kapoor and R. K. Dhavan, close aides of the Prime Minister herself, as the main link among them. It is doubtful if Indira herself was unaware of the nefarious activities of this combine and the use of all kinds of threats and temptations of wine and women that were used to raise whatever funds were required for the coming elections, for Lalit Narayan's manipulations in Bihar politics, as well as for whetting Sanjay's appetite for power.

At one stage there was considerable consternation among some important members of the party and a few of them, like Chandra Shekhar and Krishna Kant, even took the courage to voice it publicly. Before it could become common public knowledge, however, a decision was announced, on behalf of the party, that no Minister would collect funds directly but must send anyone wanting to contribute to the party to Uma Shankar Dikshit. Instead of correcting the evil, it opened yet another door for clandestine collection of funds. Lalit Narayan continued merrily with his own collection without any let or hindrance. At the same time he managed to mute all references or criticisms in newspapers of his activities by his charming public relations with New Delhi's press corps, many of whose members were flooded with extensive gifts from the generous Minister. He even broke a tacit rule that no Congress Minister should throw drink parties. More difficult to deal with were the journalists belonging to papers aligned to a leftist ideology. In the case of some of these newspapers, direct links were established with their higher ups and occasional financial assistance to them, individually or institutionally, ensured their silence. In the process he also acquired a progressive image for himself that was as false as that of Sanjay in the role of an industrial and engineering genius.

For once Indira was not stayed for funds during the mid-term elections to the Lok Sabha in March 1971, despite the ban on company donations to political parties. Most of these funds came from the unaccounted accumulations with businessmen and industrialists because of widespread evasion of taxes and proliferation of the highly profitable smuggling in luxury items of foreign origin. Such activities, detrimental to the economy of the country, had been encouraged even in the past by unscrupulous party bosses wishing to perpetuate their own personal power through a command of unlimited resources and even men amenable to various kinds of clandestine activities. All manner of operators in the shady financial world now started making tentative overtures to the new power elite. They achieved some success in this enterprise, at least with some who, perhaps, held no particular political position directly, but were near the seat of power. The life-styles of the latter underwent as a result a qualitative change; they became the trend setters of a kind of high living, which had been looked down upon in the past. A certain degeneration thus set in among this kind of power elite, resulting ultimately in the downfall of the entire power structure headed by Indira. The structure became morally hollow from inside, and, in the historic elections six years later, it simply collapsed like a house of cards.

To the people at large, particularly in rural India, Indira was dear as the daughter of that beloved leader Nehru and also a charismatic leader in her own right. Stories about intrigues and corruption around her had not reached them yet, being still confined to a handful of industrialists and politicians, who had been the direct victims of the new style of political functioning at New Delhi. But they were disturbing enough to influence most newspapers in the country to gradually persuade their owners to adopt an increasingly anti-Indira policy. Thus, two surprisingly contradictory situations developed at this time. While Indira's popularity reached its peak among the masses, her appeal among the intellectual elite touched rock bottom. The latter phenomenon was evident from the fact that almost every big newspaper opposed her and did its best to work for defeating her in the elections. The doyen of the newspaper world in those days, the late Frank Moraes, carried on a virulent campaign against her day in and day out in his famous column, 'Myth and Reality'. Despite all such opposition, Indira swept the polls beyond all expectations of even the most optimistic of her supporters. While most pollsters gave her from a minimum of 220 to a maximum of 300 seats in a house of 520, she, in fact, returned with a clear two-thirds majority securing 350 seats. This massive majority was a clear vindication of her stand in her fight against the party bosses two years earlier and a victory over those very people once again in a 'Grand Alliance' with parties like the Jana Sangh, the Swatantra and the Socialists.

This historic mid-term election established Indira as the undisputed leader of India.

Dramatic results witnessed in Indian elections have often baffled political scientists, particularly from the West. They usually apply the same norms to analyse Indian elections, as they adopt in their own countries. Such analyses fail, because the Indian electorate is very different psychologically and reacts differently in conditions that appear similar to those in their countries. Irrespective of the economic backwardness of the majority of the voters, an average individual, even in a village, is quite conscious of the power balance around him. Taking the village as a unit, the various caste groups act and react on one another as the main power groups. Usually a number of caste groups join together, for no single caste is in an absolute majority.

The other important factor that determines the behaviour of the average Indian voter in a particular region is the economic development of that region. For instance, the more developed and educationally advanced coastal states have undergone a silent social revolution over the last thirty years, as a result of which power has gone out of the hands of the upper castes like the Brahmins and the Rajputs. The power pattern is now determined in these states by a delicate balance of the haves and have-nots not only in economic but social terms as well. It is a continuous process, with the have-nots pushing from below and changing the overall balance at the end of every new election.

The six elections, that India has had since independence, have brought out certain social realities into sharp focus. First, the caste Hindus do not form a majority as is often mistakenly assumed. Second, ever since Mahatma Gandhi gave recognition to what were then known as the untouchables and renamed them as Harijans, they have acquired a separate identity and form the largest minority in the country along with *adivasis* or the aborigins. They do not like to be included among the Hindus any more, for then they would no longer be an important power group in their own right. They also know that they can get social acceptability only if they acquire political power. This realization has dawned upon them as a result of the discrimination they continue to suffer from even after getting highly educated. Even the law, declaring practice of untouchability as a cognizable offence, has not helped. Only when any one of them acquires political prominence and power, does he find even the highest caste Brahmins willing to join him at his table. No amount of money can give them the kind of social acceptability that political power does.

Again, like Harijans, the Muslims who are a clear ten per cent of the total population, also constitute a very important power group. Most of them vote *en bloc* according to the *fatwa* issued by their religious leaders. In quite a large number of constituencies, particularly in northern India, their vote can make a radical difference to a party. For instance, during the election in March 1977, the entire Harijan and Muslim votes in the northern Hindi belt went against the Congress. As a consequence, the Congress did not win a single seat in that region. As against this, in 1971 these two power groups supported Indira and she was returned with a massive majority. Then there are smaller minorities like the Sikhs in the north, the Christians spread all over the country, the Parsis concentrated in the two western states of Gujarat and Maharashtra, and the Buddhists in the remote north-eastern and north western tribal areas. By themselves all of them are important power groups and in combination with one another, or with the bigger power groups like the Hindus, the Muslims and the Harijans, they can affect the power pattern in the country.

It is by taking account of this power division as a dominant factor that an election in India should be judged and not merely on the basis of percentages of votes polled by various parties. Usually, the winning party in India — till 1971 the Congress and now the Janata Party — is never a clear-cut political party in the sense understood in the West. It is a broad combination formed by the best permutation and combination of the various power groups, as described above, attracting all kinds of people. That is why many a foreign observer is baffled on seeing that even Communists in India fight elections on the basis of caste and community rather than on ideological slogans.

One cannot say whether it was by accident or design that Indira Gandhi had behind her the most formidable power combination in 1971. This combination came into being during her fight with the party bosses in 1969. While the party bosses, who combined against her during the years just prior to the split in the party, represented mostly the upper class haves who had enjoyed political power in the previous two decades, the leaders who joined her represented the have-nots in the country. This was very clearly reflected in the highest policy-making body in her own Cabinet, known as the Political Affairs Committee. To wit, Indira herself represented the enlightened upper-caste Hindu. Next in importance in the committee was Jagjivan Ram, the most important Harijan leader in the country, with a definite following of his own. Then came Fakhruddin Ali Ahmed representing the big Muslim minority. The next, Y. B. Chavan represented the Maratha community in Maharashtra, consisting of the majority of the small farmers corresponding to the jats and ahirs of north India. And lastly, there was Sardar Swaran Singh, representing a very important minority. Had there been a suitable Christian or a Parsi available, he could also have found a place in the committee.

The same combination of power groups pervaded right down to the state, district and village levels in Indira Gandhi's party after the split. In contrast, this effective element was missing both in the Organization Congress as well as in the alliance of four parties that came into being in 1971. So long as this formidable combination, representing the various important power groups in the country, endured, Indira was invincible and was able to face any challenge to her authority — economic or political. In those days rumours used to be floated off and on that one of the above-mentioned senior leaders was about to be dropped from the Cabinet; but it never came about, until Fakhruddin Ali Ahmed was persuaded eventually to occupy the Rashtrapati Bhavan. Even then the strength, emanating from the combination, would have endured, had she not started throwing out people like Swaran Singh and distrusting colleagues like Jagjivan Ram and Chavan. In time, she herself destroyed her greatest asset and therefore suffered as a result in the sixth election in March 1977.

Until the 1971 elections, Indira's relations with Jagjivan Ram and Fakhruddin Ali Ahmed were excellent. She also trusted Swaran Singh a great deal. Only about Chavan did she harbour suspicions because her sycophants had dinned into her mind that he was a scheming politician who alone posed a threat to her in the party. She started feeling distrust in Jagjivan Ram also soon after the 1971 elections. Jagjivan Ram, the then Congress President, had made a wrong assessment of the margin of victory of his party. In fact, no one in those days thought that Indira would get such a massive majority in the Lok Sabha, since she had persuaded the party into entering an electoral alliance with the Communist Party of India leaving for it as many as 76 seats. The Congress put up only 442 candidates and it was beyond the imagination of anybody, with the entire national press carrying on a virulent anti-Indira campaign, that 350 of these would return. Therefore, if Jagjivan Ram, as the Congress President, went wrong in his assessment, it was no surprise. A common topic of speculation then, it was generally believed, that Indira's party would get just a bare majority, or even a few seats less, and might be forced to enter into a coalition with the C.P.I. Another cause of friction was the selection of candidates in Jagjivan Ram's own home State of Bihar where, to the detriment of his influence, a greater share was given to Lalit Narayan Mishra. Not only had he to swallow that, but had also to lump the adjustments with the C.P.I. in Bihar that Lalit Narayan Mishra had arrived at on his own.

As soon as the polling was over, Jagjivan Ram was tricked into making a statement by a newspaperman that has been held against him as indicative of his real ambition — to displace Indira at the slightest opportunity. He was asked if he would allow his party to enter into a coalition with the C.P.I. in case the Congress failed to get a clear majority. Pat came the reply that he was not 'a sleeping President'. The General Secretary of the Congress at that time, H. N. Bahuguna, had come very close to Jagjivan Ram. He had also earned the wrath of the Prime Minister for extending his own personal influence among the rank and file in Uttar Pradesh. He had been the only leader from that state to openly criticize interference by Yashpal Kapoor in the State Congress politics in Prime Minister's name. His proximity to Jagjivan Ram was made another reason for sowing the seeds of suspicion in Indira's mind.

With the announcement of the election results, she found herself for the first time in an impregnable position; and she made it known in no uncertain terms that she had not liked either Jagjivan Ram's statement or Bahuguna's political manipulations in Uttar Pradesh. It was conveyed to Jagjivan Ram, who was also the Defence Minister, that he would have to choose between the party post and the ministership. He could not continue to hold both offices. Jagjivan Ram decided in favour of remaining in the Cabinet and promptly sent in his resignation from the presidentship of the party.

For the important position thus vacated, she favoured D. Sanjivayya, another Harijan leader from Andhra Pradesh. Sanjivayya had been the Chief Minister of his State at a comparatively very young age, and had also been the Congress President and a Union Minister. Indira inducted him once again as the Congress President. It was widely interpreted as a clever move on her part to counterbalance Jagjivan Ram by promoting another Harijan leader in the party. But Sanjivayya died within a few years. She tried also to build another all-India Muslim leader to counter-balance Fakhruddin Ali Ahmed, who had become indispensable to her as the only Muslim leader of all-India stature in her party. She brought Moinul Huq Choudhary from Assam into her Cabinet, but he failed to survive in Delhi's politics of intrigue and backbiting. She, then, tried to build up G. M. Sadiq, the then Chief Minister of Jammu and Kashmir, but he was a sick man and died soon. His successor, Mir Qasim, though a capable politician, was too young and had still to acquire an all-India image. At one stage in her prolonged negotiations with Sheikh Abdullah she even toyed with the idea of persuading him to play a part in the national politics through the Congress. But his heart was set on Kashmir, and he wanted to be rehabilitated in power there from which he had been forcibly thrown out in 1953. It was something of an article of faith with him. He made it quite clear that he was not interested in coming to the Centre in any capacity. The only person she could not displace, from his unquestioned leadership of Maharashtra, was Y. B. Chavan, and it was not for lack of trying.

All this goes to show that from the very beginning Indira was conscious of her over-dependence on these senior leaders. Having fought and won against one set of party bosses, she did not want to be beholden to another set. That was one reason why she failed to establish rapport with her senior colleagues and gradually got isolated from them. It was also in keeping with her strategy of never having the same set of persons too long around her lest they combine and pose a threat to her own position. Dinesh was the first casualty. He had already been demoted from the External Affairs Ministry in the last reshuffle of the Cabinet. After the election he was not even invited to join the Government. His cup of humiliation was full. At one time head of her so-called 'Kitchen Cabinet' and the most influential individual next to her, he had been pushed into oblivion. Others in the 'Kitchen Cabinet', too, had to pay in some way or the other. Inder Gujral survived but not in the prestigious Information and Broadcasting Ministry. He was shunted to the Works, Housing and Supply as a Minister of State under a full Cabinet Minister, Uma Shankar Dikshit, who was brought into the Cabinet for the first time. Until then Dikshit was one of the three General Secretaries of the Congress, incharge of disbursing election funds to the party candidates.

While consideration of personal power was always predominant in all her dealings with individuals and the organization, in her public utterances she carefully maintained an ideological stance that added to her personal popularity as a progressive leader. For instance, speaking at the time of the dissolution of the Fourth Parliament and calling for mid-term elections for the Lok Sabha, she referred to the Supreme Court's striking down the Presidential order derecognizing the princes as yet another instance of obstruction against implementation of radical measures. She warned the country against 'economic difficulties and the growing impatience of the people who are being exploited by political elements'. She used to talk in those days of violent activities of the right reactionaries, meaning the Jana Sangh and the R.S.S., and left adventurists like the Naxalites. This typically Communist phraseology had become a fashion with her and the political elite. It also indicated the growing influence of the radicals in the party, with a Communist past, under the leadership of Mohan Kumaramangalam, a new entrant to the Union Cabinet. He, along with Siddhartha Shankar Ray, brought a more sophisticated style of functioning at the Centre. They even discarded the khadi uniform of the Congress. A Minister dressed in impeccable western style became a common sight. These two were also the only ones not over-awed by the Prime Minister's position or personality and could talk to her on equal terms. Those were the days of the radicals.

But, true to her policy, never to be totally identified with any rigid policy or set of individuals, Indira took the first opportunity after the dissolution of Parliament to indicate that her radicalism was more pragmatic than was ordinarily believed in those days. Addressing a press conference on December 29, 1970, first she made a frontal attack on 'the vested interests and business groups' who were holding up investments to force the Government to change its policies, and then immediately tried to placate the big business by maintaining that 'further nationalization of private industry was not on the agenda'. She also announced that if returned to power, she would put through constitutional amendments to promote the interests of the 'many' against the few. 'We are not in favour of curtailing Fundamental Rights. We do not even want to take away the right to hold and enjoy property' she declared at the same time.

Just about this time, with J. C. Shah as the Chief Justice, the Supreme Court revoked the Chief Election Commissioner's decision to award the election symbol of the yoked bullocks of the united Congress to the New Congress. This added to the annoyance of the leaders of the ruling party, but they soon reconciled themselves to the reality that the old united Indian National Congress, as it had been known since the independence struggle, had ceased to exist. Its place had been taken by a new party, with a younger and dynamic leadership which tilted towards radicalism as a popular stance but remained for all practical purposes only slightly left of the centre. The Organization Congress, on the other hand, acquired a conservative, but what its leaders claimed to be a Gandhian outlook, except in

Tamil Nadu where Kamaraj maintained a slightly progressive outlook.

It is interesting to note at this point that after the split the two leaders, among all the older ones, who continued to command respect and following in their respective states and the country at large, were Morarji Desai and Kamaraj. All others not only lost their states in the Assembly elections the following year, but also their own followings. The Organization Congress survived as a force only on Gujarat and Tamil Nadu, but the leaders of these two states, Morarji and Kamaraj, never saw eye to eye on future political alignments. As years rolled by, Kamaraj openly started a dialogue with Indira for a possible *rapprochement* between the two Congress parties. But Morarji refused to have anything to do with her to her party and inevitably moved towards the four-party alliance which ultimately emerged as the Janata Party under Jayaprakash Narayan's inspiration. The Janata Party was to be like the Congress of old, not a mere party but a movement of diverse political groups with differing ideologies, brought together by a common cause — that of saving democracy in the country.

On the eve of the 1971 elections, however, there was no people's movement yet. Only a four-party alliance came into being on February 14 in order to fight the elections on the very limited programme of removing Indira from power. At that time neither had she acquired the public image of a ruthless authoritarian leader, nor were the people enthused by the coming together of the disparate political groups as a viable alternative to the Congress. No one took this 'Grand Alliance', as it was called then, seriously for they had not yet acquired the revolutionary fervour that Jayaprakash imparted into the Janata Party later. This was in spite of the fact that their leaders had claimed to be fighting against forces 'which, to achieve absolute power, are raising seductive slogans to mislead the country and take it away from the democratic path'. As was expected, the Grand Alliance was completely swept off its feet by the Indira wave all over the country. It was partly due to the fact that none of the four constituents in the Alliance was prepared at that time to merge its identity in a single party. Nor could they agree on a minimum economic programme. The only agreement they had among themselves was on the single slogan of 'Indira Hatao' (remove Indira). Such a slogan was hardly able to counteract the current popular slogan 'Garibi Hatao' (remove poverty) of the Congress. This call of the Congress spread like wild fire in the countryside, burning away all opposition and prejudice against Indira and her party. A common quip in those days was that even a lamp-post would win with a thumping majority on a Congress Ticket.

An essential part of Indira Gandhi's election strategy was to give the Opposition the least amount of time to prepare for and face the election. But she had known in her own mind for quite some time that she would call for a mid-term poll. People close to her had already been assigned various tasks, like collection of funds, screening of important candidates and assessment of the party's chances. But it was all done rather surreptitiously from the Prime Minister's house. Perhaps, the A.I.C.C. office and its secretariat were only vaguely aware of what was on. Uma Shankar Dikshit was the only one in the organization in complete confidence of the Prime Minister. And he was given the important task of doling out funds to party candidates — on an average Rs. 25,000 to each candidate. The Congress President came into the picture only after the elections had actually been called. Despite these prior preparations, the formality of selecting the candidates proved quite a hectic affair. On top of it needing attention was the question of arriving at adjustment of seats with the C.P.I. in West Bengal, Kerala, Bihar and Uttar Pradesh. Even till the deadline for filing nominations, some candidates were asked telegraphically to file in their nominations only tentatively, pending the final selection.

If this was the condition in the more organized ruling party, one can well imagine the plight of the four-party alliance, which formally came into being only about a month before the elections were to be held. Naturally, the task of adjustment of seats among the four constituents in various states, the pulls and counter-pulls within the different parties, the paucity of funds compared to the Congress and the lack of good candidates — all added to the difficulties of the Grand Alliance. Even so it managed to field as many as 543 candidates for a total of 515 seats. In 76 constituencies all the four constituents of the Alliance had put up candidates, because there was no time left to arrive at an adjustment among themselves. It was quite remarkable that in the remaining constituencies they were able to agree on a single candidate for each constituency. Thus, the Organization Congress put up a total of 237 candidates, the Jana Sangh 152, the Swatantra Party 62 and the Samyukta Socialist Party 92. This also goes to prove that it was not just the division of the

Opposition votes that gave the Congress the fantastic two-thirds victory. There was much more to it, apart from the all-too-obvious popular support enjoyed by Indira herself. The Organization Congress was the biggest loser of the four constituents of the Grand Alliance — winning only 16 seats as against the 65 it had had in the previous Lok Sabha.

The Grand Alliance disintegrated immediately after the election, with each constituent asserting its own separate identity in Parliament. The Organization Congress Working Committee attributed the sweeping victory of the New Congress to the latter's easy access to vast sums of money, misuse of Government machinery during elections, partisan use of All India Radio and such other factors. The Swatantra Party leader, C. Rajagopalachari, remarked on March 12 that democracy had been 'fatally wounded by this unscrupulous hustled mid-term election'. But the popular mood at that time was such that people dismissed these and similar remarks lightly as the rantings of aging and frustrated individuals who should have long retired from public life but still nurtured ambition of being in power.

Handing over charge to his successor, D. Sanjivayya, on April 3 at the Delhi A.I.C.C. Session, the outgoing Congress President Jagjivan Ram struck a note of warning that 'the party is at the cross-roads of history. It has aroused the hopes and aspirations of the people. Their tolerance has reached a breaking point. If we allow it to burst, the Opposition parties will accuse us of having broken our pledges to the people.' That is exactly what started happening from 1973 onwards and reached its climax with the total rout of the Congress in 1977.

It was no mere accident of history that simultaneously, in almost all South Asian countries, popular leaders swept the polls, as Indira had done in India. Mrs. Bandarnaike was thus returned in Sri Lanka. In Pakistan, too, after a military regime of nearly 13 years, a comparatively fair election had thrown up two popular and strong leaders in the two wings of Pakistan, Sheikh Mujibur Rehman in East and Zulfikar Ali Bhutto in West Pakistan. Both of them had swept the polls in their respective regions, the Awami League under Mujibur Rehman securing all the 201 seats in East Pakistan and Pakistan People's Party under Bhutto's leadership getting in West Pakistan the remaining 99 seats in the National Assembly of 300. It was this division of seats that created the situation leading Mujib to declaring independence for Bangladesh. The next twelve months proved to be a nightmare for the people of Bangladesh and a time of serious political and military decisions for India. During those critical days, all internal differences in the ruling party and the country were pushed to the background and as at that time the Jana Sangh leader Atal Behari Vajpayee put it, India became 'one country with one leader, Indira Gandhi, to save the honour and integrity of the nation'. How that came about is in itself a fascinating story.

Some ominous developments were, however, already taking place behind the scenes unknown to the outside world, and were to have far-reaching consequences for the country and Indira Gandhi herself. The first of these was the coming into being of a combine or, as it came to be known later as a caucus, around the ambitious son of the Prime Minister, Sanjay Gandhi, who started interfering, at first in a small way, in the transfers and appointments of personnel at various police stations in and around Delhi. He had already begun building his Maruti factory on the land allotted to him by Bansi Lal. Complaints about interference in the local police administration reached the Principal Secretary to the Prime Minister, P. N. Haksar, through the Home Ministry. Some resentment was expressed by a few senior officers, both in the local administration and in the Home Ministry, at this uncalled for interference by somebody who had no *locus standi* in the hierarchy of power except that he was the Prime Minister's son. Haksar had occasion to talk about it as an elder belonging to the same community, not only to the Prime Minister but to the young man himself.

Instead of having any taming effect, this talk only created powerful enemies against Haksar in circles close to the Prime Minister. He had already annoyed important politicians, like Uma Shankar Dikshit, Lalit Narayan Mishra and Yashpal Kapoor, by objecting to their manner of political manipulations divorced from any ideological necessity. He soon realized that it would be better for him to fade out before he was pushed out. He therefore asked for his retirement in the normal course on September 4, 1971, for reasons of health. He was allowed to go without any fuss, partly because he was considered dispensable in the presence of D. P. Dhar, India's former Ambassador to the Soviet Union, as the Chairman of the Policy Planning Committee in External Affairs Ministry and T. N. Kaul as the Foreign Secretary. With these two available for dealing with the day-to-day developments on the Indo-Pakistan borders in the wake of the Bangladesh war of independence, Haksar's going away was not considered too much of a loss. That he had to be recalled within three months to his old position in an honorary capacity is proof enough of how indispensable he had become for Indira and the country in those critical days.

Haksar's going away at that juncture produced quite a bit of relief for those who had found him as an irritant and a stumbling block in their designs to acquire authority and power, not necessarily legitimately. His replacement, Professor P. N. Dhar, was more an academician than an administrator. Haksar had maintained his independence, despite being so close to the seat of political power and at times being called upon to even exercise it. The impact of Professor Dhar in this important office was almost nil, partly because he had come at a time when some unscrupulous persons, with a political base of their own, had taken over the main task of advising the Prime Minister and acting on her behalf. P. N. Haksar, having a broad intellectual grasp of the world events, was able to give the very necessary ideological turn to Indira's personal fight for power with the party bosses earlier. He had also helped her to project a new relevance of India's non-alignment policy in international relations, with the Super Powers on the one side and the Third World on the other. It was also his idea to keep the door open for a dialogue with China, even if it did not lead to an immediate response. Again it was his thesis that India should have a direct dialogue with the Shah of Iran with a view to establishing long-term economic ties, even if that country continued to back Pakistan on Indo-Pakistan disputes.

Although Haksar had retired from the scene for the time being, Mohan Kumaramangalam, who had joined the Union Cabinet as Steel Minister, and Siddhartha Shankar Ray continued to advice the Prime Minister on the need to maintain the ideological stance she had assumed on both national and international planes. They, too, had noticed that some politicians and individuals around Indira were indulging more and more in politics of manipulation and warned her at that time against encouraging such elements. But she apparently listened to their advice only to the extent it helped her to ward off any Opposition attacks on her; and she continued to ignore the criticism, that had started already, of what was being done in the name of setting up a small car factory by her son. She even helped Sanjay to get the necessary letter of intent from the Industrial Development Ministry, contrary to the earlier decision of the Government not to allow a small car project in the country. While the attention of the whole country was concentrated on the Bangladesh developments and the difficulties facing India as a consequence, there was a slight undercurrent of dissatisfaction discernible within the party with the way certain things were happening in the party in the name of the Prime Minister. Lalit Narayan Mishra's interference in Bihar politics had become quite open and blatant. He was the one pulling strings against the state leaders through the use of 'money power', much to the dislike of a very influential section in the Congress Parliamentary Party. The same role was now being played more openly by Yashpal Kapoor in Uttar Pradesh. In other states, too, leaders, who had no base of their own and would have to look to Indira for survival, were being propped up. In other words, a calculated move was set in motion on behalf of Indira to displace anyone acquiring prominence or strength in his own right in any state. The idea was to have everywhere only those leaders who were loyal or beholden to her for their positions.

As a first step in that direction, it was necessary for Indira to establish a hand-picked Central Election Committee, which was due to be constituted at the A.I.C.C. Session at Simla on October 8, 1971, for selecting candidates for the coming Assembly elections. While all the members of the Central Parliamentary Board were its members, there was also a panel of elected members in it. The stormy petrel of the past A.I.C.C. Sessions, Chandra Shekhar, once again put himself up for election to the C.E.C. much against the wishes of the Prime Minister. It became a prestige fight for her, and the High Command threw in all its weight along with that of the Chief Ministers in favour of an agreed panel in which Chandra Shekhar did not figure. The main organizers of this election were Lalit Narayan Mishra, Bansi Lal and Yashpal Kapoor. Despite their cajoling and threats to the delegates they could not prevent Chandra Shekhar's victory. This was a big blow to the caucus that had started operating in the name of the Prime Minister.

Chandra Shekhar's victory also indicated that the so-called radicals, who claimed proximity to the Prime Minister at that time and who considered themselves as the new power elite, including Chandrajit Yadav, one of the General Secretaries of the Congress, had no popular base of their own in the organization despite the important positions held by some of them in the party and the Government. Chandra Shekhar, on the other hand, had displayed, ever since the Bombay Session of the Congress in 1969, that he commanded respect in the rank and file of the party and could win any election to the Working Committee or the C.E.C. Besides, his main reason to put himself up for election to these bodies was to expose attempts, in the name of Indira Gandhi, to stifle inner party democracy. He had always disagreed, whether in the Congress Paliamentary Party, of which he had been a duly elected Secretary one term, or in the A.I.C.C., to fixing elections by mutual understanding among the party leaders behind the scenes. They had fought against similar method of functioning of the 'Syndicate' under Indira Gandhi's leadership in 1969, and did not wish to see its revival in the New Congress — that, too, in her name. Chandra Shekhar had become the leader of those in the Congress who thought this way. He was therefore not liked by the power-wielding clique.

Naturally, the entire Socialist Forum, now controlled by the former Communists, turned against him under the inspiration of Lalit Narayan Mishra and Yashpal Kapoor, to denounce him as disloyal to Indira personally and as being in league with his former colleagues in the Socialist Party allegedly in order to destroy the Congress from within. With him were identified Krishna Kant, Mohan Dharia, Ram Dhan and some others. In due course, Chandra Shekhar become one member of Parliament in the Congress of whom everyone in power of authority was afraid. Overtures to win him over by dangling temptations of a seat in the Cabinet failed to tame him. Although he never broke the party discipline, in forums like the Working Committee he could be uncomfortably outspoken.

The war with Pakistan that was looming large on the horizon kept these simmering differences in the party under control; they did not burst out into the open till much later. Meanwhile, Indira had emerged as the undisputed leader of the country and her finest hour was in the offing.

CHAPTER VI

HER FINEST HOUR
(March 1971 to December 1971)

WITHIN seven days of her swearing in as the Prime Minister, Indira was faced with a major threat to the country's security. The threat came indirectly from the military rulers of Pakistan, who let loose a reign of terror in East Pakistan against Bangla nationalism that had assumed, for the rulers, threatening proportions under the inspiring leadership of Sheikh Mujibur Rehman. India had full sympathy for the people of Bangladesh in their struggle against tyranny of the aggressive West Pakistani rulers. The President of Pakistan, General Yahya Khan, perhaps in one of his drunken moments, had promised return to civilian rule following an election for a National Assembly, little realizing that Bangla nationalism would help Mujibur Rehman to sweep the polls in East Pakistan. They thought they would be able to neutralize his influence through political patronage and, failing that, through downright threats of repression. But the elections held on December 7, 1970, for a National Assembly virtually divided the country into a dominant Bangla section, with all the 201 seats in East Pakistan going to Mujib's Awami League, and a group of 99 from West Pakistan under the leadership of Zulfikar Ali Bhutto, in a house of just 300. The results were shocking to the ruling class of West Pakistan. Although General Yahya Khan himself hailed Mujibur Rehman, leader of the victorious Awami League of East Pakistan, as the future Prime Minister of Pakistan, an ambitious Bhutto, who, too, had swept the polls in the West, was determined to see that no one from the backward East Pakistan was foisted on Pakistan as the Prime Minister, however popular and charismatic that leader might be in his own region. The two regions of Pakistan, divided by one thousand two hundred miles of Indian territory in between, had nothing in common except Islam. Their language, culture, dress and food were entirely different. For the West Pakistani ruling class treating East Pakistan as a colony was essential for the prosperity of the better-developed West. These tensions between the aggressive Punjabi rulers and the growing Bangla nationalists had grown for some years. In fact, India was often accused by the Pakistani rulers of encouraging Bangla nationalism in East Pakistan, not only through direct propaganda from Calcutta Station of All India Radio, but also through clandestine help to the nationalists across the border. It had also been a calculated strategy of Pakistan over the years to fan an anti-India campaign in that country whenever it faced any economic or political trouble of its own. This time they did not have to resort to that, because there was already a tension between the two countries following the break-up of a very big Pakistani ring in Jammu and Kashmir, called the 'Al Fatah' organization, in January 1971. The announcement of the break-up of the spy ring on January 18 was followed with the expulsion of the First Secretary in the Pakistan High Commission, Zafar Iqbal Rathod, for involvement in the spy ring and its sabotage plans. Pakistan retaliated by expelling one of our diplomats of equal rank on grounds of alleged espionage.

That was not the end of the matter, however. Two members of the spy ring, who had evaded arrest, managed to highjack to Lahore an Indian Airline's Fokker Friendship plane on January 30, while on a scheduled flight from Srinagar to Jammu with 28 passengers on board. The highjackers demanded the release of all 'Al Fatah' saboteurs who had been arrested in India, and on February 2, they blew up the plane on the tarmac at Lahore airport in full view of Pakistani troops. Following this incident, Indira, in an election speech at Berhampur in Orissa the next day, warned Islamabad that 'Delhi was strong enough to meet any challenge'. Sheikh Mujibur Rehman, who had gained a clear majority in the National Assembly and had been hailed as the future Prime Minister of Pakistan by President Yahya Khan himself, also condemned the highjacking and the blowing up of the plane in Lahore. But Bhutto, the leader of the West Pakistan group of 99 in the National Assembly, maintained that Pakistan was not responsible for the act, claiming that the highjackers were 'Kashmiris struggling against Indian imperialism'. This was clearly indicative of the attitude of the man who was one day to be the Prime Minister of Pakistan.

India retaliated by disallowing overflights of two military aircrafts of Pakistan to the eastern wing on the day the Indian plane was blown up in Lahore and followed it up by banning all overflights of all Pakistani planes, commercial and military, two days later, when Pakistan refused to hand over the two highjackers to India. This was about the time when Pakistan had ordered a hectic airlifting of troops to the eastern wing as a precaution against a possible revolt of Bangla nationalists. This fear arose from the fact that the West Pakistan power elite was in no mood to hand over power to Mujib, even though he had won the National Assembly election with an overwhelming majority. Yahya and Bhutto had maintained a facade of negotiations with the Bangla leader on how they should go about framing a Constitution for the country. As these negotiations got bogged down on the question of autonomy, the meeting of the National Assembly had to be postponed a number of times. The last round of talks was held in Dacca, when Bhutto turned down any proposal which even remotely promised a possible ascendance of an East Pakistani as the country's Prime Minister. Ultimately, the talks broke down on Mujib's demand for complete autonomy for the two parts of Pakistan except on Defence, Foreign Affairs and Currency. While the talks were still in progress, widespread rioting started in some parts of the eastern wing.

On March 25, General Yahya Khan imposed martial law in East Pakistan and appointed Lt. General Tikka Khan as the Chief Martial Law Administrator. Following India's ban on overflights by Pakistani planes, troop movement from the Western to the Eastern wing had been considerably hampered. Even so Pakistan had managed to move about three divisions by this time using military and civilian aircraft flying via Ceylon. Meanwhile, Pakistan complained to the U.N. Security Council against India for banning the overflights. It had also persuaded several Islamic and West European countries to intercede with India on her behalf to get the ban on overflights of Pakistani planes through Indian airspace lifted. But none of them offered mediatory services, nor were they surprised at India's polite rejection of their suggestions to that effect.

With the breakdown of negotiations in Dacca, General Yahya Khan returned to Islamabad on March 26 after issuing orders to General Tikka Khan to take the necessary steps to tame the recalcitrant Bengalis. On March 28, a clandestine radio, which came to be known in the subsequent critical months as the 'Voice of Indepedent Bangladesh', announced to the world that 'Bangabandhu' Mujibur Rehman had declared independence of Bangladesh. It was no more a part of Pakistan. Thus, even before Indira had time to settle down with her new Cabinet after the elections of 1971, the country was faced with a major development on its eastern borders threatening to swamp the area with an unending stream of refugees running away from the repression let loose by an army gone berserk.

In the beginning it was only a trickle of refugees, but as the weeks passed, it became a torrent, soon to deluge the entire eastern region of India. At the height of suppression there were as many as ten million refugees living in camps hurriedly provided by India despite her own meagre resources. By the time the conscience of the world was aroused at the plight of these people, India had already been spending at the rate of nearly Rs. 2 crores per day for looking after their stay in this country. By the middle of April the East Bengali civil servants, diplomats and army personnel started revolting against the ruthless terror let loose against their people by the Pakistani Army. The first such diplomat to denounce and disown Pakistan was their Deputy High Commissioner in Calcutta, M. Hussain Ali, who moved to Delhi with his family. He later played an important role as a liaison between the Government of India and the Provisional Government of Bangladesh that was set up somewhere near the border. Soon followed the defection of two other diplomats, K. M. Shahbuddin and Amjadul Haque, from Pakistan High Commission in New Delhi. Pakistan retaliated by harassing the Indian diplomats in Dacca. At this point Pakistan wanted to convert its war against Bangla nationalists in East Pakistan into an open military conflict with India in order to divert the world attention from its atrocities against its own people and to shift the blame on to India. As a consequence, the number of clashes on the eastern border between India's Border Security Force and Pakistan Army increased considerably. There was a major border clash in West Bengal on April 26-27 in which several B.S.F. constables were reported killed. Simultaneously, the number of refugees coming to India, too, had increased considerably. On May 10 the Prime Minister had to warn Pakistan publicly that India was undeterred by any of her threats. 'If a situation is forced on us, we are fully prepared to fight', she declared.

As the weeks passed, the situation in East Pakistan became grimmer and grimmer. While the other leaders of the Awami League had escaped, Mujib was taken into custody and for quite some time there was no information about his whereabouts. Meanwhile, a large number of young people, students and others, had organized themselves into a voluntary army of freedom fighters under three Bengali Pakistan Army Majors who had left to fight for their people. This volunteer force, which became famous as the 'Mukti Bahini', grew steadily, acquiring arms and ammunitions from Pakistan troops themselves through guerilla tactics in that land criss-crossed by innumerable rivers and rivulets. It made the heavily equipped Pakistan Army almost immobile and unable to control the fleet-footed Bangla youths who enjoyed the sympathy of the local population and lived on the land itself. Many a heroic tale is still told of these four Majors — one of them today is the Chief Martial Law Administrator of Bangladesh — and their unkempt and ill-clad hordes of inspired youngsters, many in their teens only, taking on the whole might of a highly modern armed machine.

India watched these developments with increasing concern, for, her leaders knew that if the Pakistan Army failed to subdue the youthful 'Mukti Bahini', it would then try to convert its frustrating conflict into an open military confrontation with India. India had given asylum to a number of wounded and fleeing volunteers of the 'Mukti Bahini' in camp hospitals hurriedly set up to care for the lakhs of refugees that had flocked into the Indian side of the border. Already Pakistan had launched a barrage of propaganda against India, accusing her of not only training and arming the 'Mukti Bahini' volunteers, but also sending in her own troops in mufti to help the guerillas. While it could not substantiate its charge, President Yahya Khan threatened on July 19 to declare a war against India 'if she made any attempt to seize any part of East Pakistan'. This was a clever way of telling the world that what was happening in the eastern wing was of India's creation, and she was trying to take over East Pakistan in the name of Bangla nationalists.

India's protests would have had no meaning, had not the world press rushed to Dacca before the borders closed and started exposing the atrocities being committed by the Pakistan Army. For a short while the Martial Law authorities just did not know what to do. Foreign newspapers, particularly in Britain and the United States, which had always shown a bias in favour of Pakistan as against India, started carrying stories hardly complimentary to the military regime of Pakistan. The world public opinion was, for once, with India with the Bangla refugees pouring in daily in their thousands. Gradually the Pakistan authorities woke up to the damage that had been done by this worldwide publicity of virtual genocide perpetrated on Bangladesh people. They started expelling inconvenient correspondents and intercepting their messages. Instead, some friendly correspondents were flown directly from London and Washington to Karachi for a background briefing before they were taken to Dacca on a conducted tour. Even they could not close their eyes to the reality of the situation. Some of them wrote far more damaging dispatches than even those who had been expelled earlier. For once the world mass media endorsed what India had been saying, but Washington could not care less for what was happening in that remote country, as it felt obliged to Pakistan for the help in opening the door for its direct negotiations with China. The rulers in America were willing to turn a blind eye to the atrocities being perpetrated in Bangladesh so long as Pakistan continued to play their game in the international arena. A loyal friend, however ruthless and undemocratic at home, was far more important to them than an honest non-conformist. The then Secretary of State, Dr. Henry Kissinger, had come to New Delhi earlier in the year, but had shown no reaction to Pakistan's intransigence even when it was brought to his notice with irrefutable facts, because he was on his way to achieve the great breakthrough in Sino-U.S. relations and could not be bothered about the genocide of a whole nation or sufferings of a few million people. From Delhi Kissinger went to Islamabad from where he disappeared for a couple of days. He was stated to be on a holiday at a remote hill-station in Pakistan, when, in fact, he had flown to Peking to talk to the late Chou En-lai, the then Prime Minister of China. It was a major breakthrough for him personally and for Richard Nixon in the White House. They could not be bothered about what happened in South Asia, where the major country, India, had always been a constant irritant to the American policy-makers. There was much more sympathy for India and Bangladesh in some of the West European countries like Britain and France, but they could not afford to deviate too much from the line laid down by the Americans on international problems. Thus, India found herself pressed, on the one side, by a ruthless enemy bent upon transferring to her its unwanted surplus population in East Pakistan, and, on the other, almost completely isolated politically in the international forums which could have been expected to bring pressure on Pakistan to make her desist from ruthless suppression of Bangla nationalists.

For all the sympathy that the people of the United States showed for India and the suppressed people of Bangladesh at that time, their

Government showed utter lack of understanding of the seriousness of the situation. A very senior State Department official suggested to the author, during a meeting with him in Washington, that Yahya had got rid of his surplus population in East Pakistan, which had really caused the disparity between the seats secured by the Awami League of Mujib and then by the People's Party of Bhutto. Once there was a parity between the population in the two wings of Pakistan, he added, a fresh election could be held to correctly reflect the power pattern in Pakistan. He further argued that India could do nothing but to lump the so-claimed 10 million refugees (he did not believe there were so many!), and that it would hardly make any difference to her with over forty per cent of her own five hundred and sixty million people living below the poverty line. He indicated that his country would, of course, be quite generous if India did not take recourse to arms to settle this problem. In any case he felt convinced, as were most officials in Washington at that time, that militarily Pakistan was far too superior to India to leave her any choice in the matter. Such was the sad state of understanding in Washington of a very serious and volatile situation in South Asia. The White House was apparently confident that, before much damage was done, the United States would be able to force a ceasefire in the eventually of an open military conflict. What the U.S. could not prevent was the type of guerilla movement that had developed in Bangladesh in the name of the 'Mukti Bahini'. The State Department and the White House were angry at the adverse publicity their ally was getting and so they started accusing India of giving sanctury to armed guerilas. This was the only thing they could find against India, which had so far maintained a very correct public stance on the whole issue.

Meanwhile, General Yahya Khan continued to threaten India that he would declare a war 'if India made any attempts to seize any part of East Pakistan'. In his reply on July 20, India's Foreign Minister Swaran Singh cautioned Pakistan's military rulers against using the freedom struggle in Bangladesh as a pretext for launching an attack on India. For the first time India's intelligence on Pakistani troop movements and plans was perfect. If Yahya made one move in the East or the West, India immediately made a counter-move in terms of its own troop movements on the border. As is well known all over the world, the game of international politics is played at two levels: the diplomatic level where the most polite language is used to convey the harshest of intentions, and at another level, where no holds are barred so long as the objective is clear. A situation had arisen on India's Eastern borders where there was no escape from an open armed conflict. Harassed by the continuing activities of armed guerillas, Pakistan military commanders now started thinking of sealing their sanctuaries, or suspected concentrations, in the adjoining Indian territory. If it provoked an open military conflict between India and Pakistan, they and their masters in Islamabad thought that that would serve their purpose far better in international forums. Thus attacks on India's Border Security Forces guarding the various border posts suddenly escalated in the ensuing months.

Indian intelligence services had already informed the Government of the possible Pakistani intentions and therefore an army alert was ordered, accompanied with considerable troop movements towards the two borders of Pakistan. But the army commanders were strictly instructed to keep in the background and come to the aid of the B.S.F. only if the enemy crossed into our territory. Simultaneously, the Prime Minister, who used to have regular meetings in those days with the three Service Chiefs, General Manekshaw, Air Chief Marshal P. C. Lal, and Admiral Nanda, asked them to keep contingency plans ready just in case an open conflict did develop in the next few months. Her strict instructions were that the plans in the east should aim at the fall of Dacca within two to three weeks and in the west to aim at mainly a holding operation. But if Pakistan were to pierce into any part of India, a larger chunk was to be seized from the enemy.

On the international plane, special envoys were dispatched to friendly countries to explain India's point of view. During these diplomatic contacts, it was made quite clear that unless international pressure was brought to bear upon Pakistan to ensure the release of, and negotiation with, Sheikh Mujibur Rehman, India would have no alternative left but to intervene in Bangladesh to end the agony of the people there and to send back the huge refugee population she had had to receive as a consequence. While the western capitals remained lukewarm to India's case and advised against a military solution, the Soviet Bloc promised full support in any eventuality. It was also suggested that India should enter into a twenty-year treaty of peace, friendship and co-operation with the Soviet Union. D. P. Dhar, who had been India's most successful Ambassador to Moscow, was now the Chairman of the Policy Planning Committee in the External Affairs Ministry and formed with P. N. Haksar, Principal Secretary to the Prime Minister, and T. N. Kaul, Foreign Secretary, the trio who really initiated all foreign policy moves. This trio was convinced that signing of a friendship treaty, which, according to them, had no military overtones, at this juncture would be politically of great help to India in international forums like the Security Council, where she appeared isolated on the Indo-Pakistan issue. Anticipating a possible military conflict with Pakistan, which could not, in any case, be expected to go on for more than a week or two before international pressure was brought to bear upon both parties to agree to a ceasefire, it was felt very desirable to have a super power and permanent member of the Security Council backing India at the crucial moment. Whatever little doubt there might have been entertained at that time about Soviet Union's political support in the Security Council, it would certainly be dispelled with the signing of the treaty. Besides, the treaty would have an immediate and far-reaching impact internationally, it was argued by the trio.

The Soviet Union had been pressing India for quite a number of years to sign such a treaty and much groundwork had been done on it when D. P. Dhar was India's Ambassador in Moscow. But it would be wrong to assume that any of the trio had any misconceptions about the Soviet Union. For them national interests were far more important, and, at that critical moment, it appeared to them that signing that treaty would serve the national interests most. The question was discussed in detail in the Union Cabinet, and it was unanimously agreed that it would be in India's immediate interests, particularly with Pakistan threatening a war every now and then. The agreement was accordingly signed in New Delhi on August 9 between the Soviet Foreign Minister Andrie Gromyko who had come specially for this purpose and India's Minister for External Affairs Sardar Swaran Singh. The treaty envisaged immediate consultations between the two countries to counteract any threat to the security of either country and to take 'appropriate, effective measures' to ensure peace. In the talks Gromyko had with the Prime Minister and Swaran Singh, assurances were offered to India about Soviet readiness to supply sophisticated weapons to strengthen India's defences. It provided a very timely warning to the military rulers of Pakistan and their friends in China that India was not alone.

The agreement was hailed in Parliament from all sides, and even by the leaders of those parties which had always had reservations about the Soviet Union and its ultimate intensions towards India. Even in some foreign capitals like Washington, London and Paris, the first reaction was a sigh of relief that the Soviet Union would now be able to restrain India against starting a military adventure. But after a few days, when the provisions of the treaty had been fully digested by experts in those capitals, there arose a feeling among them of having been outmanoeuvred by the Soviet Union in the subcontinent. For the first time military experts in those countries started taking detailed interests in the respective strengths of Pakistan and India and the possible outcome of a short and sharp conflict between the two.

China's reaction, too, was not very happy. There was reason to believe that in a conflict that country was likely to make some noises, but now would not dare to actively participate on the side of Pakistan for fear of retaliation by the Soviet Union under this treaty. India, naturally, felt considerably relieved on this count. Even so our military experts wanted assurance that a conflict, if it was forced on India, will take place at the time of their choosing and not when Pakistan wanted it. They did not want such an eventuality to occur until the northern passes were snowbound. Besides, Indian troops were still at their bases far away from the borders. Their movement alone would require a clear six to eight weeks. It is a moot point that if Pakistan had launched its attack two months earlier than on December 3, 1971, India might have been caught on the wrong foot, particularly on the western front.

By September the number of refugees from Bangladesh had gone up to about nine million, stretching India's resources to the maximum. The stories of horror and atrocities perpetrated by Pakistani troops, against students and other intellectuals as well as on the poor people in the countryside in Bangladesh, had gradually woken up the conscience of a few humanitarian organizations in the world and some foreign aid had started flowing in. But it was only a trickle compared to the burden that India had to bear. Meanwhile, the number of clashes on the eastern borders had increased perceptibly. There was no indication from Islamabad that the problem of East Pakistan would be settled politically, nor was there any information about the whereabouts of Sheikh Mujibur Rehman. Repeated inquiries on behalf of different powers in Islamabad yielded no information. It was at this stage that Indira decided to undertake a tour of various world capitals to personally inform the leaders there about the situation in the subcontinent and to tell them in no uncertain terms that unless international pressure was brought to bear on Pakistan to seek earnestly a solution of the Bangladesh problem through negotiations with Sheikh Mujibur Rehman, India could not remain for long a mute spectator to actions that had resulted in her having to care for millions of refugees. The first capital she decided to visit was Moscow on September 27. Her plane landed in Moscow just about lunch time and official talks at the Kremlin, where she stayed as the State guest, were due to begin at four in the afternoon. But Brezhnev, who was also to be present at those talks, could not return that evening from a visit to Sofia. The Russian Prime Minister Kosygin suggested to Indira that the talks might start without the Secretary of the Communist Party of the Soviet Union, for President Podgorny would be present. Indira's reply was that she had come to discuss matters of great importance to her country's security and integrity and therefore she would prefer the top three of the Soviet hierarchy to be present when the talks begin. Formal talks were thus postponed till the next morning. This was interpreted in the Indian official circles as the Russian way of testing how serious the Indian leader was and how determined to stand up to Pakistan even militarily.

Apparently the next day's talks progressed smoothly. While India was advised to show some more patience and assured that the Soviet Union would do all that was possible to persuade Pakistan to settle the political problem in East Pakistan, India on her part, made it quite clear that she could not wait indefinitely and carry the crushing burden of the eight million refugees for very long. International aid had to come in a big way to help look after these refugees. Indira also managed to get an assurance from the Russian leaders that in case of an open military conflict, the Soviet Union would not only help India with sophisticated weapons, but would also extend political support to the country in the United Nations and other international forums. The talks were described by D. P. Dhar, who had accompanied the Prime Minister along with T. N. Kaul, as very successful from India's point of view. Later that very evening, at a banquet held by the Indian Prime Minister, Kosygin made a statement to Indian correspondents accompanying the Indian delegation, which, in a very clever way, equated India and Pakistan and tried to project a neutral public stance in regard to the Bangladesh developments. This led to considerable consternation in the Indian camp and the Indian reporters were persuaded to delay their dispatches overnight. Next day, September 29, Kosygin had come to see the Indian Prime Minister off at the airport and when he noticed the group of Indian newspapermen, he made a beeline for them. He plunged straightway into an explanation of his previous night's remarks even before any of the reporters had formulated a proper question. In any case the Indian officials heaved a sigh of relief. One or two papers carried both the statements separately, but without causing much damage to Indo-Soviet relations or any misunderstanding among their leaders.

While Indira's visit to Moscow had been quite encouraging from India's point of view, the situation on the eastern border was becoming grimmer and grimmer as the days passed. Jagjivan Ram, who was India's Defence Minister in those days, on October 17 made the first categorical statement on a possibility of war with Pakistan. This statement was based on definite information India had obtained through its intelligence sources of Pakistani troop movements and of plans being hatched in the Pakistan Army Headquarters for provoking a war on the western front if the situation in the eastern wing continued to deteriorate. There was another purpose behind the Defence Minister's statement. It was to convey to General Yahya Khan that India had a very accurate idea of what he had in mind and was fully prepared to meet any eventuality. The fact, however, was that India had still not moved her troops to the western borders. Orders were immediately issued for the forward movement of troops from their bases. The troop movement on the eastern region had already been made. A massive operation was undertaken by the Indian railways to ensure that our troops reached their forward bases on the western front within the next six to eight weeks. Jagjivan Ram's statement, as was expected, led to a suggestion from General Yahya Khan offering talks which, of course, was rejected outright by Indira herself, saying that 'you cannot shake hands with a clenched fist'.

On the eastern side now the 'Mukti Bahini' operations had become a major headache for the Pakistani military commanders, who openly alleged that Indian troops in mufti had been sent in masquarading as Mukti Bahini volunteers. Of course, the Provisional Government of Bangladesh, which had been operating from a small village settlement on the border of West Bengal, had been given all facilities by the Government of India to run a school near by for giving a six-week crash training to young volunteers of the 'Mukti Bahini' recruited from among the refugees spread in temporary camps all along the border. Representatives of the Provisional Government of Bangladesh used to visit these refugee camps in search of such volunteers. Many of them were university students who had been hounded out by the Pakistani troops. The Provisional Government also made arrangements to secure arms for these volunteers. A stage had been reached where India was actively engaged in helping to raise the 'Mukti Bahini'. Many a foreign correspondent wrote heroic accounts of these bands of young volunteers operating in a country writhing under the oppression let loose by a ruthless military machine. The rape and murder of hundreds and thousands of Bangla girls in the trenches by the Pakistani soldiers only resulted in redoubled determination of the 'Mukti Bahini' volunteers to take revenge. When they got the chance, they were equally ruthless with Pakistani soldiers.

Six weeks were over since Indira had visited Moscow. She had promised the Soviet leaders to do nothing during this time except await their efforts to persuade Islamabad to see reason. Their efforts had apparently failed. Indira now planned a tour to six Western capitals to make a last effort to secure their good offices for persuading Pakistan not to precipitate a military conflict. She left for Europe on October 24; visited six capitals including Washington, London, Paris and Bonn and returned on November 13, not very happy with the outcome of her visit. Before leaving she had been keenly missing her former Principal Secretary, Haksar, and requested him to rejoin in an honorary capacity in the same post on a token salary of Rs. 750 a month. At that time away in Geneva for rest and medical treatment, Haksar joined her party on her way to the world capitals. While Indira found some understanding and sympathy for India's problem in Bonn, Paris and London, in Washington she had the most disheartening experience with Nixon and herself talking at completely different levels. She returned to New Delhi a thoroughly disillusioned but a wiser person convinced that whatever might happen in the next few months, the blame would always be placed at India's door, partly because she was the biggest country in the subcontinent and partly because she was looked upon with suspicion on account of her special relationship with the Soviet Union.

However, in her own way, Indira had conveyed to the Western leaders, as she had done to the Soviet leaders a few weeks earlier, that the situation involving the burden of nearly ten million refugees and the irritation due to constant sniping at her borders was too serious for India to brook any further delay while hoping for international pressure to build up on Pakistan for sorting out the political problem in Bangladesh. The Americans did not take her too seriously, except insofar as they suspended all shipments to India of arms and strategic materials which had been ordered much earlier. The quantity of these materials was so small that it did not matter much to India, except for its publicity value. The British, the French and the West Germans were quite sympathetic, but advised further restraint and hoped India would rather depend on her friends in the U.N. and the Security Council to force Pakistan to come to the negotiating table with the Bangladesh leaders. They agreed that the first problem was to get some information about Mujib, as to whether he was still alive, and that he had not been tortured into signing something not acceptible to his people. Such were legitimate fears of his colleagues in the Provisional Government of Bangladesh. Indira, in her turn, made it quite clear that she could wait only for a maximum of six weeks for international efforts to try and get Pakistan military leaders to see reason. But she was not very hopeful, and wanted to leave behind a distinct impression that while, in case there was a military conflict, it would not be because of India's choosing, still India was determined to see to it that Pakistan did not get away with the bullying tactics.

On return to India on November 13, she apparently advised the three Services Chiefs to be ready for any eventuality, both on the eastern as well as on the western borders, at short notice. It was on November 22 that Pakistan precipitated an open conflict in the east by sending four Pakistan Saber jets into West Bengal on a mission to destroy alleged sanctuaries of the 'Mukti Bahini'. This was the first direct attack on the Indian soil and India retaliated by shooting down three of the four attacking planes and hitting the fourth one which, however, managed to escape towards Jessore cantonment in Bangladesh. The next day Pakistan declared a State of Emergency and followed it up with an attack on Indian border post, again in West Bengal, with a mechanized column including Chafee tanks, 14 of which were destroyed in the operation undertaken to repulse the attack. The regular units of the army, which had been placed behind the Border Security Force, were now moved up to take on the primary responsibility for guarding the border in the face of regular attacks by the Pakistani troops on the other side. While the war had not been formally declared, fighting started all along the border in the east with daily clashes. The orders to the Indian troops were not to move into Bangladesh, but to repulse every attempt of the Pakistanis to make the Indian soil as the fighting arena.

On the western front, too, there was an ominous movement of Pakistani troops all along the ceasefire line in Jammu and Kashmir, along the Indo-Pakistan border in Punjab and across the border along the Rajasthan desert going right down to the Runn of Kutch which had already been the target of an attack earlier in 1965. For once our intelligence reports had predicted accurately that General Yahya Khan's public threat of war within ten days, made on November 24, was a real one. The Pakistan plans, according to the intelligence reports, were to make a pre-emptive air strike at almost all the forward airbases in India on December 3 to mark the beginning of the war, which was soon to start, with a massive thrust at Chhamb-Jaurian sector in Jammu with the purpose of attempting a breakthrough into Kashmir, and with thrusts via Haji Pir in Poonch and down south in the deserts of Rajasthan. Based on her own earlier clear-cut orders to the three Services Chiefs, Indira gave them a blanket order to start retaliating in any manner they thought fit the moment such an attack started from the other side. She had also taken her Political Affairs Committee of the Cabinet into confidence on this matter. As the time approached on December 3, she herself made a plan to be away in Calcutta to address a large public meeting. Two of her other senior colleagues, Jagjivan Ram and Y. B. Chavan were also away in Patna and Bombay, respectively, when the Pakistani planes launched their attack on seven of India's forward airfields exactly at 5.47 in the evening on December 3 when it was already quite dark, as had been anticipated to the minute by our intelligence sources.

In New Delhi that evening there was no air-raid practice which had been going on every alternate day for the past few weeks. As the situation was rather grim, there used to be a formal briefing of the world press at six every evening in the spacious hall of the Press Information Bureau. The official spokesman used to be the Secretary of the Inforamtion and Broadcasting Ministry R. C. Dutt himself. That particular evening the entire press corp, nearly three hundred in all, had gathered for the usual official briefing, when at about 6 p.m., while it was just getting dark, an air-raid warning was sounded and the street lights switched off. Everyone thought perhaps it was one of the surprise exercises. But the air-raid alarm went on and on for quite some time, with no sign of the official spokesman anywhere. Everyone gathered there realized that it was something more than just an air-raid practice. Even the officials of the Press Information Bureau did not know what was on, except that they had been warmed to keep the press people waiting for an important announcement. It was an hour and a half later that a grim R. C. Dutt, accompanied by a Joint Secretary of the Defence Ministry and the Principal Information

Officer, entered the hall and without wasting any time in formalities announced: 'Gentlemen, this is not an air-raid practice, but an actual attack by Pakistani planes on almost all the airfields of India.' Making the announcement more dramatic, he went on: 'Just this time bombing is on over Srinagar, Pathankote, Amritsar, Ambala, Agra, Jodhpur, Faridkot, Avantipur (J & K) and Uttarlai (Rajasthan) airfields.' He then gave details of the number of planes employed by Pakistan in this so-called pre-emptive, but unsuccessful, strike, for not a single Indian plane was hit on the ground. He also announced that ground troops had attacked all along the ceasefire line across the Punjab and Rajasthan borders.

In Calcutta, news of the air attack reached the Prime Minister about six in the evening at the Maidan just as she got up to address the huge gathering which had assembled to hear her. Her first words, as reported in Calcutta newspapers next day, were: 'As I stand here to speak to you, Pakistan has unleashed a massive air attack on our country.' Indira returned to New Delhi by about eight in the evening. So did Jagjivan Ram, but Chavan could not reach until two in the morning next day because his plane had to be diverted as there was a night-long attack on Jodhpur airfield. The Union Cabinet met on her return at about nine and took a formal decision to retaliate. By midnight our planes were pounding most of the important airbases in Pakistan. In a mid-night broadcast to the nation the Prime Minister described this 'wanton attack' as a 'full scale war launched by Pakistan'. She assured the nation that the unprovoked aggression would be 'decisively and finally repelled'. These were brave words carrying a ring of refreshing determination behind them. For once, India had the finest of leadership at all levels, starting from the political down to the administrative and military, and the chain of command was very clearly defined.

The attack by Pakistan was also the signal for the Indian troops to move into Bangladesh to end the agony of the people of that country in the shortest possible time. The Prime Minister had asked the three Services Chiefs, particularly the Chief of the Army Staff, General Manekshaw, to finish the operation in Bangladesh in the shortest possible time, in any case in not more than three weeks. Preparations had begun much earlier. Now started the implementation of the plan with a four-pronged move of Indian troops towards Dacca. The Pakistan Army defences were made in the traditional manner, the first ring of defensive fortifications around the border, the second midway, because the rivers of East Bengal provided a natural obstacle to an attacking force reaching Dacca, and the last around Dacca — the capital — itself. Trained in the traditional British copybook style of military manoeuvres, the Pakistanis expected the Indians to follow the same style, for the two armies were almost identical in training and discipline. The one thing they overlooked was that the Indian army commanders had not been spoilt by political power and had concentrated in the past twenty years solely in improving their professional competence.

After having studied the terrain, the Indian military strategists worked out a strategy of movement, avoiding frontal confrontation with well-trenched Pakistani troops in and around their cantonments. Instead, they were bypassed and then attacked from behind by a small column, the rest moving on towards the capital. The capitulation of Dacca was the main objective. The Air Force played a very important role in this war of movement, first by clearing the skies over Bangladesh of all Pakistani military aircraft, then by dominating the skies and finally by helping the movement of the ground forces with helicopter airlifts in a difficult terrain, criss-crossed with innumerable rivulets apart from three major rivers. Except for the northern Hilly area and across West Bengal near Jessore Cantonment, this war of quick movement succeeded excellently. Just when the Indian troops were poised for a breakthrough towards Dacca, the U.S. aircraft carrier *Enterprise* started moving towards the Bay of Bengal. This was an open threat by the Americans. Only thirty-six hours were left for the *Enterprise* to reach the port of Chittagong. Two of the Indian columns, one from Agartala side and the other from Sylhet in the north, had reached the outskirts of Dacca. The third column was about to cross the river from Khulna side and the fourth had come down menacingly near via Faridpur, when General Manekshaw made his first offer asking the Commander of the Pakistani troops in Bangladesh, General Niazi, to surrender in order to save the loss of life and property in an all-out attack on Dacca. This was an attrition at its best, helped further by a most accurate rocket attack on the Government House in the heart of Dacca by Indian Air Force boys, scaring the provincial Governor and his Cabinet out of their wits. The surrender came at about four in the afternoon on December 16, exactly fifteen days after the war had actually begun. Dacca had fallen a few hours ahead of the arrival time of the U.S. naval squadron led by *Enterprise* in the Bay of Bengal.

Ever since the war had started, the United States had brought forward resolution after resolution in the U.N. Security Council calling on the two parties for immediate ceasefire. And every time the resolution came up, it was vetoed by the Soviet Union. China was every time with the U.S. Britain and France had remained neutral, watching the situation as it developed in Bangladesh particularly. When they were convinced that Dacca would fall, they decided to sponsor a joint resolution on December 16.

India's and Indira's finest hour came at about 4.30 in the afternoon that day when in a hushed Lok Sabha, especially called for that purpose, Indira announced the fall of Dacca amidst thunderous applause from all sides. While the House was packed, the visitors' galleries were almost empty. The timing of this special session had been changed thrice since lunch time. When the actual announcement came, even the usually packed diplomatic gallery was almost empty but for the chief of the political section of the U.S. Embassy in New Delhi and an officer from the U.K. High Commission. After the announcement, these diplomats speculated with some journalists about what India's next step would be. Would the Indian Army which was doing equally well in its holding operations on the west, apart from occupying a huge chunk of desert land across the Rajasthan desert, now move into West Pakistan the way it had done in the east to finish the Pakistani military machine? At least that was the impression Washington had been given. It therefore came as a big surprise to the western diplomatic circles in New Delhi when, within an hour of the fall of Dacca, India's Prime Minister offered unilateral ceasefire to General Yahya Khan from eight in the evening next day. There was terrific diplomatic activity between London and Washington and pressure was brought to bear upon Islamabad to accept the ceasefire offer.

By then it had become clear to everyone that Pakistan stood no chance against India in the face of the blasting of the Karachi harbour by Indian patrol boats, the sinking of the big Pakistani submarine, *Gazi*, outside Vishakhapatnam harbour and of two destroyers outside Karachi and the destruction by the Indian Air Force of its oil installations in and around the harbour and the penetration of the huge armed column across the Rajasthan desert towards Longewala. The Indian army had also occupied 3,500 sq. km of Pakistan territory, adjoining the desert of Rajasthan, right up to the railhead at Naya Chor. Pakistani rulers had themselves realized that they had been truly beaten, with nearly 90,000 of their troops in Bangladesh taken as prisoners of war, and their entire air force in the eastern wing completely destroyed. It would have been suicidal for Pakistan at that moment to continue the war.

From India's point of view the unilateral ceasefire offer was very important politically. It forestalled a joint move that evening by Britain and France to bring a ceasefire resolution in the Security Council. The Soviet Union would have found it very embarrassing to veto it, because the basic objective of their ally had been already achieved and they could not possibly be a party to any further military adventure by India. India, on her part, was determined not to have a ceasefire at the behest of Security Council. She had had a not very happy experience of the ceasefire in Jammu and Kashmir called by a resolution of that august body. For the first time that ceasefire line had been changed and India was in no mood to allow U.N. interference, as in the past, on what came to be known later as the new line of actual control. India had thus taken the whole question of the Jammu and Kashmir ceasefire line's supervision out of the hands of the U.N. military observers. These observers still continue to stay in Srinagar and on the other side in Pakistan, but India does not allow them now to go to the line of actual control. Nor does she bother to report to them any ceasefire violations. These questions are now taken up directly with the sector commanders of the opposite side.

At one stroke India had inflicted a major military defeat on Pakistan and outmanoeuvred its political allies in the West, particularly the United States. Later it was, of course as expected, made out in certain western quarters that India had been pressurized by the Soviet Union, whose special representative was present in New Delhi, to call for the ceasefire against the wishes of India's Defence Minister Jagjivan Ram who allegedly wanted the Pakistani military machines to be finished for all times. Perhaps, the Defence Minister had expressed such an opinion in the heat of the battle. But when he realized the tremendous political advantage India stood to gain by calling for a ceasefire on her own, he wholeheartedly agreed with that decision. Another point which should not be overlooked in this context was that the ceasefire decision was taken at a meeting of the Cabinet immediately after the announcement in Parliament of the fall of Dacca. The Prime Minister, or her aides, had hardly any time to receive any advice on this issue. The year 1971 saw the emergence of India as a middle power in her own right in South Asia and of Indira Gandhi as a statesman of international reputation. It was the peak of Indira's achievement as Prime Minister, never again to be matched, even though she stayed in power thereafter for another six years.

CHAPTER VII

THE DECLINE SETS IN
(December 1971 to January 1973)

THE euphorbia generated by the magnificent victory against Pakistan overshadowed any premonitions on the economic and political difficulties that were to follow in the next six months. Perhaps, the Government was aware of what the cost of the war would be in terms of inflation; but this was not the time to spoil the glow in which the country and its leaders were basking. In a memorable function held, a day after the ceasefire became effective, in the historic Central Hall of Parliament leaders of all political parties attributed India's victory to the 'wise and courageous leadership' provided by the Prime Minister. They also paid well-deserved tributes to India's Armed Forces and the 'Mukti Bahini', and attacked the U.S. administration for its 'blatantly partisan role and for sending a task force of the Seventh Fleet, led by the nuclear-powered aircraft carrier *Enterprise*, to the Bay of Bengal in a vain bid to bail out the Yahya regime'.

The Prime Minister's memorable words on this occasion were: 'World admires a deed well done, and with all modesty I think we have done this action well.' But she warned: 'Let us not forget that the road ahead is still long and very steep and we have many peaks to scale.' She went on to add amidst loud applause that 'we will go from peak to peak, raising our nation to greater heights of quality and excellence.' As a fitting tribute of a grateful nation, President Giri conferred the 'Bharat Ratna' award on Indira.

While India was basking in the glow of a victory well earned, Pakistan was naturally passing through a very traumatic experience. There were widespread demonstrations in that country against General Yahya Khan. He was forced to resign the presidentship on December 20, and the leader of the Pakistan People's Party, Z. A.

Bhutto, who had more than a year earlier swept the polls for the National Assembly in West Pakistan, was sworn in as the new President and Martial Law Administrator. A civilian Head of State had taken over in Pakistan after thirteen years of military rule. But the language he used in the first few weeks of his ascendance to power was hardly that of the polished politician he turned out to be later. Bhutto's first public statement, two days after he took over as the President of Pakistan, was to promise to his countrymen 'to take revenge' for the humiliation that India had inflicted on Pakistan. In a broadcast over Radio Pakistan he claimed that 'East Pakistan (which had now been recognized by many countries as independent Bangladesh) is an inseparable and unseverable part of Pakistan'. This was, perhaps, only a public posture of a politician who wanted to entrench himself before he took any initiative towards accepting the new reality in the subcontinent. He also held talks with Sheikh Mujibur Rehman, who had been under arrest in West Pakistan, in a vain bid to persuade the later to retain some links, however slender, between the two erstwhile wings of Pakistan. But the father of Bangladesh was in no mood to oblige. Ultimately, on January 8, 1972, Sheikh Mujibur Rehman was taken to London in a Pakistan International Airways plane and released there. The Sheikh's first and most historic statement on release in London was that 'Bangladesh was an unchallengeable reality'. Two days later he arrived in New Delhi, on way to Dacca, and was accorded a very warm welcome by President Giri, Prime Minister Indira Gandhi and a huge crowd of admirers who had gathered at the airport to receive the 'Bangabandhu', as he was now affectionately called.

The popularity of Indira as the Prime Minister had soared sky high. But, there was a simmering of discontent in her party at the growing concentration of power in a single hand. She had become the most powerful leader the Congress had had since Independence. Her handling of the rebuffs from the United States and her slogan of self-reliance, coined at that time, became the keynote of the general elections to the State Assemblies that were due in March. In the normal course, the elections to the Lok Sabha, too, should have taken place at this time. But she had preferred to hold them a year ahead of schedule, thereby delinking the Assembly and Parliament elections. Only Tamil Nadu, which was under the DMK rule, and Orissa, under the Swatantra Party, had called for elections the previous year along with the Lok Sabha elections. Uttar Pradesh and Haryana had had mid-term polls and were due to go to the elections at that time. Only the authoritarian Chief Minister of Haryana Bansi Lal decided to dissolve the Haryana Assembly also and go for fresh elections. Thus, elections were held in thirteen states and four Union Territories. Not unexpectedly, the Congress, under Indira's leadership, swept the State Assembly polls as well.

As during the Lok Sabha elections, Indira set a most arduous pace for herself during the three-week electioneering. In all her election speeches she kept herself above local and partisan issues and took full advantage of India's magnificent victory in the 14-day war against Pakistan. One of her recurrent theme was that she needed her hands to be strengthened still further both to be able to carry through her radical programmes inside the country as well as to consolidate peace outside. She took particular pains to explain to the people that the termination of hostilities with Pakistan had not ended the crisis, and that she still needed total support of the nation to ensure lasting peace in the subcontinent.

A direct result of the massive victory that the ruling party had scored in the state elections as well was to further consolidate Indira's personal power over the party and the country. She made sure that the Governments in the states were headed not by individuals elected by the Assembly Parties in their own right but by those nominated by her personally, irrespective of their political strength. The Union Education Minister, Siddhartha Shankar Ray, who had been a close adviser to the Prime Minister, was asked to move to West Bengal as the Chief Minister. He was senior enough to control the party in that difficult state. But others, like P. C. Sethi in Madhya Pradesh and Ghanshyam Oza in Gujarat, who were originally Ministers of State in the Union Council of Ministers, or Barkatullah Khan in Rajasthan, Devraj Urs in Karnataka and S. C. Sinha in Assam, were comparatively junior. They had been foisted on the state parties by the Prime Minister in the hope that she would be certain of their total loyalty, for their survival as Chief Ministers depended on her constant support. A time came soon when nobody mattered in the party except Indira; everyone had to run to her for survival. Only Haryana and Maharashtra had intrinsically strong Chief Ministers. Bansi Lal of Haryana used to proclaim even then his total personal loyalty to the Prime Minister, partly because he had already acquired considerable influence in the Prime Minister's house through her ambitious son, Sanjay. V. P. Naik of Maharashtra, too, had developed a direct rapport with her ever since he had played in 1966 a crucial role in her fight to succeed Lal Bahadur Shastri. Concerning the handling of Maharashtra, D. P. Mishra, her political mentor in those days, had advised her to keep herself away from the Maratha politicians who, in his view, always combined in the face of a challenge from outside, but who, if left alone, would end up fighting among themselves, thereby providing her with an opportunity to support a candidate of her liking. It was much later in 1975 that she got such an opportunity to install a Chief Minister of her own choice, S. B. Chavan, but only to find, as a result, all the other Maratha leaders combining against him. But for the Emergency, S. B. Chavan would not have survived the time he did. Indira's biggest headache was Bihar, where no political stability had been possible since 1967. It was partly due to lack of a leader of stature and partly because political corruption had reached the limit in this state. Even for obtaining a small appointment or posting one had to pay the political masters a fee commensurate with the possibility of making extra money in the position sought. For instance, a promotion to the job of a Chief Engineer was openly auctioned for anywhere near Rs. 50,000 to Rs. 75,000. It was the people's discontent with this kind of rampant corruption that gave Indira's Congress a victory in that state, perhaps, in the hope that her party would at least provide political stability and, therefore, might reduce the extent of corruption.

Little did the Bihar people realize then that politics based on money power had corrupted the Congress as well, with Lalit Narayan Mishra displacing all other state leaders including Jagjivan Ram. Instead of different political groups manipulating the politics of the Samyukta Vidhayak Dal, it was now Lalit Narayan who manipulated the state's politics sitting in New Delhi. He would make or unmake a Chief Minister at his whim and fancy. Once he had made up his mind against an individual, he would spend money like water to see that person lose his seat of power. Even after voting for the Congress, therefore, the people of Bihar only got the same kind of instability that they had experienced since 1967, while, in fact, corruption seemed to have increased even more. At one stage, Indira Gandhi did think of sending Lalit Narayan, who was the real boss of Bihar, as the Chief Minister; but he preferred to operate from the safe distance of New Delhi rather than be caught up in the prevailing quagmire of corrupt politics of Patna. Bihar had three Chief Ministers within a span of two years after the 1972 elections, none of them capable of standing on his own merit or political strength, and each one was toppled at Lalit Narayan's instance the moment he tried to show some independence. In the process, Lalit became the symbol of all that was corrupt in the body politic of the country, and as such, the first target for attack by the Sarvodaya leader, Jayaprakash Narayan, on taking up the challenging task of re-establishing clean and democratic norms in public life. But that was a year later. In the meanwhile, Lalit Narayan remained the state boss even if his way of functioning had disillusioned the people of Bihar.

This kind of disillusionment also grew in Gujarat, because Ghanshyam Oza, who had been imposed there by the Centre, had no following of his own and was soon the target of attack by unscrupulous group leaders who felt that he had usurped the Chief Ministership. Their machinations soon forced the Chief Minister to resign. He was replaced by Chimanbhai Patel, a very cunning and allegedly corrupt operator, who had the audacity to defy even Indira at the Centre. Naturally, when he was threatened by the students' 'Navnirvan Samiti' movement, the Centre did little to help him weather the storm. In fact, it watched the whole drama being enacted with considerable glee, for Patel had earlier toppled its chosen man, little realizing that the threat was not just to Chimanbhai Patel, but much more in time to come to Indira herself. As Jayaprakash Narayan has admitted, it was the Navnirvan Samiti's movement that gave him the idea of his own movement in Bihar later and also subsequently the inspiration for his 'total revolution' directed at Delhi. That came, of course, much later. Suffice to say that the new style of imposing leaders from the Centre was responsible for the first simmerings of discontent in the various states, soon to develop into a popular storm of resentment in the wake of inflation resulting in rising prices, aggravated further by the failure of the monsoon. This was the first drought after a number of good seasons, and the country had a sudden shortfall of 15 million tonnes in the kharif production. The impact of these developments was still abuilding. Meanwhile, Indira's main preoccupation was to clear the debris left behind by the Bangladesh developments and the war with Pakistan and to attempt an establishment of durable peace in the subcontinent.

With 90,000 prisoners of war and 30,000 square miles of Pakistan territory under India's occupation, Indira had all the trumps in her hand for securing the best possible peace terms with a recalcitrant enemy, who had attacked the country four times since Independence.

India had also to ensure that she did not find herself doing anything that would hurt the newly created State of Bangladesh. There were powers who had not relished India's emergence in South Asia as a middle power in her own right. They were bent upon creating all kinds of suspicions in the minds of the new leaders of Bangladesh against India's intentions. India's army was still present to help the new Government of Bangladesh in establishing law and order and to repair the damage to bridges and other installations done by the Pakistanis. It was against this background that India decided to withdraw her troops from Bangladesh on March 25, exactly a year after the crackdown there by the Pakistani army. In fact, the withdrawal was completed on March 13 — thirteen days ahead of schedule. That day Sheikh Mujibur Rehman took the salute at a ceremonial parade by the last two Indian battalions before their departure for India. This was again hailed as an earnest of India's declared policy to let Bangladesh evolve her own destiny. The world applauded the move, but India's detractors described it as a mere propaganda gimmick.

Simultaneously, in a letter to the U. N. Secretary-General, Dr. Kurt Waldheim, dated February 14, India's Prime Minister made an offer to Pakistan for direct talks without any preconditions to ensure lasting peace between the two countries. In response, Bhutto made a conciliatory statement four days later agreeing to India's formal offer of talks at any time, at any level and at any place. At the same time he denounced his predecessor, General Yahya Khan as 'a drunken irresponsible man' appealed to the United States for arms supply to make good the losses Pakistan had suffered during the 14-day war. India was quite conscious of the two faces of the Pakistani leader, but it was generally believed among the close advisers of the Prime Minister on Indo-Pakistan affairs, particularly the trio, D. P. Dhar, P. N. Haksar and T. N. Kaul, that it would be easier to have a deal with a politician like Bhutto rather than a rigid military man. The initiative for direct talks was taken at their behest. And now Bhutto had made a positive response.

India, therefore, made the next move early in April, when Indira, in a statement in Parliament, called for a summit meeting between herself and President Bhutto on a mutually convenient date. In the meantime, it was suggested, emissaries of the two leaders could meet to prepare the agenda for the summit meeting. Bhutto agreed to the emissaries meeting on April 12.

After a couple of meetings in New Delhi and Islamabad between the respective emissaries, D. P. Dhar of India and Aziz Ahmed of Pakistan, it was announced on April 30 that the two countries had agreed on a summit meeting between Indira Gandhi and Z. A. Bhutto at the end of May or the beginning of June at New Delhi on a specific date to be announced later. Within fifteen days of this announcement, however, Pakistani troops attacked some posts in the Tithwal area in Jammu and Kashmir, ostensibly to regain some of the ground they had lost earlier in this region. There were two more ceasefire violations in Rajauri and Poonch sectors. In fact, there had been in all twenty violations since the ceasefire. India had an impression that all this was being done before the summit meeting to regain the old line of ceasefire which, according to India, had ceased to exist the moment Pakistan had crossed it on December 3, 1971. India's Defence Minister Jagjivan Ram, speaking about these violations in Parliament, made it quite clear that so long as there was no assurance of permanent peace there would be no disengagement of forces. He warned: 'If Pakistan does not learn, we will teach them how to behave.'

While talks were on for fixing the date and the agenda for the summit meeting, other developments in the country diverted Indira's attention and caused some concern in the ruling circles. The first was the sudden death of the Congress President D. Sanjivayya after a heart-attack on May 7 at the comparatively young age of 51. On May 11 the Working Committee met to elect his successor, Dr. Shankar Dayal Sharma. Till then Dr. Sharma had been one of the General Secretaries of the Congress.

The second development, which caused considerable concern in the Prime Minister's circle, was the scathing attack the President of the Jana Sangh, Atal Behari Vajpayee, mounted against her personally at the Bhagalpur Session of his party on May 6. For the first time he talked of Indira as encouraging a personality cult in the country and attributed the recent overwhelming victory of the Congress in the Assembly elections to the fact that the Congress had 'just one candidate (Indira) for all seats', and its only manifesto was her request to the electorate 'to strengthen my hands'. Vajpayee warned that the Prime Minister's personality cult threatened to inflict 'a new kind of authoritarianism on the country'. Added to this personality cult, he said, were 'tons of black money amassed through immoral methods, massive misuse of Government machinery and appropriation of all the credit for Bangladesh victory to turn the tide of electoral battle in favour of the Congress'.

Vajpayee also advocated a tough line in negotiating a peace settlement with Pakistan. He warned against 'weakness of misplaced generosity', which, he feared, would not only undo 'the achievements of our Jawans, but it can wreck forever our cherished desire for an era of lasting peace. Our negotiations with Pakistan should aim at stable peace and friendship. This cannot come about until Pakistan unreservedly accepts the realities of the new situation and refuses to act as a tool of foreign powers'. These were strong words which caused dismay in the Government circles at a time when all had been set for a summit meeting on June 28 in Simla. Vajpayee had been one of those leaders of the Jana Sangh for whom there was great respect in the ruling circles. But, from Bhagalpur onwards, his attack on Indira personally and her away of functioning assumed a strident note that came as a shock to her personally.

Yet another development of importance here was the rapid deterioration in the economic situation in the country. While presenting the Budget for the year, the Finance Minister, Y. B. Chavan, had talked of 'the resilience of the economy', which had helped it to withstand the strain of looking after the Bangladesh refugees for nine months and of the 14-day war against Pakistan. The war alone had cost the country nearly Rs. 200 crores. The Economic Survey for the year emphasized that despite 'the remarkable responsiveness of the economy in meeting the challenges of refugees relief and the war, the budgetary deficit has turned out to be much larger than anticipated'. The Survey noted with dismay the 'disconcerting increase in the money supply with its pressure on prices' and underlined the Government's confidence, which proved to be misplaced, that the resilience in the economy could be channelized for a faster and self-reliant growth. In other words, it was a tacit admission that there was an inflationary spiral in the economy and the prices were shooting up.

The popular enthusiasm of only a year ago for Indira and her radical policies was thus slowly turning into sullen resentment against her Government. This popular resentment was to assume alarming proportions in the coming six months, threatening the very existence of the so-called elected Governments and Assemblies in some of the states. For the present it was merely as mood of frustration among the people and had not yet been properly channelized. It was thought it could be pacified provided Indira could come out with a peace settlement with Pakistan on the one side, and some radical reforms in the economic sphere on the other. At least that was the diagnosis of the situation by some of her advisers who now included D. P. Dhar and Mohan Kumaramangalam at one level and D. P. Mishra and Uma Shankar Dikshit at another. The latter two were not particularly enamoured of further radicalization of the Congress. They preferred its working as in the past and shot down all proposals to make the party cadre-based. Instead, they suggested that the organizational elections, which had not been held since the New Congress came into being in December 1969, should be held to give an opportunity to people who had harboured a feeling of having been left out and ignored by those at the helm of affairs in the party.

The split and all the radicalization of the party had apparently not changed the character of the Congress or the style of its functioning. The moment the decision to hold organizational elections was announced, party men started their old game of enrolling bogus members. Those, who could produce the largest list of such members, automatically qualified for active membership and all that went with it in terms of a better standing in the party hierarchy. The organizational elections also opened the flood-gates to factionalism and Indira, who had become the supreme leader, was engulfed by complaints of bogus membership from all over the country. The people were further disillusioned by this unseemly scramble for power and influence within the party that had ugly repurcussions also on the newly formed Congress Governments in the states. They had expected some of the radical programmes of the Congress, like ceiling on rural and urban lands, to be implemented. Instead, the new party leaders were seen to be no different than what the Syndicate bosses and their followers had been. They were more interested in perpetuating their own power rather than in implementing the party's programme.

Just about this time the report of the committee on direct taxes, headed by N. N. Wanchoo, further added to the growing disenchantment with the party in power. The report very clearly stated that since company donations to political parties had been banned, black money had become the main source of funds for all political parties, the party in power getting the major share. It was also stated that such donations were made to the ruling party for policy concessions and to the opposition parties for creating powerful lobbies in Parliament to pressurize the Government. Wanchoo committee also stated that since farm income was exempt from income-tax, it was often used as a camouflage for black money. The committee, therefore, strongly recommended levying of tax on farm income in keeping with taxes on other incomes, so as to eliminate the scope for evasion of direct taxes. Not many of the committee's recommendations were palatable to the Government. The ban on company donations still continues and even on the eve of March 1977 elections to the Lok Sabha, huge amounts of black money were collected by important persons close to the Prime Minister, including Sanjay Gandhi and P. C. Sethi, at that time Treasurer of the party, under threats of raids by income-tax authorities and officials of the Directorate of Enforcement. Anyone defying such directives or refusing to give advertisements costing fabulous amounts for party souvenirs that were never brought out immediately faced such a raid. Some relatives of the Ministers of Indira's own Cabinet were humiliated thus for not donating towards party funds. Such collections of funds, derived from the proliferation of black money, continued unabated even during the Emergency, although some economic offenders were booked under MISA and other laws. It became an accepted style of raising party funds from 1971 onwards, although some well wishers of the Prime Minister had warned her of undesirable elements growing around her as a consequence.

In other words, it was not as if she were unaware of what was happening in her name. Only she preferred to keep her eyes closed to anything that might reflect on her own integrity. As the popular disenchantment increased at the way of functioning by her close advisers, like Lalit Narayan Mishra, Bansi Lal, Yashpal Kapoor and even Sanjay Gandhi, she tried, not too successfully, to divert attention of the party and the public by speaking again and again of continuing threats from abroad and making her Party President, Dr. Shankar Dayal Sharma, openly denounce the Central Intelligence Agency of the U.S.A. for involvement in Indian politics. Even if there had been some basis for such allegations, that was certainly not the proper way of dealing with the situation. Intelligence and espionage have become an accepted part of international politics and have to be counted by means other than open denunciation, unless such denunciation is calculated for some major political end. In India, at that time, it appeared to be a diversionary move so that popular resentment could be kept under control. Simultaneously, frantic efforts were set afoot to secure a peace agreement at the forthcoming Summit meeting (June 1972) between Indira and Bhutto at Simla so that it could also be utilized to project a popular image of the Prime Minister in the face of the mounting opposition attacks on her personally and on a small caucus around her.

The Simla Summit naturally attracted world attention. The agreement, which has since guided Indo-Pakistan relations, was evolved after much hard bargaining by both sides. In fact, on the last day Bhutto all but announced at his press conference the failure of the Summit. 'But for a last-minute initiative by India's Prime Minister herself', he said, 'I would have announced now the failure of our talks.' This was at about five in the evening. At midnight, after a banquet hosted by the Pakistan President in honour of India's Prime Minister, a brief meeting between them was followed by an announcement that an agreement had been reached. The details of the agreement were to be announced simultaneously from New Delhi and Islamabad on the return of Pakistan President to his capital. The agreement had been held up mainly on the question of the formulation of the Kashmir issue. It is interesting to note here that Pakistan's attempt all along had been to somehow get the ceasefire line in Jammu and Kashmir under the supervision of the U. N. observers. But India maintained that the ceasefire line, that had come into existence as a result of the U. N. Security Council resolution in 1949, had ceased to exist the moment Pakistani troops crossed it at Chhamb in Jammu in December 1971. A new line of actual control had come into being as a result of the unilateral ceasefire by India and, therefore, U.N. observers had no role to play any longer in its maintenance. This was a major setback for Pakistan, for she had often used border violations for her own propaganda purposes in the world forum through U.N. observers' reports. That propaganda opening was being closed now for good. There was also some talk between the two leaders about a possible acceptance, in the distant future, of the line of actual control in Jammu and Kashmir as the final international border between the two countries. At that moment, it was appreciated on both sides that neither could Bhutto accept publicly such a proposition, nor Indira sell it in her own country. A compromise was finally reached whereby the line of actual control was accepted by Pakistan with the proviso that it would be 'without prejudice to the recognized position of either side'. It is under this proviso that Pakistan continues to insist on the role of the U.N. observers and often threatens to raise the issue in the Security Council. In the step-by-step agreement, mention of a final settlement on Jammu and Kashmir came almost last.

While the Simla Agreement was hailed all over the world as an act of statesmanship on the part of India's Prime Minister, and while Bhutto himself described it in his farewell message as 'a breakthrough in our relations', the Jana Sangh leader, Atal Behari Vajpayee, characterized it as 'a sell out'. He said that instead of a 'package deal', Indira Gandhi had promised the country, she had been tricked into 'a step-by-step agreement'. In the process, important issues, 'such as vacation of Pakistani aggression in Kashmir, war damages, settlement of pre-partition debt, evacuee property and compensation for the burden of looking after the refugees before the declaration of independence of Bangladesh, have been bypassed'. Accusing the Government of losing on the negotiating table what the brave jawans had won on the battlefield. Vajpayee called it a 'black agreement', through which the Government had replaced into a state of 'self-delusion under ritualistic homage to peace, non-interference and friendship'.

It was rather a strong indictment of the agreement, which was hailed by most other leaders in the country as a statesmanlike act on the part of Indira. But soon she was to realize that what Bhutto was interested in primarily was the withdrawal of Indian troops from 3,000 square miles of Pakistan territory they had occupied and the release of 90,000 prisoners of war, who had unconditionally surrendered to the Indian Army in Dacca. The very first act under the Simla agreement — the delineation of the line of actual control in Jammu and Kashmir — was stalled. Pakistan was not keen on this delineation and was trying to waste time until the deadline of September 15, when, according to the agreement, the withdrawals of the troops from the two sides were to begin. Even a visit by India's Chief of Army Staff to Islamabad and talks with his counterpart failed to break the impasse on the question of the delineation of the line of actual control. It was then that India's Defence Minister announced that there was no question of any withdrawal of troops from occupied territory until the delineation was completed. It was this pressure which again started the work on delineation, but Pakistani negotiators continued to display considerable reluctance to come to terms on delineating the line of actual control on the respective maps of the two countries. On November 15, a complete deadlock on the implementation of the Simla Agreement was reached and even Indira publicly expressed her doubts about Pakistan's sincerity about the accord. Under the original time schedule, the delineation of the line of actual control should have been completed by September 4. Talks between the officers of the two countries on this question had begun on August 25. And if the timetable was to be kept, the withdrawal of troops had to be completed by September 15.

Internally, too, Indira faced serious problems, particularly on the economic front. The Reserve Bank in its annual report had talked of 'disconcerting rise in prices from March 1972 onwards'. The economy was obviously drifting towards a disaster with the failure of the monsoon. She now brought in D. P. Dhar into her Cabinet as Planning Minister and T. A. Pai as Railway Minister. Hanumanthaiyya and Moinul Huq Choudhury were dropped, and the Planning Minister C. Subramaniam was shifted to Industrial Development. D. P. Dhar, C. Subramaniam and Mohan Kumaramangalam, the Steel Minister, thus become the main advisers on economic policy. It was at this time that the idea of a widespread public distribution system was mooted at Dhar's initiative, and incorporated in the economic policy resolution passed at the Gandhinagar Session of the A.I.C.C. on October 9. By then it was clear that the country had had a major drought and the kharif crop had fallen short by 15 million tonnes. P. N. Haksar, who, as already related, had been recalled on the eve of the war with Pakistan in an honorary capacity, was requested to continue in his post not only to clear the debris created by the war but also to help the Prime Minister in facing the growing economic and political challenges.

Within the party a tussle had grown between the radicals and a group of members of Parliament who had set up an organization known as the Nehru Forum under the leadership of A. P. Sharma of Bihar, in order to provide a foil to the Socialist Forum. The Nehru Forum, enjoying the blessings of the Union Minister for Health, Uma Shankar Dikshit, was meant to checkmate the growing tendency among the radicals to get near the seat of power. Two of the radical leaders, Mohan Kumaramangalam and Chandrajit Yadav, were already holding influential posts — the former being the Union Steel Minister and main adviser with D. P. Dhar on economic policy, and the latter as the seniormost General Secretary of the Congress. In fact, Yadav had become even more important than the Congress President, Dr. S. D. Sharma, because he had greater access to the Prime Minister. The politics, as it was developing in New Delhi at that time, was on the basis of one's proximity to the main of seat of power, concentrated in one individual, Indira Gandhi. Nothing could happen, either in the Government, or in the party, or even in the states, except through her direct involvement or that of someone known to be close to her. Although surrounded mainly by the so-called radicals at this moment, she had brought Uma Shankar Dikshit, an old and trusted friend of the family, into the Cabinet. Gradually, he started exercising considerable influence on her. Since Dikshit was also close to D. P. Mishra and had taken both Bansi Lal and Lalit Narayan Mishra under his wing, his position *vis-a-vis* Indira had become very strong to the utter dismay of the radicals.

New centres of power had thus developed about this time. The Chief Ministers ceased to form the political cabinet of the Prime Minister unlike as in the past. On matters of economic policy, the trio, comprising D. P. Dhar, Mohan Kumaramangalam and C. Subramaniam, was most important. This trio was helped by the Law Minister, H. R. Gokhale, whose main task was to mould the legal system as a 'fit instrument to bring about socio-economic change'. He did it with such total dedication and loyalty to the Prime Minister that a time came when he could not any longer discriminate between what was only for socio-economic change and what was meant merely to perpetuate the personal power of Indira Gandhi and the small ruling coterie around her. A judge of the High Court and fairly well respected in his profession at one time, Gokhale became the victim of radical slogans behind which was concealed a naked power hunger.

On the political front, D. P. Mishra and Uma Shankar Dikshit continued to be the advisers, but the former's importance had already been curtailed. Time was fast approaching when Mishra would be quitely pushed out by people who had already started creating suspicions between him and Dikshit — the two who had so far worked in close co-operation to ensure complete political supremacy for Indira. Ambitious younger people, such as Lalit Narayan Mishra, who had become the Party's main fund raiser and Bansi Lal, the ruthless Chief Minister of Haryana, had reduced to a great extent the importance in New Delhi of old leaders like D. P. Mishra. Another centre of power, that had developed at about the same time, was that of a set of officers around P. N. Haksar, Principal Secretary to the Prime Minister, and Professor P. N. Dhar, Economic Adviser in the Prime Minister's Secretariat, who was, ultimately, to succeed Haksar himself. All major initiatives, whether in the economic sphere, or in international relations, or even in political matters, started coming from the Prime Minister's Secretariat. It become a separate rival centre of power over and above the various Ministries. Such was to be the manner of governance adopted by Indira Gandhi for the remaining years of her rule. The Prime Minister's Secretariat and its adjunct, the Cabinet Secretariat, assumed powers far beyond what they were originally meant to have.

Despite all this permutation and combination of the power elite in New Delhi, senior leaders like Jagjivan Ram, Y. B. Chavan, Fakhruddin Ali Ahmed and even Swaran Singh retained their political importance and usefulness. So long as the character of the Congress remained what it was, they continued to have a lot of political weight despite repeated rumours, set afleat intentionally, that one or the other of them was either to be dropped from the Cabinet or demoted. Indira Gandhi, perhaps, realized, that they represented important power blocs in the country and the party, and had provided her one of the strongest power combinations which could not be easily displaced, unless it was disturbed from within. As it happened much later, this power combination did get fatally disarranged when Fakhruddin Ali Ahmed sent to the Rashtrapati Bhavan and Swaran Singh dropped from the Cabinet. That, in fact, marked the beginning of the end of Indira's own power. In those earlier days, however, their positions in the Political Affairs Committee of the Cabinet and in the Working Committee of the party had remained intact. But other power centres were concomitantly built up, as described above, to initiate policies, which came to the Political Affairs Committee or the Working Committee, only at the last stage solely for their concurrence and approval. For the people at large, all these senior leaders seemed very important in the power hierarchy; whereas, in fact, their power had been eroded. Fully conscious of the situation, they chose to keep quiet for reasons best known to themselves. Only at the fag end did Fakhruddin Ali Ahmed, perhaps, try to stand up to unscrupulous individuals who had steadily captured power without any constitutional sanction, and Jagjivan Ram sought for and found an appropriate opportunity to cut himself off from them; but by then the country had paid a very heavy price. None of the senior leaders are likely to be excused by history for allowing the drift towards an authoritarian rule of the worst kind.

As we have seen above, while Pakistan was showing no signs of implementing the Simla Agreement in its true spirit, the country had got caught in a serious economic crisis. Conflicts developed within the Cabinet on radical policies like compulsory bonus for workers. The policy formulated at the Gandhinagar Session of the Congress to create a widespread network of public distribution system and to introduce State trading in wheat — both being brain-children of D. P. Dhar — remained on paper, because implementation at the state levels was found to be almost impossible. This was party due to the leaders in the states not having either the political following or the personality to ensure proper implementation. As a consequence, the initiative started slipping out of the hands of the Government. The opposition parties, with militant trade union leaders, began mobilizing popular resentment to give a direct fight to Indira. It marked the beginning of the challenge that was to assume alarming proportions under the guidance of Jayaprakash Narayan two years later. There was a crisis of confidence in the country focussed on the charismatic Indira herself.

As the economic situation deteriorated, there began open clashes between the so-called radicals and those who held the radical policies as primarily responsible for the difficulties causing the sullen mood of the people against their party. Differences and suspicions developed even between Indira and her senior colleagues such as Jagjivan Ram who was attacked in the Working Committee by a junior like P. C. Sethi, who was merely a creation of the Prime Minister. But for the timely intervention of D. P. Mishra, there might have been an open rift between them at that moment itself. The real cause of Jagjivan Ram's annoyance, however, was Lalit Narayan's operations in Bihar intended to cut his senior colleague's roots in their home state. Everyone knew it was being done deliberately with the full knowledge of the Prime Minister who wanted to control that state herself. In the process, Lalit Narayan became the unscrupulous boss of that state, operating mainly through money power.

Another senior leader, who, in spite of his loyalty to Indira, came in for some criticism and failed to have his way, was Kamalapati Tripathi, the then Chief Minister of Uttar Pradesh. He resented political manipulations in his state by some individuals in the name of the Prime Minister. He pulled up Yashpal Kapoor and complained to Indira Gandhi against Kapoor's operations through the two Pradesh Congress Committee secretaries for mounting a campaign against the Chief Minister in order to force a dismissal of some of the U.P. Ministers for purely factional reasons. But he failed both in stopping Kapoor from meddling in U.P. affairs as well as in getting the two P.C.C. secretaries changed. Naturally, he was resentful of this undermining of his authority as Chief Minister, when he was also a very senior member of the Congress Working Committee.

In other words, all these identified as conservative old style leaders of the Congress were under attack; some of them gradually disappeared from the scene in the next few years. The first to move away from Delhi was D. P. Mishra, realizing that his usefulness to Indira was over. She did not repose confidence in his judgment any more. Jagjivan Ram and Kamlapati Tripathi managed to survive by simply lying low for the time being. Uma Shanker Dikshit was still important and influential with the Prime Minister and was to stay on for another year, until differences developed between him and two powerful younger men, Lalit Narayan Mishra and Yashpal Kapoor. At one time Dikshit had to go so far as to ask Kapoor to stay away from the Prime Minister's house; but, ultimately it was Dikshit himself who had to leave Delhi for a gubernatorial post, chased by some gossip concerning funds collected by his daughter-in-law acting as his private secretary. One by one Indira managed to shake off all those senior colleagues who had once stood by her loyally during her fight with the 'Syndicate'. They had not deserted her because they had begun to dislike her — rather they still considered her the best leader for India in those critical days. They did not desert her of their own volition; they were, in fact, hounded out by unscrupulous persons around her. Some of them, who again surrendered like Tripathi, were rehabilitated only as ornamental pieces.

The radicals still enjoyed influence. Their leader, Mohan Kumaramangalam, in collaboration with D. P. Dhar, called the tune on economic policy. Chandrajit Yadav looked after the party organization as the most important General Secretary. But their days, too, were numbered.

CHAPTER VIII

DISENCHANTMENT GROWS
(February 1973 to January 1974)

EVERYTHING seemed to be going wrong with Indira Gandhi and her Government in the new year. With alarming rise in prices and all-round shortages of essential commodities, a serious economic crisis confronted the Government. Widespread disillusionment reigned among the people. There was no knowing at this stage if the drought of the previous season, leading to a shortfall of 15 million tonnes in the last kharif crop, would not be repeated. As it happened, the country suffered in some parts another drought in 1973 as well, leading not only to a shortage of foodgrains, but also to a widespread shortfall in power generation. Most of the hydroelectric projects were starved of water supply, resulting in a sharp drop in industrial production. Naturally, the Opposition, which was already playing on the people's disillusionment, utilized the economic crisis to organize agitations and strikes by Government employees and industrial workers all over the country.

On the international plane, too, the Government was finding it difficult to normalize the situation in the subcontinent. After the completion on December 11, 1972 of the delineation of the line of actual control in Jammu and Kashmir, considerably delayed by Pakistan, it appeared that Pakistan had lost all interest in implementing the remaining provisions of the Simla Agreement. The question of the 90,000 Pakistani prisoners of war was hanging fire because Bhutto had not yet reconciled himself to Bangladesh having a say in their release. India could not but adopt a posture of 'wait and watch', ignoring pressures to secure the release of the P.O.W.s from some third country like Iran. Pakistan probably argued, that India would have to release the P.O.W.s sooner than later, and therefore Islamabad need not succumb to New Delhi's pressures to have the reality of Bangladesh recognized and to have a tri-lateral exchange of P.O.W.s, the Bengalis stranded in Pakistan, and the Pakistanis in Bangladesh. Bangladesh, too, was determined to try some P.O.W.s for war crimes and had, for this purpose, prepared a list of 195 officers of the Pakistan Army, which had surrendered in Dacca to the Joint Indian and 'Mukti Bahini' Command Indira was also coming in for some criticism for having vacated the occupied Pakistani territory without a prior overall agreement on all outstanding issues including P.O.W.s, recognition of Bangladesh and return of the Bengalis stranded in Pakistan. This criticism grew with growing recalcitrance in Pakistan on any further step-by-step approach to the settlement agreed to at Simla.

It was, however, the economic situation that chiefly engaged the attention of the Government. The new economic policy advisers, D. P. Dhar and Mohan Kumaramangalam, came out with a scheme for setting up a widespread public distribution system on the one side, and for taking over of the wholesale trade in foodgrains — to start with in wheat — on the other, in order to meet the difficulties being experienced by the people at large in gettting their daily requirements at reasonable prices. The scheme was first mooted at a meeting of the State Food Ministers called by the Food and Agriculture Minister, Fakhruddin Ali Ahmed, on December 15, 1972. While all the State Food Ministers agreed to increase their procurement targets for the coming rabi crop, which was expected to be good, they had reservations on a takeover of the wholesale trade in wheat from that season. They were anxious to ensure that the changeover took place without any dislocation, and did not cause any unemployment. As it was, unemployment had already reached alarming proportions and was causing considerable unrest in the country. Also adequate storage capacity had first to be made available and the distribution machinery streamlined.

On the political front, too, trouble erupted between the Telangana and Andhra wings of Andhra Pradesh and, despite a five-point formula given by the Prime Minister herself, the demand for separate states grew, leading to widespread agitation and violence in the state. What was happening in Andhra Pradesh was only a reflection of the growing weakness of the Centre in controlling fissiparous tendencies, faned by factions within the ruling party itself. It was reflected in other states, too, with the organizational elections bringing out dormant conflicts among established leaders and the new entrants whose style of functioning was totally different. In almost all the states the so-called radicals were in conflict with the old generation Congressmen who had either stayed behind during the split or had since returned to the new Congress. It was this conflict in the party that the Congress President Dr. Shankar Dayal Sharma referred to in his address to the Annual Session at Bidhan Nagar in Calcutta on December 28, 1972, when he alleged that the 'old Syndicate men and even Jana Sanghis and Swatantrites have sneaked into the organization'. He also warned the party against 'the re-emergence of the forces of vested interests, grand alliance and other reactionary elements'. Dr. Sharma did not make these allegations on his own accord. His address had been approved earlier by Indira herself. Perhaps, he was also hitting at people in the party who had objected to his being declared elected unanimously as the Congress President even before the organizational elections were over. There was considerable dissatisfaction in a section of the party against similar methods, as adopted in the past by the 'Syndicate', being used now to stifle inner party democracy. It was against these very trends that they had fought under Indira's leadership. If the party were to function again in the same manner, then what, they openly asked, was the point in precipitating the split?

It was also at this session that differences arose in the Working Committee on the state's taking over of wholesale trade in wheat. C. Subramaniam had reservations about the whole scheme and proposed a phased programme of the takeover spread over three to four years. But D. P. Dhar, who was the author of the scheme and who had vociferous support among the radicals in the party, insisted on its immediate implementation. That it was a disastrous failure is obvious from the fact that the Government had to scrap it within a year. At that moment it had become the rallying point of the radicals who had been under pressure for sometime and were fighting back for their survival in positions of influence and authority in the party. Dhar argued that free market in foodgrains could be permitted only 'at our peril'. Unless the foodgrain dealer was eliminated, the Government could have no control over food distribution. The country would have to move gradually to a situation where total rationing in towns, coupled with an efficient public distribution system, became inevitable. After this strong advocacy, the Working Committee adopted a time-bound programme of action for the implementation of the scheme within the next fifteen months. This was taken as a major victory for the radicals, although P. N. Haksar, who was often identified as their mentor, felt that such a scheme should not be implemented in a year of scarcity but in a year of plenty. That particular time was not the right one, so the scheme was bound to fail, as it did ultimately.

Another victory for the radicals was scored when for the first time, D. P. Mishra was dropped from the list of the elected members of the Working Committee and was put among permanent invitees. This was done at the initiative of the elected members of the Working Committee and was put among permanent invitees. This was done at the initiative of the Prime Minister herself and was interpreted as the end of D. P. Mishra's influence over her. Instead, she got P. C. Sethi, Chief Minister of Madhya Pradesh, elected in his place. When she had sent Sethi to head the Government in Madhya Pradesh, D. P. Mishra was not very happy, but had promised her not to do anything to disturb her protege. Mishra lived up to his promise even after he found that he was no longer welcome in New Delhi. The Calcutta Session marked the end of D. P. Mishra. It also marked the emergence of Lalit Narayan Mishra as one of the closest advisers until his death in January 1975. The latter now become an elected member of the Working Committee for the first time in his career. The only person whom Indira could not prevent from getting elected to the Working Committee once again was Chandra Shekhar. Two other important younger leaders, dropped altogether from even the special invitees' list, were Nandini Satpathy, Chief Minister of Orissa, and H. N. Bahuguna, Union Minister for Communications at the time and later to be a powerful Chief Minister of Uttar Pradesh. Although Nandini Satpathy had enjoyed considerable influence with Indira for a long time, while she was in the Union Council of Ministers, differences had developed between them ever since she had been sent to Orissa as the Chief Minister; for Indira could not tolerate as assertive Chief Minister in any state. Chandrajit Yadav advised Nandini to lie low for a time instead of annoying the people around the Prime Minister. But Nandini's difficulties continued to grow until she was finally toppled in Orissa and decided to come out of the party with Jagjivan Ram and Bahuguna in early 1977.

Another incident, not specially related to party affairs, gives an insight into the differences that had been growing between Indira and Jagjivan Ram, as the Defence Minister. Soon after the magnificent victory in the 14-day war against Pakistan, a proposal was mooted, apparently at the initiative of Lalit Narayan Mishra who was very friendly with General Manekshaw, that the General be promoted as the first Field Marshal of the Indian Army. The proposal originated formally from the Prime Minister's Secretariat. It was proposed that the honour should be conferred on the Indian Chief of the Army Staff on the Republic Day in January 1972 immediately following the victory. The Defence Minister and his Secretary, K. B. Lall, learnt of the proposal only when it came to them formally for their comments, if any. They thoroughly disliked this procedure and managed to shoot it down on the ground that it would not be proper to give the Army Chief a status higher than that of the Defence Secretary. Besides, they commented further, the Chiefs of the other two Services had done excellently in the war, too, and deserved to be honoured, if at all, in equivalent measure. This unseemly controversy tarnished the image of General Manekshaw who was, in any case, due to retire and did not know about his future till the last day when he was asked to stay on in his job indefinitely by a Presidential order. Since reports about his promotion as Field Marshal had already leaked out, it was explained semi-officially for public consumption that the promotion had been under serious consideration, but the Government had chosen to delay its announcement in order to avoid giving the impression of gloating at the time of a great victory over Pakistan. Whatever the reason, the promotion had been successfully stalled for the time being.

The proposal was revived exactly a year later. By then, of course, General G. G. Bevoor had been named as the next Chief of the Army Staff, and was to formally take over on January 15, 1973. It was on January 2 that General Manekshaw was made Field Marshal of the Indian Army. The honour was conferred on him in his personal capacity at a ceremony held at Rashtrapati Bhavan in recognition of the outstanding and meritorious services rendered by him during the Indo-Pakistan war. Simultaneously, the then Defence Secretary, K. B. Lall, was also promoted to the rank of Principal Secretary. He was the third one to be so designated. The other two were the Principal Secretary to the Prime Minister and the Cabinet Secretary. At that time it was not very clear what this honour, conferred on the retiring Chief of the Army Staff, implied. According to British traditions, a Field Marshal never retires and continues to draw his full salary and enjoy all other privileges until his death. It was thought the same would be the case in India. But soon it became clear that it was just an honour conferred on him in his personal capacity, and carried no executive position or responsibility — only a slightly enhanced pension and a few privileges. It may not be out of place to mention here that the Chiefs of the other two Services, too, were granted a slightly enhanced pension. Besides, both the Air Force Chief and the Navy Chief were called back to service in different spheres — one became the full-time Chairman of Indian Airlines and the other Chairman of the Shipping Corporation of India. Only Field Marshal Manekshaw failed to get anything substantial, for a Field Marshal never retires! In the beginning he was, of course, held in high esteem. But gradually, the gloss of his position started fading on account of his making certain inadvertent remarks later in London, which were considered politically unwise, coming from India's first Field Marshal, even if made in a lighter vein.

This whole episode illustrates the mutual lack of confidence in the higher echelons of the power structure in those days; not only the politicians but even senior officers from the civil service as well as the armed services suffered from it. Such politicking by career officers had resulted from two developments. One was the tendency to play favourites among politicians. A new thing at the Centre — most civil servants had had a foretaste of it in the states they had served. The second, and the more important, was the Prime Minister's decision to keep the civil servants out of important cabinet meetings. This was a slight that had undermined the prestige of the civil service as a whole; and the bureaucrats tried to regain some of their importance by coming personally close to politically important Cabinet Ministers, such as the Prime Minister herself, Jagjivan Ram, Chavan, Lalit Narayan Mishra and to some extent Swaran Singh and Fakhruddin Ali Ahmed. The bureaucrats in New Delhi knew very well that the other Ministers did not count so far as the real power hierarchy was concerned. Persons like Mohan Kumaramangalam and D. P. Dhar were indeed important but only at Indira's pleasure.

The Opposition parties, which had fought the Congress in 1971 and 1972 elections collectively as a 'Grand Alliance', again started exploring the possibility of jointly providing a viable alternative to the Congress. They also realized that the critical situation developing in the country provided the best setting for the emergence of an alternative to the Congress — an objective towards which they had been working since 1971. George Fernandes, Chairman of the newly united Socialist Party, addressing its first conference at Bulandshahr in U.P. on January 5, talked of the role of money in elections and alleged that over Rs. 40 lakhs had been spent in the Cuttack by-election in November 1972 to get the Orissa Chief Minister, Nandini Satpathy, elected. He also contended that nearly Rs. 1 crore had been spent in the by-election to the Lok Sabha from the Darbhanga constituency in Bihar, from where Lalit Narayan Mishra had been returned. Till then Mishra had been a member of the Rajya Sabha. For these and various other reasons, George Fernandes was highly critical of the Congress, of Indira Gandhi and of the English-speaking elite, which had identified its own interests with those of the ruling party.

Similarly, at the Jana Sangh Session at Kanpur on February 9, the new President of the Party, L. K. Advani, sought to project an image of his party as one 'committed to egalitarianism and change, but not to any economic dogma'. The tone and content of his address underscored an obvious effort by the party to respond, in its own way, to the challenge posed by the radicalization of Indian politics. Advani took pains to emphasize that the party's stance had remained the same as in the past, calling for appropriate curbs on concentration of wealth, for taxing consumption to prevent ostentatious expenditure and for pragmatic monetary and fiscal policies. He declared that in the Sangh's view the right to property was not absolute. He further added that the Government had to play a key role in shaping the economy in a manner so as to subserve the twin goals of growth and social justice.

As is obvious from Advani's address and the newly united Socialist Party's stance, the two major constituents of the later-born Janata Party were already moving towards each other policy-wise. And it was not long after that the Organization Congress leaders saw similarity in the pragmatism of these two parties and that of their own as against the doctrinnaire approach adopted by Indira's Congress. Their coming together was thus inevitable after their earlier efforts to form a grand alliance. The process was accelerated by the growing economic and political difficulties in the country and widespread disenchantment of the people with Indira who had failed to implement, even partially, her popular slogan of 1971 of 'Garibi Hatao' (End Poverty).

The political challenge to Indira's authority, though already simmering at various levels, had yet to take a definite shape. Meanwhile, she was kept busy and harassed by the troubles in Andhra Pradesh in the wake of a separate Telengana movement and by widespread disturbances in universities and by industrial workers. Ultimately, she was forced to impose President's rule in Andhra

Pradesh, keeping the Assembly in suspended animation. President Giri, in his address to the nation on the eve of the Republic Day, reflected the Government's concern at these developments. He proposed talks with the so-called separatists in Andhra Pradesh on the future of the state without pre-conditions or reservations provided normalcy was restored in the quickest possible time. He condemned violence and destruction of public property 'which only created bitterness and acted as stumbling blocks' in realizing one's objectives.

President Giri, as a former labour leader who was held in high esteem in all trade union circles, repeated his suggestion to workers and employers to agree to a self-imposed moratorium on strikes and lockouts for three years. He said that developing countries like India could not affort to waste available industrial capacity and resources. He also talked of the increasing unemployment and felt that 'the present unrest among students is attributable to a large extent to their apprehensions as to their future when they complete their education'. The President had thus warned the nation against the difficult times that were ahead, but his suggestions found no response, either from trade unionists, or employers or students. The unrest in factories, in public undertakings, among Government employees and in university campuses became more intense in the following months.

Just about this time, Mohan Kumaramangalam, the main ideologue of the radicals in the Union Cabinet, pushed through nationalization of coal industry against stiff opposition from some of his Cabinet colleagues. Soon after, there was yet another major Cabinet expansion, in which Uma Shankar Dikshit was shifted to Home, Lalit Narayan Mishra was given full Cabinet status as Railway Minister and the Bihar Governor, D. K. Barooah, was brought in as Petroleum and Chemicals Minister, apparently at the recommendation of Mishra. The induction of other new entrants to the Cabinet was for a definite purpose. The inclusion of another senior Harijan leader, Bhola Paswan, from Bihar as full Cabinet Minister along with six other Harijans, tribals and backward people in the Council of Ministers, was apparently to counter Jagjivan Ram's claim to be the sole representative of such sections of the society in the Government. Similarly, by bringing in five Muslims into the Council of Ministers, Indira hoped to reduce her dependence on Fakhruddin Ali Ahmed as the top Muslim leader in the Congress at that time. Although this was clever move on her part to show to these leaders that she was not totally dependent on them, she did not disturb the balance in the

Political Affairs Committee on the Cabinet. Not even the new Home Minister, Uma Shankar Dikshit, was included in it. This was an indirect admission that those senior leaders were still very important for her own political survival in the power pattern of those days. The slight intended through the expansion of the Cabinet did not go unnoticed by those against whom it was directed.

On the international plane, Indira's main worry, as pointed out above, was the complete standstill obtaining on the implementation of the Simla Agreement between India and Pakistan. Ever since India had withdrawn its troops from the occupied Pakistani territory, Pakistan seemed to have lost all interest in any further implementation of the accord. Bhutto was only using the P.O.W.s, hold in India, as a big stick to beat India with in international forums. At one stage, even the International Commission of Red Cross had to make a firm representation to Pakistan objecting to her distortions of its report on the conditions in the P.O.W. camps in India by quoting it out of context purely as an anti-India propaganda. Pakistan got some more propaganda material when four P.O.W.s were killed in an escape bid from a camp in Uttar Pradesh. The incident caused considerable uproar in the Pakistani Press.

Despite all this, Indira herself wrote to Bhutto on January 24 offering further steps towards normalization of relations under the Simla Agreement. He rejected the offer in his reply sent late in February, saying that any steps towards restoring normal relations between India and Pakistan must wait until the P.O.W.s returned home. He wanted the release of the P.O.W.s before he would consent to deal with the third step specified by the Agreement, namely resumption of communications — by land, sea and air, including overflight — and trade and co-operation. While India was still in the midst of these exchanges, the United States announced her resumption of arms supply to Pakistan. Nixon rejected India's protest, saying 'India's military superiority is so enormous that the possibility of Pakistan being a threat to India is absurd'. This was one more instance of tilt towards Pakistan to help her get the best terms in any peace negotiations. India's relations with the U.S.A. had not been very cordial ever since the U.S. Seventh Fleet Task Force had been sent to the Bay of Bengal during the war for liberation of Bangladesh. It was pointed out, on behalf of India, that she saw in the latest American move once again a 'grave threat to India's security' and a hindrance to the prospects of durable peace in the subcontinent. India reiterated her opposition to the American concept of balance of power in the region.

Despite these setbacks, India persuaded Bangladesh to make a joint-offer to Pakistan on April 17 for a simultaneous settlement of the subcontinental humanitarian problems left over by the 1971 war. It was a three-point package plan requiring simultaneous implementation. It called for the repatriation of the 90,000 P.O.W.s and the civilian interness in India, the repatriation of the Bengalis, estimated at 300,000, forcibly detained in Pakistan, and the repatriation of Pakistanis, mostly of Bihari origin and estimated at 260,000, left in Bangladesh, to Pakistan. Left out of its scope were 195 Pakistani officers who were to be tried by Bangladesh for war crimes.

The Pakistani reply, sent within three days, asked for clarifications on the offer's implications and invited Indian officials for talks. At the same time Pakistan did not accept Bangladesh's competence for trial of P.O.W.s for war crimes. Instead, it was suggested that Pakistan herself would constitute a judicial tribunal for the purpose. India's reply, despatched on May 11, was that Pakistan should accept, in principle, the essentials of the declaration. And the matter rested there until August 28, when finally an agreement was signed between the two countries, after a series of talks, liquidating the bulk of the humanitarian problems. This was the biggest breakthrough towards normalization of relations in the subcontinent since the Simla Agreement of July 1972. P. N. Haksar, who was the main negotiator and signatory of the agreement on behalf of India, paid a big tribute to Sheikh Mujibur Rehman on the occasion. He said that although Bangladesh had not been represented, but for the statesmanship shown by her Prime Minister, the agreement would not have been possible. One of the main points of the agreement was that the 195 P.O.W.s, marked out for trial, would be retained on the Indian soil and would not be tried during the three-way repatriation. A major problem was thus out of the way for Indira, only to plunge her more deeply into the growing economic and political troubles in the country.

In the midst of rising prices, the Railway Budget came out with higher fares and freight rates and the general budget introduced a much higher rate of taxation. Naturally, a spiral of higher wage demands chasing higher prices set in. On top of it all came the recommendations of the Third Pay Commission for the Central Government Employees effective from March 1, 1973, threatening to cost the exchequer an additional Rs.144.60 crores. This was over and above the three instalments of interim relief already granted by the

Commission, which had cost the exchequer Rs. 175 crores a year. As a result, State Government employees also started agitating for higher emoluments. Agitations calling for 'work-to-rule', go-slows and work stoppages began to occur in various state undertakings, the worst hit being the Railways. While the Congress Working Committee, in a resolution adopted on April 17, warned 'the reactionary and adventurist forces' that they would not be allowed to succeed in their major offensive to thwart the progress of the nation towards her chosen goals, the Organization Congress in its Annual Session accused Indira of having taken the economy in a steady downtrend ever since she had become the Prime Minister seven years earlier. The latter party decided to launch a countrywide 'peaceful, non-violent direct action' to fight the 'autocratic and dictatorial government at the Centre'.

While Nandini Satpathy had already got Orissa under President's rule following difficulties in her legislature party, other Chief Ministers, such as P. C. Sethi in Madhya Pradesh and Ghanshyam Oza in Gujarat, too, were facing difficulties with their Assembly parties. Oza had soon to make way for a scheming colleague, Chimanbhai Patel, against Indira's wishes. And Patel had to pay for it, ultimately with expulsion from the party on charges of indiscipline. That, of course, was later. The state which really got rocked by disturbances was Uttar Pradesh. It had been witnessing student rowdyism for sometime culminating now in a revolt of the Pradesh Armed Constabulary. It all happened suddenly on May 21, when Lucknow University was closed for an indefinite period and troops were called in to the campus as mobs of students started setting ablaze a row of university buildings and burning records in the office of the registrar. A battalion of the PAC had been posted in the campus earlier; but, the students and the PAC reached an understanding and took out a midnight procession together. Next day the PAC men were asked to go to the lines; and that was the signal for the revolt of PAC battalions all over the state. The situation that developed looked like a virtual civil war between the PAC on the one hand and the troops of the Border Security Force and the Central Reserve Police, wherever available, or armymen, where no other force was available, on the other. The situation improved after two days, when a large number of the PAC men surrendered. In all the clashes 37 persons had died, 22 of the PAC and 13 of the Army and 101 had been injured, 56 of the PAC, 42 of the Army and three civilians. Three battalions of the PAC were disbanded, followed by a wholesale transfer of officers. The Chief Minister, Kamlapati Tripathi, took the whole blame and tendered the resignation of his ministry. He said that the PAC revolt was the result of unprecedented strain because of a very serious drought, scarcity of many essential commodities and shortage of power, making large sections of people restive. It was an unprecedented development that shook even the Centre for a while.

The Congress suffered yet another blow when in the prestigious by-election to the Lok Sabha from the Banka constituency in Bihar Madhu Limaye of the Socialist Party won against a C.P.I. candidate who was his nearest rival. The Congress candidate trailed far behind in the third place. While the party was still recovering from these shocks, Mohan Kumaramangalam died in an air-crash in Delhi. This was the biggest blow to Indira personally and to the radicals in her party with no one of their own left now in the Cabinet close enough to the seat of power. The spurt in prices was continuing unabated and the deficit in the budget was mounting day by day. Lalit Narayan Mishra was facing special problems in the Railways. He therefore got the Government to invoke the Defence of India Rules on May 26 so as to ban strikes in the Railways for six months. In some sections of the Railways, mass absenteeism by loco staff had seriously disrupted the movement of trains and food specials further aggravating the economic crisis in the country. The loco drivers' strike ended after six days and Mishra heaved a sigh of relief for the time being.

It was against this background that the National Council of the Socialist Party gave call from Bangalore on July 1 to work towards a 'credible alternative' to the ruling Congress. The Council authorized its President and the General Secretary to initiate discussions with other Opposition parties with this end in view. The resolution, however, cautioned the party against forging any 'hotch-potch' united fronts or alliances and directed its workers to remain ever active in agitational struggle. The plan of action proposed at this session was to direct the party's trade unions to support the proposed strike by the All India Railwaymen's Federation on August 27; to intensify struggle for need based minimum wage and payment of bonus to all categories of workers and to organize a countrywide strike on the issue of rising prices. Thus preparations had already begun to forge a united front of all opposition parties and to paralyse the economy of the country by a total strike in the Railways. The strike came not in August, as was being planned, but in May of the following year. The ruthless manner in which it was suppressed left gaping wounds which had not healed even as late as March 1977, when Indira was finally displaced from power.

Another issue, that became a matter of serious controversy all over the country, was the supersession of three senior judges of the Supreme Court the day after the Courts had pronounced a majority judgment upholding Parliament's right to change the Fundamental Rights. These three judges, J. M. Shelat, K. S. Hegde and A. N. Grover, had given a dissenting judgment. The very next day, President Giri, on the advice of the Government, broke a convention by appointing a judge junior to these three as the Chief Justice of India. There was a countrywide furore at this, following the resignation in protest by the three superseded judges. S. M. Sikri, the retiring Chief Justice, described the supersession of the three judges and the appointment of the new Chief Justice as 'a big blow to the independence of Judiciary'. He told newsmen that 'it seems politics is involved in the decision. I am very pained and depressed since then'. The Bar Association strongly condemned the Government's action and called it 'a blatant and outrageous attempt at undermining the independence and impartiality of the Judiciary and lowering the prestige and dignity of the Supreme Court'. This act of the Government was to have very serious repercussions on the future of Indira Gandhi herself, apart from playing a part in the rout her party suffered in the sixth Lok Sabha elections. Indira's anger against the Supreme Court had been growing over the years. She and many in the ruling Congress had started feeling that the Supreme Court did not reflect the socio-economic needs of the country, for it had been striking down measure after measure of, according to these people, progressive legislation. Only a few days earlier the Supreme Court had held Section 17A of the Maintenance of Internal Security Act (MISA), authorizing detention of a citizen without reference to an advisory board for a period exceeding three months but not exceeding two years, as a bad law because it did not satisfy the requirement laid down in Clause 7(A) of Article 22 of the Constitution. This, along with the judgment in the Keshavanand Bharati case holding that Parliament had no right to change the basic structure of the Constitution, apparently annoyed the Government as unnecessary and unfair interference in the functioning of the Executive. Had the supersession taken place at some other time in keeping with the recommendation of the Law Commission, of which S. M. Sikri himself was a member, perhaps, the motives of the Government would not have been questioned. But, as Sikri himself put it, 'those who decided against the Government in the Fundamental Rights case, though senior, were superseded'. It smacked of the political Executive's vendetta against the Judiciary. It signalled the start of an open warfare between the political Executive of the time and the Judiciary all over the country. The main spokesmen of the Judiciary were great legal luminaries such as N. A. Palkhivala and Soli Sorabjee, but they also had had political differences with Indira's Congress for a long time as votaries of the Swatantra Party. So, when a former Chief Justice of the Bombay High Court and former senior colleague in Indira's own Cabinet, M. C. Chagla, joined them in denouncing the methods adopted to curb the freedom of the Judiciary, the reaction in the country grew really adverse. No amount of radical talk now could counter the general feeling, assiduously fanned, that the motives behind the supersession were entirely different, and that their hidden logic would inexorably lead to an authoritarian rule as actually did it come to pass.

The argument that with all the independence of the Judiciary Justice was weighted in favour of the rich and the influential did not cut much ice then. No one cared that the process of seeking justice was so expensive and time consuming that by the time one got the verdict, it was not worth having. For the rich and the influential the legal process was a method to get things done as they wanted. Justice did not come into it. What was more important was the process of law, which could be manipulated to delay justice to such an extent that sometimes it became infructuous, because the parties concerned in the dispute might have long died in the normal course. Any number of such cases could be cited in favour of the argument, that the whole judicial system had become archaic and needed to be changed. While the legal luminaries agreed with the drawbacks and weaknesses of the system, they still maintained that in the present circumstances, it was the best even if it was weighted in favour of the rich and the influential. Besides, they argued, the Executive's action in superseding three judges of the Supreme Court was not motivated by any desire to improve the system but to curtail the independence of the Judiciary and to rear a 'captive and committed judiciary'. In the beginning, people gave the benefit of doubt to Indira, but as time passed and her Government came forward not only with dracenian laws like the amended MISA, but also introduced drastic amendments in the Constitution to curtail the power of Judiciary, it became apparent to everyone that the motive of the Government had never really been to accelerate the process of socio-economic change, as was so often proclaimed, but to maintain and perpetuate the power of one individual, Indira Gandhi. She was beginning to feel threatened from all sides, including legally through the election petition against her by Raj Narain in the Allahabad High Court. A stage had been reached when she thought that all the legal, political and moral challenges she was facing could be met by a sufficiently drastic administrative action. And that is where she made her biggest mistake.

Indira's most vociferous supporters in the party at this juncture were the radicals, largely because, with the sudden death of Mohan Kumaramangalam, they found themselves orphaned in the highest echelons of policy-making. Haksar, too, was on his way out, acting now only as a special envoy of the Prime Minister on major foreign policy initiatives. For instance, he opened a dialogue with the Shah of Iran, a close political ally of Pakistan, for forging economic ties with a view to neutralizing in course of time the Shah's bias in favour of Pakistan. The radicals, therefore, felt a strong need to look around and find someone near enough the seat of power to give them protection. They found such a person in Lalit Narayan Mishra who himself needed an active group in Parliament. Chandrajit Yadav, who, as General Secretary of the Congress, had at one time wielded considerable influence with the Prime Minister, had been pushed to the background. Nandini, too, had lost her influence. K. D. Malaviya was fine as an adviser on matters pertaining to oil and for obtaining Soviet assistance in this sphere, but he exercised no influence politically, either on Indira or on the powerful gang that was gradually growing around her.

The radicals had never accepted the Gandhian philosophy of means being as important, if not more, as the end itself and, therefore, had no difficulty in getting quickly adjusted to the politics manipulation through money power that had become the recognized hall-mark of Lalit Narayan's functioning. Besides, the radicals, and even some of those, who had come to exercise considerable influence in the Prime Minister's house, had developed the basic weaknesses of high living — wine and women. While members of the Congress continued to pay lip service to the policy of abstinence, prohibition and khadi, in their own personal lives they violated all these principles with impunity. Even the general public was becoming increasingly aware of their double life — one for projection in public and the other for their personal practice. Addiction to the best of imported or smuggled liquor and cigarettes was very common in those days among Ministers and party functionaries. No one could have taken exception to what one did in one's personal life, had not the Congress made total prohibition an article of faith. The whole moral fibre of the party had been corroded over the years through such double standards. One of the reasons was that Mahatma Gandhi had put public men on a high pedestal, which ordinary human beings that all politicians are, could not live up to. Most politicians, therefore, started life in politics with a basic lie — they did not believe in wearing home-spun khadi clothes, they did not believe in abstinence and they wanted to have a gay life like any successful individual, but in public they posed as saints. This was one of the main reasons of the downfall of the Congress. Indira Gandhi should have been aware of what was going on among the so-called new leaders of the Congress. Either she turned a blind eye on these weaknesses, or did not take too moralistic a view so long as these weaknesses were kept hidden from the public view or might even have found them useful for controlling over ambitious individuals. Where she went wrong was in assuming that such doings can remain out of sight of the people. In an open society, as in India since independence, nothing can ever remain hidden from the public view. The hypocracy of it all was so patent that the people simply developed a kind of cynicism against anyone wearing khadi and proclaiming to be a Congressman. The uniform of the independence struggle had become the dress of a new corrupt aristocracy.

As the economic situation continued to deteriorate, despite strict credit curbs by the Reserve Bank, the demand for higher pay packets by Government employees and higher wages by industrial workers increased in intensity. President's suggestion for a three-year moratorium on strikes and lockouts, repeated in his message on Independence Day, got no response whatsoever from militant trade unionists. They thought the economic situation ideal to whip up an all India political agitation. In September the situation seemed to be really going out of hand. The Congress President, Dr. Shankar Dayal Sharma, alerted the party at the Delhi A.I.C.C. Session against the danger of vested interests joining Hindu and Muslim communalists to obstruct the process of economic recovery.

It was the Prime Minister's speech at this session which really gave an indication of how worried she was. Parliament Sessions, since the beginning of the year, had only been severe trials of patience, for she had to face increasing allegations of corruption involving different Ministers, Chief Ministers like Bansi Lal and her own son in the Maruti affair. Various other scandals were also raked up with no satisfactory explanation forthcoming. Perhaps, it was against this background, that she described the situation in the country being very similar to that in Chile, when the Marxist leader Salvador Allende, sworn in as the duly elected President on November 3, 1970 was overthrown by a military coup on September 11, 1973, with the help of some right wing guerillas. He was found dead in the Presidential Palace after the coup. Indira talked of similar danger in India of 'collusion between certain elements in India and outside forces to threaten the country'. Without naming any particular country she said: 'We know which countries were taking an active interest in the elections held in 1971, or for that matter, in the leadership contest in the Congress Party in 1966.' This was meant primarily to divert attention of the people from internal troubles she was facing to a possible threat of subversion from outside. How far the information in her possession justified these remarks would probably be never known. But she utilized her privilege as the Prime Minister to create among the people a fear of a possible threat to the country from outside intelligence agencies without ever giving precise information or naming any particular individual or country.

The economic policy resolution, adopted at the session, called for stringent measures to curb inflation and urged a comprehensive strategy to check the menace of black money in the country. Without spelling out what the strategy would be, the resolution also admitted that the implementation of land reforms, particularly ceiling on land holdings, had been very tardy. Congressmen returned from this session rather shaken and unnerved. Even the decision to hold fresh elections in U.P. and Orissa did not help to lift their mood of depression. It was, therefore, decided to send to U.P. a young and dynamic leader who could see the elections through. The Union Communication Minister, H. N. Bahuguna, was selected for this purpose, not because Indira was particularly enamoured of him or because powerful people around her liked him but because none else seemed capable of performing the transformation required in that state after the fiasco attended by the revolt of the PAC in collusion with the students.

At one stage the job was, in fact, offered to K. C. Pant who had proved himself to be an able administrator. With a fund of goodwill for his father, Pandit Govind Ballabh Pant, the first Chief Minister of that state after Independence, it was hoped, he would be able to manage this difficult and massive state. But he himself declined, fearing that he would not be able to survive in the factional politics of Uttar Pradesh. Bahuguna was, therefore, the inescapable choice, and as events proved subsequently, turned out to be the best Chief Minister U.P. had had after the senior Pant. That was also his undoing; for Indira did not really relish the growth of a strong and able Chief Minister who could stand on his own strength and merit. She wanted to control particularly her own home state herself. That was not going to be possible with Bahuguna heading the State Ministry. Ultimately, he, too, was toppled; but, of course, many things preceded and caused that.

Instability stalked other states as well despite the majority enjoyed by the ruling Congress. This was because every state had a weak leader imposed from the top and not elected by the legislature party itself. This denial of inner party democracy was creating a great deal of unrest and factionalism in almost all the states, Rajasthan had in Barkatulla Khan an able and good successor to Mohanlal Sukhadia; but he died prematurely and was succeeded by Harideo Joshi. It was also decided to revive popular government in Andhra Pradesh where separatist agitation had in the meanwhile settled down. But before a stable government could be established, the controversial former Chief Minister, Brahmananda Reddy, who still wielded considerable influence in the State Party, had to be removed from the scene. There was no question of his re-ascendance to the Chief Ministership. So, he was called to join the Central Cabinet, while Vengal Rao was selected to head the State Government with the help of the rival faction.

On the industrial front the situation suddenly improved with the able handling of the famous Indian Airlines strike by its new Chairman, Air Chief Marshal P. C. Lal. It was the first feather in the cap of the Government in a year, which had proved otherwise most difficult. It had its repercussions in some other public undertakings as well, like the Life Insurance Corporation, where, too, a lockout could be lifted after an amicable settlement with the workers. But the various sectors of the Railways continued to be disturbed, for the simple reason that till then the Government had preferred to settle disputes piecemeal with various craft unions instead of having a dialogue with the apex body. At the moment the situation had not really gone out of control. But the resolution adopted even by the C.P.I. National Council in December at New Delhi showed that the situation on the labour front was far from good and most likely to aggravate in the coming months. The C.P.I. National Council decided that a sharp struggle for leftward shift in Government policies was needed to properly realize the possibilities opened by the Indo-Soviet agreements reached during a recent visit of the Soviet leader, Brezhnev, 'in view of the proven bankruptcy and crisis of the policy of centrism of the Congress Central leadership'. If C.P.I., an ally of the Congress, could be on war path, the other parties in the Opposition could be expected to be far more militant.

It was just about this time Jayaprakash Narayan, till then a Sarvodaya leader in Acharya Vinoba Bhave's Sarva Seva Sangh that had pledged not to take any part in active politics, decided to fire his first salvo against 'a corrupt and authoritarian Government'. He, along with some of his colleagues in the Sarva Seva Sangh, decided to withdraw from the Sangh to enter active politics. In his view, democracy had been stifled in the country and, as a consequence, there was rampant economic and political corruption. His first step was to give a call to the people and the youth to fight against this political and economic corruption. It was in December 1973 that Jayaprakash Narayan gave his call for 'people's democracy' for reorienting the Indian polity and economy towards decentralized and community controlled system of society. For this purpose he went round the country calling upon the intelligentsia and the youth to form organizations like 'citizens for democracy' and 'youth for democracy'. It was just the beginning of his movement for a 'total revolution', which took the country by storm within a year. JP himself was not very clear in his mind at that time as to what precisely he wanted and how he proposed to go about it. His movement built up with the flow of time on its own in a manner, perhaps, he himself had not quite anticipated. The response he got from his old colleagues in the Socialist Party was most heartening. But much more heartening to him was the response from the intelligentsia which had got disillusioned with unfulfilled promises of Indira Gandhi.

So far the Government did not feel very much bothered by Jayaprakash Narayan's moves. They hoped to curb and control the movement through pressure on the Sarvodaya leader, Vinoba Bhave, and some workers in the Sarvodaya movement favourably inclined towards Indira Gandhi. But little did they realize that JP was determined to go ahead with his movement even at the cost of a split in the Sarva Seva Sangh. Acharya Vinoba Bhave, while not approving of Sarvodaya workers taking part in active politics, was not prepared to see the Sangh split on this issue. He, therefore, kept it dormant for a period and himself took a vow of silence (*Maun Vrata*) for a year. His opinion was conveyed in writing, and interpreted as it suited the party concerned. A large number of people, who had been close to Vinoba Bhave, were sent to him by Indira to get him to denounce JP's movement. But the efforts did not succeed — not even Indira's personal visit to Paunar.

From January 1974 onwards, JP's movement acquired menacing proportions. He started openly denouncing corrupt practices by Ministers of the Union Cabinet and State Ministries. Lalit Narayan Mishra and his methods came in for open attack, creating an atmosphere hostile to the boss of Bihar in his own home state. According to some people who had been close to Jayaprakash Narayan in those days and had had discussions with him, he might not have carried the movement further, had Indira dropped Lalit Narayan from her Cabinet. But far from showing any desire to listen to JP's demand, she started depending more and more on Mishra for political advice, and to get him to perform unpleasant tasks which she herself could not perform.

The question, whether Lalit Narayan Mishra was really the evil genius, as he has been painted, or was merely a captive of unscrupulous persons around the Prime Minister, will forever remain unanswered. Only one thing stands out in bold relief. The methods used to raise funds continued to be the same even after his death, only the reprisals in case of non-conformity became more ruthless. Indira knew now that the challenge to her political and moral authority had begun in right earnest and unless it was crushed well in time, it might assume threatening proportions. Unfortunately, just at about this time she lost her judgement that political and moral challenges can never be successfully met by administrative action, however ruthless; and further, that the price to be paid for such ruthless administrative action can be really high. Indira's grip on power had started slipping. No amount of force could save her.

CHAPTER IX

A PEOPLE'S MOVEMENT
(February 1974 to June 1975)

THE year 1974 can well be described as the year of Jayaprakash Narayan, though Indira Gandhi, too, had a large list of achievements to her credit during this period. The Sarvodaya leader had already cut himself off from the Sarva Seva Sangh of Vinoba Bhave to lead a people's movement against what he described as widespread corruption in the country. He was not yet sure how he would go about it, except that, as a first step, he started contacting intellectuals at various centres in the country primarily to exchange ideas on what had gone wrong with India's democracy and what ought to be done to save the country from corrupt politicians. Jayaprakash Narayan had watched, with growing apprehension, the phenomenal rise in prices in the previous two years, siphoning away of funds earmarked for development by corrupt politicians in league with contractors, growing frustration and consequent misdirected indiscipline among students and youth at large due to the lack of gainful employment opportunities.

While on his tours of various centres in the country, he did expound certain ideas among the intellectuals; but, as often happened in the past, his ideas were considered either impracticable or destabilizing politically. He did not find much response until the Navnirman Samiti (Society for Reconstruction) of students in Gujarat succeeded in forcing the Centre to dismiss the State Government, headed, according to the Samiti, by one of the most corrupt Chief Ministers. Here was youth power channelled to achieve something concrete — a phenomenon unthinkable till then.

This eye-opening occurrence followed four weeks of statewide food riots, in which 48 people were killed in police firings. Students played a leading part in the whole agitation, which began in a college as a small protest against price rise and food scarcity. Chimanbhai Patel's handling of the situation was ruthless, and its reaction was correspondingly strong. The movement spread like wild fire all over the state so much so that the Centre had no choice left but to impose President's rule. The mistake the Centre committed, however, was to keep the Assembly in suspended animation, perhaps, in the hope that the Congress Government could be revived under a new and more acceptable leader as soon as the students' movement subsided. It was a very superficial assessment of the situation, because, within a few weeks, further agitation built up demanding dissolution of the Assembly and fresh elections. In this the Gujarat Organization Congress leader, Morarji Desai, played a crucial part by going on an indefinite fast on March 11. The students had, by then, evolved the technique of pressurizing their representatives in the Assembly to resign their seats. The movement had grown to such an extent that even 17 Congress M.L.A.s, led by the former Deputy Chief Minister Kantilal Ghia, felt compelled to hand in their own resignation from the Assembly to the Congress General Secretary Chandrajit Yadav, declaring also their own support to the demand for the dissolution.

At Delhi, however, the assessment was that the anger of the people of Gujarat was directed only against the Chief Minister, Chimanbhai Patel, whom Indira herself had not liked and who had come to power despite her by toppling Ghanshyam Oza sent by her personally to head the State Government. She felt, therefore, no sympathy for Patel and when pressure mounted, she had no hesitation in dismissing his ministry. But she was not prepared to give in to the popular pressure for dissolution of the Assembly. The moment President's rule was imposed on the state, large quantities of foodgrains were rushed to Gujarat to meet food shortages. But all this only exposed the double face of the Central Government and led to a further intensification of the struggle to force the members of the State Legislature to resign, if it was not dissolved. There was every likelihood of violence breaking out again, when Morarji decided to undertake his indefinite fast.

In a telegram to the Prime Minister he warned that the situation in Gujarat had become volcanic. He further stated that as the Centre was not conceding the 'legitimate, popular and universal' demand for immediate dissolution of the Assembly, he had been left with no alternative but to undertake an indefinite fast so that the heroic struggle of the people was strengthened without any resort to violence and loss of more lives. Morarji had to undertake another fast exactly a year later to demand immediate elections in that very state. During the intervening period he, too, like Jayaprakash Narayan, had acquired a moral halo that marked him out as the future leader of the Janata Party which was to come into being under JP's inspiration on the eve of the 1977 elections.

Paying a compliment to the students, Morarji said that his fast was meant to supplement the strength of the popular agitation. He felt prompted to undertake it as he was convinced that efforts to crush the struggle and kill the spirit of the students were being intensified. Referring to the Home Minister Uma Shankar Dikshit's stand that dissolving the Assembly at a time when legislators were under duress to resign 'would be a bad precedent', Morarji reminded the Centre of the 'bad precedent' it had already set by dissolving the Kerala Assembly in 1959 during the communist regime. On that earlier occasion, the dissolution had been carried out at the insistence of the then Congress President, no other than Indira Gandhi herself, even though Prime Minister Nehru was against it.

On the sixth day Morarji broke his fast following the Centre's announcement of the dissolution of the State Assembly. He described it as 'victory of the people's struggle', and exhorted the students to carry on their planned 'reconstruction' work with courage and patience but without violence. He welcomed the Navnirman Samiti leaders' proclamation that the youth would give a 'prolonged fight for true democracy after successfully agitating against the price rise and corrupt government'. It was a fantastic victory, significant not only for the students, who had galvanized themselves into effective action, but also for the Opposition. It had been feeling frustrated with its suffocation in Parliament and its helplessness against growing corruption and authoritarianism in high places. Any number of motions in Parliament on blatantly unexplained cases, like that of Nagarvala, or of allotment of government land for Sanjay's Maruti factory against all known norms for such allotment, or even of the import licence scandal hardly ever yielded any result. Evasion and prevarication from the Treasury Benches sometimes created the impression that the frustrated Opposition had now sunk so low as to be reduced to indulging in character assassination. Subsequently, it came to be an established part of the Government propaganda to plug this line, presumably, to destroy the Opposition's credibility. Instead, in course of time, the Government's own credibility got lost to a large extent; to wit, even people on the streets readily assumed that Lalit Narayan's death had been stage-managed because he had become a liability to certain persons in important positions.

For Jayaprakash Narayan, in search of a method to fight corruption in high places and to establish a type of democracy that ensured for the people an effective voice, the Gujarat developments provided just the inspiration he had been waiting for. Gradually he started moulding the students of his own State of Bihar also for the struggle, he was to launch soon, to get the State Government dismissed and the Assembly dissolved. But the Opposition parties had not yet recognized the potentiality of JP's movement. They were still operating through Parliament and Assemblies. Their main objective then was to make the functioning of these institutions impossible. For instance, while the Jana Sangh abstained on February 18 from the joint session of Parliament, which was to be addressed by President Giri, other Opposition groups, like the Marxists, the Samyukta Socialist Party, the Forward Bloc and the Akali Dal, precipitated a scuffle with some Congress members right in front of the Presidential dias by preventing the President from reading his address. After shouting slogans for sometimes they walked out of the Central Hall of Parliament to register their protest against the situation in the country. Similar disturbances were created in most of the states when Governors came to deliver their formal addresses before the respective legislators. But such tactics of the Opposition parties went against them rather than in their favour. The general feeling in the public was that Parliament members and legislators in the states ought to show more decorum and refrain from insulting the Head of the State.

The Jana Sangh was particularly annoyed with the Prime Minister who had been reported as having alleged during one of her election speeches in Uttar Pradesh, where a mid-term poll had been called later in the month, that the Jana Sangh had paid money to a Muslim youth in Delhi to promote the Muslim League in the country. Atal Behari Vajpayee reacted sharply and described it as 'false and baseless propaganda'. He accused Indira of diverting attention of the people from the real issues of rising prices and corruption by raising the bogey of national security. In politics, of course, half truths are often used to condemn one's opponent. But for a Prime Minister to make such public allegations, which were openly denied, was something new and unheard of so far. There had been occasions in the past when the Prime Minister either came forward with full and exact information which he or she should normally have, or apologized in public for having made a wrong statement. Unfortunately, Indira had stopped bothering about such niceties in public life. She was obviously very angry against some of the Opposition parties for harping on instances of apparent corruption in her Cabinet and around herself; and she was finding it difficult to erase the doubt thus created in the public mind about the integrity in general of people in power. This anger, perhaps, made her forget that a leader has not only to be above board, but he should also appear to be so all the time. The Opposition had by now made it appear as if she gladly overlooked such weaknesses in persons who carefully professed personal loyalty to her. For instance, even when 117 members of Parliament and legislators from Haryana had submitted charges of corruption against Bansi Lal, she did not think it necessary to order an inquiry into them. But she had always been very quick in ordering inquiries against Opposition leaders. Not a single inquiry was ordered against any Congress Chief Minister or Union Minister, although there were charges galore. But she did order inquiries against two Chief Ministers belonging to the Opposition, Prakash Singh Badal, the Akali Chief Minister of Punjab, and M. Karunanidhi, the DMK Chief Minister of Tamil Nadu. Jayaprakash Narayan, naturally, raised the question whether there were absolutely no corrupt Ministers and Chief Ministers on the Congress side. In the case of Chimanbhai Patel an inquiry was, in fact, instituted but only after he had been expelled from the party for six years for defying the directive of the Congress President to resign the leadership of the legislature party. However, this inquiry was quashed by the successor Janata Front, because it, too, had to depend for its own survival on the support of the party floated by Patel after his expulsion from the Congress.

Taking inspiration from the success of the Navnirman Samiti movement of the Gujarat students, Jayaprakash Narayan started his own movement in Bihar with the help of disgruntled students and people at large oppressed by continuing rise in prices. He gave a call to prevent the Governor and the Legislators from reaching the Assembly on March 18, when the Governor was due to address the Legislature. In the next two days, Bihar witnessed unprecedented violence and police firings, in which, according to the Union Home Minister Uma Shankar Dikshit, eight persons were killed and 72 injured. These figures were subsequently challenged by a seven-member enquiry committee, comprising two retired judges of the High Court, a retired

District Court judge and four lawyers, set up by JP. Uma Shankar Dikshit publicly accused some of the Opposition parties and other forces, such as the R.S.S. and the left adventurists 'who do not have any faith in parliamentary democracy', of fomenting politically motivated violence in Bihar. He appealed to the people to raise their voice against what he described as 'the fascist attempts to stifle democratic life'. He also expressed concern at the 'misguided youth and lawless elements being inducted to create a situation resulting in the loss of life and property'. He admitted that during the two days of disturbances, the police had to open fire on nine occasions.

While the movement in Bihar had started under the inspiration of Jayaprakash Narayan, the various political parties, which did ultimately join him in his movement for 'total revolution', were still busy making up their minds as to what behoved them. Their obstructionist attempts inside the legislatures, such as to manhandle even Governors or to adopt other bizarre ways to paralyse the functioning of these Houses, was only getting them adverse reaction from the people. They realized more and more that no movement, which did not have the sanction and support of the people, could ever succeed. Thus, ground was being inexorably prepared for all Opposition parties to coalesce, not just into a 'Grand Alliance' of the past, but into a people's movement under the leadership of Jayaprakash Narayan. Many in the country were baffled when the Father of the Socialist movement in the country welcomed people from the Jana Sangh, the R.S.S. and even the Marxist Communists with open arms. Here was a kind of political illogicality that went way beyond the rational understanding of those who had learnt to play politics only in the western ways. It was Jayaprakash Narayan who was the first to denounce the inspiration and motivation behind the activities of the R.S.S. and the people guided by it. The same JP was now inviting them into his embrace, hoping to cleanse them of any stigma that might still attach to them for having once been identified with the murderers of the Father of the Nation. It was like raising the fallen by sheer spiritual strength. Today these elements enjoy respectability and power under his benign guidance — something unthinkable only a couple of years ago.

At the movement, the various parties, which were to join under the canopy spread by Jayaprakash Narayan, were undergoing intense introspection about their future course of action. On April 4, addressing the Jana Sangh Session, its President, L. K. Advani, opined that if the Government continued to 'mess up the economy and abort democracy, Gujarat can recur anywhere in the country and even on a nationwide scale whether one likes it or not'. He said the development in Gujarat had given a new dimension to the country's politics. In Gujarat the student wing of the Jana Sangh, along with that of the Socialist Party, was in the forefront of the Navnirman Samiti. Later they were to be in the forefront of the Chhatra Sangharsha Samiti, set up by Jayaprakash Narayan in Bihar.

The Working Committee of the Organization Congress, which had never been very happy with the attempts at *rapprochement* between Indira Gandhi and Kamaraj through the mediation of T. T. Krishnamachari, directed its Tamil Nadu unit to sever all connections with Indira's Congress and bring to an end the understanding that had been reached between the two parties in order to fight the Pondicherry election as a united front. With the defeat of the front in Pondicherry, the Central leaders of the Organization Congress felt strong enough to give this directive to the Tamil Nadu unit. In fact, there was a lot of criticism of Kamaraj for having entered into this understanding thereby spoiling the chances of the party in the Uttar Pradesh elections. But Kamaraj was unperturbed, for he had given his word to his ailing friend, T. T. Krishnamachari, who was responsible for bringing him and Indira together, that he would work towards the reunification of the Congress. After the 75-year old T.T.K. died, Kamaraj could not possibly break his promise. When he himself died subsequently, most of his followers in Tamil Nadu came back to Indira's Congress in fulfilment of the departed leader's wish. Only a few remained behind. But the Organization Congress itself had passed into the hands of Morarji Desai who wanted no truck with Indira and her party. Time was fast approaching when he would join JP's movement.

The Socialist Party had had a number of splits. One section, led by Raj Narain, had finally joined the Bharatiya Lok Dal of Charan Singh. The B.L.D. had also attracted the Swatantra Party of old as well as many regional parties based mainly in and around Haryana and Uttar Pradesh. The only other regional party to join it was the Utakal Congress of the Orissa leader Biju Patnaik. Gradually, Charan Singh was acquiring an all-India image, having forged a party wielding influence in almost all parts of the country. He truly represented the small and middle farmer and, therefore, attracted attention from the peasantry all over the country. The B.L.D. came to be known as the peasants' party, and emerged as the main opposition in U.P., the largest and the most populous state in the country. The B.L.D. had also attracted a large number of militant socialists of Dr. Ram Manohar Lohia's party, who were thrilled with the movement launched by their former leader, Jayaprakash Narayan. It was only a matter of time before they were to force their party, along with its leader Charan Singh, to join the JP movement. Raj Narain was the moving spirit behind it.

The other socialists, under the leadership of the firebrand, George Fernandes, were also followers of the late Dr. Ram Manohar Lohia. They were still in doubt if a 'hotch-potch' of disparate political parties, which Jayaprakash Narayan seemed to be forging, would be able to bring about a change in the country's government. They never talked in terms of any revolution. Their main objective for long had been to destroy Indira and her supine party which had allowed her to become a virtual dictator'. George Fernandes, who was also the Chairman of the All-India Railwaymen's Federation, had already given a call for a total strike in the Railways. Associating with the strike call was also the C.P.I.-backed All-India Trade Union Congress.

The strike began on May 8. It was followed by mass arrests of almost all the trade union leaders in various parts of the country. George Fernandes himself was arrested in Lucknow and brought to Delhi. The Government decided to crush the strike with such a heavy hand that even President Giri himself was led to protest. The then Railway Minister rejected George Fernandes's request for negotiations even from the jail. The Government accused the Opposition parties of having deliberately precipitated the strike at a time when the country was facing an acute economic crisis. It was allegedly meant to paralyse the movement of foodgrains and goods so that the economy could be brought to a grinding halt. With the ruthless suppression of the strike, which included wholesale dismissal of the strikers and arrests of activists under the Defence of India Rules and even the hated MISA, the workers were totally demoralized and the strike was formally called off exactly twenty days later on May 28. But before that, the CPI constituents of the action committee had already issued unilateral directives to their unions to come to terms with the Government on zonal basis. The C.P.I., a supporter of Indira's Government, had been prevailed upon to somehow end the strike.

According to official estimates the economy suffered a loss of more than Rs. 500 crores in the twenty-day strike. The Railways were estimated to have lost Rs. 50 crores in traffic earnings and the workers

Rs. 25 crores in wages. The railway workers had been tamed and the Government gave scant attention to George Fernandes' demand for further negotiations *de novo*. He maintained that the demands of the workers would cost the Government only Rs. 300 crores and not Rs. 700 crores, as claimed by the Railway Minister. Even this demand of Rs. 300 crores was negotiable, he offered; but no response was forthcoming from the Government side.

So the militant socialists, having been so badly mauled, felt really angry. For the moment they were in no mood to think in terms of a non-violent movement. Nor did they have any faith in parties like the Jana Sangh, as was obvious at their session at Khozikode in Kerala held as late as December 29, 1974. Speaking at that conference, George Fernandes talked about forming a radical alternative to the Congress. That objective had been adopted as an article of faith by the party already at its earlier Lucknow Session. But he dubbed parties like the Jana Sangh, the Bharatiya Lok Dal, the Organization Congress and even the Communist Party of India as 'stus quoists', who were thus unacceptable as part of the proposed radical alternative. Even nearing the end of 1974, the Socialist Party was not clear what kind of alliances it should forge, despite the people's movement already launched by Jayaprakash Narayan.

The logic of events, however, inevitably led them all in due course to merge themselves into the popular movement, from which has arisen the Janata Party of today. Indira's Congress had started feeling that the mounting challenge could not be ignored any more. In a political resolution adopted at the A.I.C.C. Session in April 1974, the Congress condemned what it described as 'the activities of para-military organizations like the R.S.S. and Anand Marg and other fascist elements' which aimed at paralysing the entire apparatus of production and disrupting the national economy. The resolution further said that 'deliberate and concerted attempts were being made to exploit the difficulties of the people to engineer violence, to misguide the youth and to impede production'. The resolution concluded by saying: 'Ostensibly, agitations were being organized to express the people's discontent, but the real purpose was to disrupt the whole economy. This is a historically familiar tactic of fascism and right reaction.'

In an obvious reference to Jayaprakash Narayan, the resolution said that even organizations and individuals, professing their faith in the principles of non-violence and in indissoluble connexion between ends and means, had openly proclaimed their intention of pulling down democratically elected governments by extra-Parliamentary methods. This, according to the resolution, had encouraged forces of violence and disorder; it was clear that 'right reaction and vested interests' had resorted to 'naked and systematic' violence, because the common people had in free elections repeatedly frustrated their attempts to capture power; the verdict of the ballot box was thus sought to be thwarted by extra-Parliamentary methods of coercion and duress, so that 'a grave economic situation had been simultaneously turned into a grave political one by the protagonists of vested interests'.

This resolution generally reflected the views of the majority of the Congressmen; but there were some in the party, such as Chandra Shekhar, Mohan Dharia and some others, who felt the Congress was equally to be blamed for the prevalent situation. Having been in the Socialist Party before they came to the Congress in response to Kamaraj's call to all the socialists at the historic Bhuvaneshwar Session of the Congress in 1962, they felt that if Indira and JP could be persuaded to have a direct dialogue, the confrontation that the two were bent upon could be prevented. Mohan Dharia, who was Minister of State for Planning, submitted a note to the Working Committee accusing the Government and the party 'of faltering on policy issues and thus creating the present difficulties'. The note said: 'Lethargy, reluctance and hesitation in implementing programmes and promises are equally responsible for the present state of affairs. We shall have to blame ourselves if Opposition parties tried to exploit these weaknesses. Increasing credibility gap could be filled in through action and action only.' Neither the note, nor the suggestion that Indira should have a direct dialogue with Jayaprakash Narayan were taken seriously. On the contrary, the loyalty of Mohan Dharia and his friends were now completely in doubt.

Indira continued her public campaign against the Bihar movement in the same strain. Addressing the annual session of the Federation of Indian Chambers of Commerce and Industry in New Delhi on April 15, she lashed out at the 'campaign of political disruption' that had been launched by a 'handful of people' who were exploiting the good intentions of idealistic students 'for nefarious purposes'. In an obvious reference to Jayaprakash Narayan, she said that 'wittingly or unwittingly, even those who swear by non-violence are indulging in activities which encourage disruptive forces'. Against this background, any attempt to bring the two leaders together was foredoomed to failure. Not only that, JP's visit to an old friend, like Chandra Shekhar who happened to be unwell, was frowned upon in circles close to the Prime Minister.

During his visit to New Delhi on April 14, Jayaprakash launched a non-political organization, wedded to non-violence and named 'Citizens of Democracy', to 'preserve, defend and strengthen democracy'. The organization was pledged to 'develop a public movement against all forms of corruption in public affairs, initiate electoral reforms, improve parliamentary institutions, ensure independence of the press, judiciary and secure recognition of the right of public dissent and defend civil liberty'. Addressing the first meeting of the organization, JP said that the Gujarat students had shown the way in taking up cudgels against large-scale corruption and spiralling prices. 'But this was only the symptom', he added.

This meeting of Opposition leaders and prominent citizens adopted a resolution welcoming the current mass movement led by the youth against corruption, galloping prices and mounting unemployment, and suggested that 'these movement should be led along constructive and peaceful lines and adequate care must be taken to avoid all forms of violence'. It also called upon the State Governments to observe restraint in dealing with these movements and 'limit the use of police force as far as possible'. It also appealed to the Government to remove the impression that no grievance would be redressed unless it expressed itself in violent forms.

As the movement in Bihar, to persuade and pressurize the members of the State Assembly to resign their seats, gained momentum, a constitutional amendment to check such forced resignations of legislators was rushed through Parliament despite Opposition protests. Until then the Speaker or the Chairman of a House had no choice but to accept a resignation the moment it reached him. Now, by amending Articles 101 and 190 of the Constitution, it was made incumbent on the Speaker or the Chairman to satisfy himself after making an inquiry that the resignation had been voluntary and genuine and not forced. The Government spokesman argued that there had been instances in the recent past of members of Legislative Assemblies being coerced to resign their membership and amendment was meant to curb that trend. The Opposition felt that since there was no provision for recall of a member by his constituency, a member had to be made to resign by his electors. The whole controversy developed into an extension of the war that was going on outside. The country was already tense with people taking extreme positions. And the report of the seven-man committee of retired judges and lawyers, set up by Jayaprakash Narayan to inquire into the firings in Bihar on March 18 and 19 and April 12 and 13, added to the tension. The report sharply brought out that the firings were not ordered out of necessity, for there was no danger to private or public property as had been alleged by the Government.

The report also brought to light a large number of cases of excesses by the police. Under the cover of curfew and the shoot-at-sight order, the Border Security Force and the Central Reserve Police particularly had unleashed a reign of terror in Patna City, breaking into several homes, caning a large number of ordinary stragglers, humiliating and misbehaving with women and threatening to enact Bangladesh in the city. The committee was firmly of the view that more people had died in the April 12 incidents than had been admitted by the Government.

Such incidents and the candid reports about them by dedicated people did much to forge the unity that was gradually taking shape among the Opposition parties under Jayaprakash Narayan's leadership. Despite their misgivings, the Socialists of all shades were attracted to their former leader and could not resist his call to save democracy. He had welcomed the Jana Sangh and the R.S.S. with open arms, which, of course, they had never expected. The former were far greater devotees of JP today than anyone else, for he had given them respectability. It was their leader Nana Deshmukh who had covered JP with his own body sustaining serious injuries, when the police showered lathi blows on the aged Gandhian while he was leading a peaceful march to the State Legislative Assembly in Patna. Their bonds had been tempered in the fire of common suffering. By mid-June it was clear that except for Indira's Congress and the Communist Party of India, all political parties had lined up behind the Sarvodaya leader, transferred now into a fiery leader of revolution.

On June 2 the Jana Sangh called upon all its Legislators in Bihar to resign their seats. Twelve of the twenty-four had already quit. But now counter-pressures, including monetary temptations, were brought to bear upon the remaining to persuade them to defy their party high command's directive. The Jana Sangh had also demanded that the Assembly should be dissolved. The Organization Congress and the Socialist Party followed suit. When eleven of the remaining Jana

Sangh members decline to honour the directive of the leadership, they were expelled from the party for indiscipline.

It was at this stage that Indira tried to isolate the Jana Sangh and the R.S.S. and held them primarily responsible for the troubles in Bihar and earlier in Gujarat. She appealed to Jayaprakash Narayan, through her speech at the A.I.C.C. Session in Delhi to extricate himself from the stranglehold of 'fascist elements of the Jana Sangh and the R.S.S.'. She also criticized dissensions in the Congress for giving sustenance in effect to the movement launched by JP in Bihar and his attempts to extend it to other states. She gave precedence to fighting inflation over corruption and asserted that the economic challenge facing the country called for hard decisions, even if unpopular with certain sections of the population. She would not agree that corruption was, at least, partly responsible for the economic crisis. While accepting that corruption should be curbed, Indira maintained that it would be a mistake to focus on it rather than on production. Despite such brave words, the credibility of her party was fast eroding, as was obvious from the resounding defeat of its candidate in her home town of Allahabad in a by-election to the Lok Sabha. Charan Singh's party won the seat in spite of the best efforts of the Congress. It was later alleged that the Chief Minister, H. N. Bahuguna, who was not in the good books of the Prime Minister and her close advisers, had sabotaged the election to humiliate her personally.

About this time, Jayaprakash Narayan gave a call to the students to stay away from their colleges and universities for one year in order to carry on their movement to a successful end. The Chhatra Sangharsha Samiti (Students' Action Committee) called upon all the Bihar universities to close down. Examinations had already been postponed once; the Government and the university authorities were now determined to hold them. It was mid-July and Intermediate examinations were due to begin on July 18. The atmosphere in the state was surcharged with apprehension and the much-expected violence did erupt at Jamshedpur and Begusarai, where three persons were reported killed and twenty-five injured. Holding the Government responsible for the eruption of violence, Jayaprakash Narayan launched the second part of his movement — the no-tax campaign, and called upon the people to 'gherao' (surround) district and taluk offices throughout the state to 'cripple the state's economy and to throw the administration out of gear'. The five-month old movement, seeking dissolution of the State Assembly, had now reached a crucial phase.

The pressure was mounting on Indira herself. The election petition filed against her by Raj Narain was taking an ominous turn. The atmosphere in the country was one of disenchantment and disillusionment, with no let up in the price spiral or in the shortages in essential commodities. The threat of strong action against hoarders and blackmarketeers remained on paper. There appeared to be on desire on the part of the administration to deal with such people with a heavy hand. A small section of community had cornered all the affluence attended with proliferation of black money and widespread smuggling. The ten-point economic programme of the Congress, with its emphasis on land reforms, particularly ceiling on holdings, too, remained almost unimplemented even after laws on them had been placed in the Ninth Schedule of the Constitution to insulate them against litigation. The country was passing through one of its worst periods after independence both economically and morally.

What was required was bold action to revive the confidence of the people in their Government and their leader. And that action came in the form of an ordinance promulgated by the President Fakhruddin Ali Ahmed. This was his first major act after being elected to that high office on August 20. The ordinance, issued on September 17, was to enable detention of smugglers and other economic offenders under Maintenance of Internal Security Act (MISA) up to a maximum period of two years. Within two days 134 smugglers, including nine top ones, whose names had been mentioned by the Minister of State of Finance in Parliament, were rounded up. While this action was hailed all over the country, some Opposition leaders felt that it could have been taken even under the normal law. But, it was alleged, the Government was afraid to bring the smugglers to open trial lest their links in the administration and the political heirarchy should also get exposed. When on November 16, by another Presidential order, the Government prevented persons detained under MISA for alleged involvement in smuggling to move any court with regard to their detention, it was described by Madhu Limaye and Atal Behari Vajpayee as a 'fresh encroachment on civil liberties'. They said the new notification was a confession by the Government that its enforcement machinery was absolutely corrupt. Before this notification was issued, a number of smugglers had secured their release from law courts for not having been given valid grounds for detention. Presumably, the Opposition leaders feared that once such blanket powers were granted to the administration, they might be misused against political opponents as well, as did in fact happen within a year.

The arrest of smugglers had a salutary effect on the economy for some time and the Government was able to divert the attention of the people from JP's movement. Earlier, on May 18, a much more resounding initiative had had the same impact. It was the peaceful implosion of India's first nuclear device deep underground in the Rajasthan desert. However, the euphoria generated by such dramatic achievements was rather shortlived, because the economic situation was inherently bad and the Government had not been able to control the relentless rise in prices. Whatever little diversion such dramatic events did bring about was soon dissipated by the single-minded determination of Jayaprakash Narayan to carry on his movement to its logical end. Popular attention could not, therefore, be diverted for long from what was happening in Bihar and what was to happen soon in New Delhi itself.

On October 14, JP had already announced a fourfold programme of action of an early formation of a parallel government from the village level upwards. On November 14, he led a massive peace march in Patna despite elaborate police arrangements involving intensive air, land and river patrolling to prevent people from coming to the city that day to participate in it. When the people in the procession were brutally beaten up by the police, he called for the Bihar Bandh (closure) next day. It was in this march that he himself received some 'lathi' blows and, but for the Jana Sangh leader Nana Deshmukh's protection, would have been seriously injured. This 'barbaric action' of the state police, as he described it, electrified the whole country and whatever goodwill had been built up for the Government, in the wake of the smugglers' arrest, vanished in no time.

Jayaprakash Narayan's next target was Haryana, the state ruled by a ruthless and ambitious Chief Minister — the final objective being the main seat of power in New Delhi itself. He went to Haryana on November 27 to set up a Chhatra Sangharsha Samiti at Kurukshetra University. Speaking at a public meeting, he blamed the Prime Minister herself for the erosion of democracy in the country and asserted that unless the trend was checked, it would soon lead to autocracy. He attacked the Central Government for most ills in the country. He regretted that a large part of the funds earmarked for development had gone into the pockets of corrupt people, including Ministers, Legislators and contractors. The reference was to Lalit Narayan Mishra who was alleged to have misused his position with the Bharat Sevak Samaj when the Samaj was given a huge contract worth crores of rupees in the Kosi Dam Project. There had been allegations of diversion of funds from this contract even in Parliament, but nothing definite could be established in the absence of a proper inquiry. Government had refused to institute any such inquiry despite repeated demands of the Opposition.

It was only on November 26 at a two-day conference of leaders of the Opposition parties in New Delhi, with Jayaprakash Narayan present, that the seed was sown for the growth of the Janata Party three years later. At that time the meeting was only meant to get as wide a support for the movement in Bihar as possible and to get people involved in similar movements in other states as well. The participants at this meeting maintained that dissolution of Assemblies could not be made the general pattern of the struggle in other states. 'The demand for the resignation of a corrupt, incompetent and otherwise objectionable Ministry in any particular state is a different matter and such a demand can be raised wherever situation calls for it.' Three days later, Jayaprakash Narayan threatened to open a new front against corruption in business. He urged upon businessmen not to make any 'underhand' contributions to political parties. If they failed to heed his request, he warned, they would be accountable to student and youth power. He said that corrupt politics and corrupt business went hand in hand, and that one could not be fought without fighting the other.

During this period, attempts were set afoot by some common friends to bring about a meeting between Jayaprakash Narayan and Indira Gandhi. In fact, one such meeting did take place in which JP went to the extent of agreeing to the Bihar Assembly being allowed to remain in suspended animation; but the talks broke down on the question of the ultimate objective. For JP, it was dissolution of the Assembly; for the Congress, it was to revive the same Assembly and have its own Government once normalcy returned to the state. The difference was a fundamental one — one side, the Congress, playing mere politics retaining all the advantages to itself, while the other, JP's, seeking a basic change in outlook and future political functioning all round. How could there be a meeting ground? The talks were foredoomed to a failure. Indira accused JP of playing into the hands of the same old 'Grand Alliance', little realizing that he had actually brought about a qualitative change. The getting together of the Opposition parties was far more basic than the alliance forged in 1971 on the single-point programme of removing Indira. It was not just Indira that was to be removed this time, but a whole system that had got corroded from inside because of a single party having enjoyed power too long. The aim was to re-establish certain norms and values in political functioning, which had disappeared over the years. Perhaps, the leaders of the Opposition parties, who had joined his movement, were themselves unaware at that time of what they had let themselves into.

Corruption had got pinpointed in the minds of the people and any one who was identified with the corrupt way of functioning, became the natural target of people's wrath. In Bihar this distinction specially fell on Lalit Narayan Mishra. He had grown very conscious of the popular disenchantment with the way the Congress had been functioning and even expressed his misgivings just a few weeks before he went to Samastipur in Bihar, ostensibly to inaugurate a broad guage line, but actually, as it turned out, to meet his end. In spite of all the security arrangements at the railway station, a bomb exploded near him on the dias. Even till today it has not been established who was responsible for this cold-blooded murder. No doubt, the tense situation, created in Bihar in the wake of JP's movement, was partly responsible for it. Perhaps, some bigger force working behind JP's movement took advantage to get rid of one grown either too powerful or too much of a political liability. Jayaprakash Narayan himself could never have wanted such an exit for Lalit Narayan Mishra, even though he had often demanded the latter's resignation from the Union Cabinet for using money power to manipulate Bihar politics.

Lalit Narayan's death came as a shock to Indira. It also seemed to have unnerved the people around her, who were gradually being exposed for corruption. Lalit Narayan died at Danapur Railway Hospital, while he was being operated upon, on January 3, 1975. His death ended all chances of any *rapprochement* between Indira and Jayaprakash Narayan. Everyone now waited for the next moves from both sides and everyone knew the moves would be drastic.

The economy had still not turned the corner despite a bumper harvest. Everyone praised the new Agriculture Minister, Jagjivan Ram, for the miracle. And yet prices kept moving up and up. Still there were shortage of essential commodities. Profiteering and hoarding were rampant. And now new fund collectors had appeared on the scene since the elections were only a year away. In Bombay Rajni Patel acquired the same position that was once enjoyed by S. K. Patil of the 'Syndicate'. A mere telephone call from Rajni Patel used to be enough to bring in lakhs of rupees, and his influence in Delhi was such that he could arrange policy concessions. The Congress Presidentship had also changed hands with D. K. Barooah taking over from Dr. Sharma. Lalit Narayan Mishra had been primarily responsible to get Barooah accepted by the Prime Minister at the bidding of the so-called leftists. Neither Lalit Narayan, who had by this time developed sharp differences with Uma Shankar Dikshit, nor the radicals wanted Dikshit as the Party chief. That was the beginning of Dikshit's fade out from the centre of power.

Events were now rolling rather fast. The election petition against Indira had already taken a serious turn. The daily proceedings of the Allahabad High Court had become big news. Indira recalled her former Principal Secretary, P. N. Haksar, to join her Government as the Deputy Chairman of the Planning Commission. That he agreed to rejoin after having had differences with her proves that when Indira wanted something, she could become the most charming person. She persuaded Haksar to take over D. P. Dhar's job in the Planning Commission because the latter had failed. Dhar was now to be shunted back to Moscow, where he had been a very successful Ambassador. That was the end of D. P. Dhar in politics. His pet policies, like the state takeover of wheat trade, had already been reversed and the public distribution system, of which he had talked so glibly, was yet to evolve. He died a few months later at his post in Moscow.

The election petition against the Prime Minister now held total attention of the public. At one stage Haksar was asked to testify. He was reluctant to tell a lie, and as a consequence he seriously annoyed some important people. At that moment they had acquiesced into his telling the court at least half the truth. These powerful people continued to feel that if Haksar could have slurred over the question as to when precisely Yashpal Kapoor was relieved from the Prime Minister's Secretariat, the judgment might not have gone against Indira. But they little realized that Indira herself, while giving evidence before the court, had tripped and made two different statements concerning the same issue. If Haksar was responsible for losing the case, she was even more so.

By this time, through a Cabinet reshuffle, the powerful Chief Minister of Haryana, Bansi Lal, had been inducted into the Union Cabinet for the time being as Minister without Portfolio. He immediately slipped into Lalit Narayan's shoes and became the boss of the powerful caucus that had grown in the Prime Minister's house around her ambitious son Sanjay Gandhi. Now her advisers were individuals who had hardly any standing in the party except, perhaps, Bansi Lal, but who had tasted a kind of high living which could only accrue from a clandestine use of power in the name of the Prime Minister.

The eyes of the world were focussed on the outcome of the election petition in the Allahabad High Court. On June 12 came the fateful judgment that completed in no time the transformation of a democratic leader into an authoritarian despot. Had she resigned at that moment and gone in appeal as a commoner — for the judgment was purely on technical grounds — to the Supreme Court, Indira, in all probability, would have come back as one of the greatest leaders of this country. Instead, she preferred to meet the challenge, now to her moral authority, by purely administrative means. And once she had slipped up on the fundamental issue of meeting moral challenges morally, there was no escape from further fatal fall.

For Jayaprakash Narayan and the Opposition leaders the Allahabad High Court judgment on the election petition came as a powerful weapon to beat the Prime Minister with. Huge rallies were organized in New Delhi to question her moral authority to continue in power. Legally she had a stay in her favour and even the Supreme Court vacation judge gave her a further conditional stay. However, the people judged her two years later, not on whether she was legally right but on whether she was morally right. She failed the final test miserably in March 1977. For in the intervening two years she took away what her father and other leaders had given to the people of India in the name of democracy. She not only imposed National Emergency, but she also got arrested in a pre-dawn swoop all the important Opposition leaders in the country, including Jayaprakash Narayan and Morarji Desai. She also arrested simultaneously Chandra Shekhar, a member of the Congress Working Committee, Ram Dhan, Secretary of the Congress Parliamentary Party, and Mohan Dharia, who was a Minister in her Council of Ministers until he rsigned a few months earlier on the question of a dialogue with JP, of which he was a strong votary. Some colleagues of these young leaders were suspended from the Congress and ultimately thrown out. Terror was let loose in Delhi and elsewhere in the country. The voice of dissent was completely muted with the imposition of the worst kind of press censorship. So were also cut her own feedback lines.

Indira had, perhaps, hoped thus to show that she was no coward and could be a ruthless leader. Only a few months earlier she had been once again humbled morally by Morarji who had undertaken another fast to force her to order elections in Gujarat. It was nearly a year after Chimanbhai Patel's Government had been dismissed. The Assembly had been dissolved also only after a similar fast. The new Assembly, too, was elected after such a fast, and Indira's Congress had suffered its first defeat against a combined Janata Front on the same day the Allahabad High Court had unseated her. Perhaps, it was a warning to her to beware of the events to come.

CHAPTER X

INTERNATIONAL RAMIFICATIONS
(1971 to 1977)

THE days of gunboat diplomacy and colonialism were over after the Second World War. But the emergence of the two Super Powers intensified the conflict for areas of influence all over the world. The newly independent Third World countries were the primary targets of this conflict between the Super Powers and the two respective groups of developed countries they headed. What they sought was extension of their areas of influence and supply of primary products. The reverses suffered by the United States in Korea, Vietnam and other countries of Indo-China brought home to them that armed intervention did not help attain the objectives and, instead, only created the risk of a possible direct confrontation between the two Super Powers. Even during the intense cold-war days, neither had wished for a direct confrontation. At best, they were willing to support small wars far away from their own frontiers. Such wars by proxy, too, had not removed entirely the danger of a direct confrontation. Besides, the emergence of China as a nuclear power in her own right had added a new dimension to the vexed question of world security and peace. The concept of detente between the two Super Powers had relevance only to the developed world. Their conflict of interests, both economic and political, in the newly independent but economically backward countries of Asia, Africa and Latin America continued unabated.

The eastern bloc, led by the Soviet Union, realized much earlier than the western powers that armed intervention to attain foreign policy objectives had lost its effectiveness to the modern world of fast communications and, in fact, became counter-productive in most cases. After World War II, no country, except Israel for a time, had been allowed to enjoy the fruits of aggression. World opinion was invariably brought to bear upon such countries, even if they had only fought wars by proxy, to withdraw from and vacate aggression in another's territory and to seek peace, either directly or through the good offices of the United Nations' Security Council. In the circumstances the Super Powers had to seek an effective substitute for the use of direct military force when diplomacy failed to achieve foreign policy objectives. It is again the eastern bloc and China, which had had a long training in subversive activities. Guerilla warfare by the so-called people's armies during liberation struggles had evolved for them the concept of subversion to attain foreign policy objectives. In this game, spying, espionage and counter-espionage played as important a part as open propaganda among receptive intellectual groups in the target country so as to create an active public opinion meant to coincide with underground clandestine activities by groups financed to destablize the country in question. There had been a tremendous hue and cry against this kind of subversion in various countries in the Third World which were of special interest to the West in the early fifties. Cuba was one example that at one stage almost became an area of direct confrontation between the two Super Powers. At the last critical moment, the leaders of the Super Powers had agreed to withdraw their nuclear armaments pointed at each other. China, too, had encouraged a number of subversive movements in its neighbouring countries by providing training and armaments to volunteers, like the rebel Nagas, Mizos and the Naxalites in India. The only objective in these cases seemed to have been to keep India weak and destabilized on its borders adjoining China and her ally Pakistan. But the Soviet Union and China had refrained from getting themselves directly involved militarily in Third World countries. Even in countries, which were supposed to be in the Warsaw Pact, such as Hungary and Czechoslovakia, the Soviet military involvement in suppressing popular revolts had had very adverse reactions the world over. Similarly, the only military involvement China had had over the years was in Korea, and that ultimately ended in a stalemate and a division of the country.

The western world also realized soon the importance of subversion as a substitute for force in attaining foreign policy objectives. The American experience, after the Second World War, was far from happy with the newly independent but highly sensitive democracies like India, which did not share any fears of communist expansionism and rejected the American policy of containment of communism. This was at the height of the cold war between the two power blocs. As things shaped, India's own policies towards the two power blocs evolved into the now famous nonalignment and peaceful coexistence which, to the Americans in those days, was nothing but apparent neutrality biased in favour of the Soviet Union. It is a sad commentary that the leaders of one of the greatest democracies of the world did not know how to deal with similar democracies elsewhere in the world, but rather found themselves very successful and quite at home with military dictators and autocratic rulers. To them a democrat like Nehru was anathema, for he had the courage to tell them where they went wrong; but, brasshats like General Ayub Khan or General Yahya Khan were individuals with whom they could strike any kind of deal without having to bother about the cumbersome machinery of a democratic government that required a proposal to move through various levels before a deal could be clinched. As self-appointed policemen of the world against the threat of communism in those days, the Americans had ceased to be democrats outside their country. From the very beginning after Indian independence, the Indians and the Americans had fallen foul of each other because of Nehru's different world view, in which even the communists, too, had a place.

In contrast, the communist world learnt fast how to pamper the patriotic and democratic sentiments of the newly independent countries and their popular leaders. It is, therefore, not an accident of history that wherever there had been a popular liberation movement or democratic regime, the Russians and even the Chinese were able to establish a rapport with the leaders far more effectively than either the Americans or their friends of the western world. For many, even in India, it appeared as a contradiction in terms not to have good and close relations with the United States and to have a treaty of friendship with the Soviet Union, whose socio-political system was entirely different from the one in India. After the reverses suffered by the Americans in their foreign policy objectives in the Third World, despite their propping up militarily of certain despotic regimes, the policy planners in Washington, perhaps, realized that the nonaligned movement of the Third World was a very clever camouflage for the identical economic interests of the underdeveloped countries. It was India, which had started a move among the latter to form cartels of commodity-producing countries to get better terms for their primary products. The inspiration for it had come from the way the oil-producing countries had used oil as a political weapon and, subsequently, as a bargaining counter for economic advancement with the developed world. This new direction was given to the nonaligned movement following the Indian Prime Minister Indira Gandhi's address to the Lusaka Conference.

India had also earned the wrath of the western world for some other developments. One such was the capability established in India, with the help of the Soviet Union, to produce most of her armaments including supersonic military planes and sophisticated naval vessels, after the debacle India had suffered against China in 1962. In fact, it was the neglect of India's armed forces till then, which, in his last two years, went against Nehru — otherwise one of India's greatest leaders and her first Prime Minister. But the change in policy had already taken place when he was still alive; for Pakistan, too, had got almost free a completely new air force through American generosity and India had no choice but to match it soon in view of the threatening noises being made by that country.

It may not be out of context to mention here how India was spurned by the western world when she went out shopping for a matching fighter to Pakistan's Sabre jet supplied by the U.S.A. India offered to buy a matching plane against payment of hard cash. But, as Galbraith has very clearly recorded in his book, *Ambassador's Journal*, America declined saying that she could supply such sophisticated equipment only to her allies in the various military alliances. But some in the State Department, perhaps, realized that as a consequence they might be pushing India into the lap of the Soviet Union, and, therefore, suggested to the British to sell their Lightning planes to India. There are various explanations why this deal could not go through. However, the impression left in India at that time was that the British, more favourably inclined towards Pakistan, were not really interested in helping India to build up her air force. The French, of course, were willing as always to sell their famous Mirage planes, but the price quoted was fabulous and beyond the means of a poor country like India. It was at this point of time that the Russians made their offer of MIG-21 planes. At first it was only to supply a squadron or two. There was tremendous resistance among the Indian experts, for it would have meant a wholesale changing of specifications and duplication of maintenance facilities. But when India persuaded the Soviet Union into helping her set up her own production facilities for this jet fighter, it created quite a ripple in the international circles. Of course, India had to pay in hard foreign exchange for all the military hardware acquired from the Soviet Union. Under the contract, the three factories to produce MIG-21 were to be set up in about three years. In actual fact, it took nearly nine years to complete them, and when the first plane rolled out of these factories, it was discovered that it was an older version. Further negotiations and some more delay made India capable of producing from basic materials what is now known as MIG-21M which has, among other things, the side-winder facility. During the years the three factories were being set up, India had to maintain a certain low profile on international issues directly concerning the Soviet Union. On many of the issues concerning the Third World, fortunately, India's views coincided with those of the Soviet Union. But on matters where India differed, she spoke out only at the risk of further delay in the setting up of these crucial aircraft factories.

Another development of concern to the West was the establishment of a highly sophisticated infrastructure of heavy industry without which no country can maintain a steady industrial development on the one side, and an armed force of the size that India had to build up over the years against the joint threat from Pakistan and China on the other. In the olden days, Nehru's voice was heard with respect in the comity of nations as a statesman, who had emerged from a great freedom struggle. But when he started talking in terms of nonalignment in the cold war context and even tried to sponsor China in the United Nations, America lost faith in him and gradually India found herself ignored in the western world, and looked down upon as a poor beggar nation with no political or economic strength of her own. India's worst plight was soon after the Chinese attack in 1962 when the Chinese withdrew on their own after giving a humiliating slap to the unprepared and ill-equipped Indian Army. The nation was, thus, forced to realize gradually that she could not have world respect merely because she had produced a Mahatma Gandhi and a Nehru, but for that she must have inherent internal political and economic strength and military capability to defend herself against any external threat. So India went ahead with her own style of planning which meant heavy investment in the basic industries even at the expense of neglecting agriculture and rural development. There were people in the Government throughout the last thirty years, who did not always see eye to eye with Nehru and his two successors on the need for laying this infrastructure of heavy industry and often delayed projects. The

Americans and the World Bank, too, could not understand the misplaced emphasis on heavy industry. But today, after the infrastructure has almost been laid and India is well on her way to being an industrialized nation in her own right, the time has come to turn her attention to rural development through agriculture-based industries. Even in agriculture, some breakthrough has already been made to increase food production from a measly 72 million tonnes in the mid-sixties to nearly 120 million tonnes in 1976-77. But India's insistence in the last two decades on the kind of economic planning that was not in keeping with the views of the western experts was held against her also as being the result of a direct influence of the Soviet Union. Not many in the western world believed that a political system, based on Parliamentary democracy, could coexist with a centralized system of economic planning. They did not like India because she would not open her doors in the heavy industry sector to their multinationals. The idea of mixed economy, popularized by Nehru, was often utilized by foreign and Indian economic interests, not in tune with the Government's policy of economic planning, to delay, if not distort, the development as visualized in various five-year plans. At one stage, India was even forced to take a plan holiday and a drastic devaluation of the rupee under pressure from the World Bank only to find herself unable for another two years to put back the planning process into full swing.

It was under Indira Gandhi's leadership that India became almost self-sufficient in her armaments manufacture, and she was able to restart the process of planning which had been disturbed after the plan holiday of 1965 during Asoka Mehta's tenure in the Planning Commission. All this would not have mattered much, had this not given India a much greater voice in the Third World, particularly after India's successful involvement politically and militarily in developments in South Asia resulting in the changing of the map of the subcontinent. That was the first development of its kind after World War II, when a country had been dismembered into two soverign states. It was a political role India had played with consummate skill, under Indira's leadership, to the great chagrin of the American patrons of Pakistan. Before that happened, the generally accepted view in the Washington official circles was that India could do nothing to prevent Pakistan from getting rid of her surplus population in East Pakistan, which had distorted the power equation in Pakistan after the elections. With her own huge population India could, according to them, well absorb another ten million without much impact; and that, if India tried to solve the problem politically, there was always the dagger of Pakistan poised on both her flanks. This assessment went completely wrong; even the morale boosting move of the task force of the U.S. Seventh Fleet to the Bay of Bengal could not prevent the unconditional capitulation of the Pakistani Army of 90,000 in Bangladesh. India had thus emerged as a middle power in her own right against all wishes of the policy-planners in Washington.

The Americans could not excuse India in the next few years for what she had achieved in South Asia. In a way, she had completely destroyed the power balance they had been so assiduously building for decades around Pakistan as the major military power in the region. The next two years saw a steady denigration of India's achievements, faced as she was with her own economic difficulties following two seasons of serious drought and an injection of international inflation in the wake of the sudden hike in the prices of crude oil, that resulted in an increase of nearly Rs. 1200 crores in India's import bill on that account. The whole idea was to hinder India from playing any significant role politically, particularly in view of her growing influence in the Third World, and the opening that she had made with Iran — the other power on which the Americans were now dependent for military balance in the region. India was not interested in obstructing Iran in her desire to become a major military power in the Gulf region. What interested India most was to develop lasting economic ties with that country, so that future political relations could be guided by mutual self-interest. India had also succeeded in opening the door to China after nearly a decade and a half of cold relations verging almost on *rigor mortis*. These were breakthroughs which inevitably gave respectability and importance to India not only in Asia but in the entire Third World. Even so, there was a certain reluctance to accepting India in the world forums as a middle power in her own right and, as a consequence, there was a deliberate attempt to ignore her views on major international issues. She had first cut the Americans to the quick by opposing their containment policy in the mid-fifties. She had, instead, urged recognition of China and her admission to the United Nations. Again India had hurt the U.S.A. by denouncing the ruthless bombing of North Vietnam and had all along urged negotiations for peace. When eventually the U.S.A. came to recognize China and to sign in Paris a peace agreement on Vietnam,

India's stand was fully vindicated; yet the Americans insisted on maintaining that it was rather due to a qualitative change in the situation that had led to the change in their attitude and not due to any recognition of a fundamental mistake in their original approach to the problems in question. Anyhow, India was to be denied credit for something she had been advocating for well over two decades.

It was only when India set off her own peaceful nuclear device deep underground on May 18, 1974, that the whole world sat up and took note of a nation which had forced its way into the exclusive nuclear club but had voluntarily renounced any desire to join the nuclear weapons club. Although not a signatory of the non-proliferation treaty, India had scrupulously followed its provision on having only an underground test ensuring that there was no radio-active fallout. No other country till then had fulfilled the requirements of this provision to the letter. But what had annoyed the western powers most was the fact that the whole operation had been carried out with such absolute secrecy in a country where nothing could remain secret. Moreover, the whole operation had been performed without much expenditure and highly sophisticated installations that had become the hallmark of nuclear nations. There were no airconditioned centres in the Rajasthan desert to trigger off the nuclear device. The countdown was done with the word of the mouth and the scientists supervising the operation stood under improvised huts in the desert at a safe distance. All this exploded the myth that it was a very expensive operation in which a poor country like India should not indulge. In any case, the very active intelligence services of all the great powers were for once taken completely by surprise. They had known for a long time that Indian scientists were capable of producing and testing a nuclear device, but they had not expected them to do that in such primitive conditions and at such a low cost. India's main reason for the explosion of the nuclear device was to be ready with the knowledge when nuclear technology ushered in a new industrial revolution and not to remain dependent for import of such technology on other countries. But no one in the world was willing to accept this explanation. They could also not understand why India had voluntarily abjured use of nuclear weapons for defence. In other words, they chose to completely distrust India on this score. Naturally, their reaction was one of anger. Canada, which had been a close friend in the Commonwealth, accused India of having misused her help for building nuclear reactors. No amount of explanations and even on-the-spot checks prevented Canada from breaking her agreement on nuclear assistance to India. There was reason to believe that she did this under pressure from the United States, which had also started raising various difficulties on safeguards before supplying nuclear fuel for Tarapore Nuclear Power Station.

All these developments occurring during eleven years' of her Prime Ministership had not endeared Indira to the Americans. The relations had really taken a downtrend in 1971 after the fourteen-day war with Pakistan. They had not been that cold before. It was only after the war that open denunciation of the activities of the intelligence agencies of some foreign countries began in India too. Authoritative persons like the Congress President himself talked of such activities and once or twice specifically mentioned in this connection the Central Intelligence Agency of the U.S.A. The Prime Minister, too, talked of threats from outside forces which wanted to take advantage of the economic difficulties and the growing political challenge to her authority. In a private conversation, she once specifically mentioned that since the explosion of the peaceful nuclear device, three countries were particularly angry with India — the United States, the United Kingdom and West Germany. She also mentioned that the intelligence services of three countries were very active in India, namely those of the United States, West Germany and, surprisingly, of South Korea. All of them were working in conjunction with one another. Beyond these stray remarks there was never any public exposure of the activities of these agencies, except that the Indians involved with them were warned against such association.

While India was passing through a challenging time, theories had been enunciated by western political scientists regarding subversion as a substitute for force in attaining foreign policy objectives, particularly in the nonaligned Third World countries. The theories delineated four stages for the use of this weapon. The first stage required 'the undermining or detachment of the loyalties of significant political and social groups within the target state, and their transference under ideal conditions to the symbols and the institutions of the aggressor. The assumption behind this is that public morale and the will to resist covert intervention are the product of combined political and social or class loyalties, which are usually attached to national symbols. Following the disintegration of the political and social institutions of the state, the loyalties may then be detached and transferred to the political or ideological cause of the aggressor.'

The author of this theory, Barry Buzan, a research scholar of the London School of Economics, working with F. S. Northedge, Professor of International Relations in the University of London, further says: 'In such an activity manipulation of public opinion becomes the most important and subtle instrument to get the desired result. The first step is to encourage a sense of self-condemnation in a people, for instance, by actively encouraging corruption at all levels. In this private trade and big cartels may play a very important role.

'The next stage is to create active public opinion against the established order through the formation and growth of interest and pressure groups accompanied by demonstrations, petitions, active lobbying, increased publicity through large amounts of relevant literature for which clandestine finance has to be found. That in its turn is bound to undermine the economy of the target country.

'The next stage can be described as the credible threats of public action. Under this groups and individuals pledge themselves to withhold taxes, to initiate and support industrial unrest, to disrupt education by encouraging youth revolt and to undertake legal or illegal methods of changing the established Government.

'The final stage is the extreme public action through large-scale internal unrest varying from widespread rioting and disobedience to authority to open revolution against the Government.'

What went on in India, particularly after the massive victory of Indira Gandhi in the Lok Sabha election of 1971 and the State Assembly elections in 1972, conforms almost step by step to the four stages of subversion outlined in the above theory. This is not to say that leaders like Jayaprakash Narayan and Morarji Desai were acting on behalf of any foreign power. Far from it. But for them, perhaps, the portentious events would have taken a turn which might have led to the demise of freedom and democracy in this country. However, the groundwork was definitely prepared over a period of time to polarize intellectuals between those, who were either pro-Soviet Union or did not consider friendship with that country a danger to Indian freedom or its socio-political structure, and those who were western oriented with a strong dislike of communism as something hateful and worthy of being shunned. Little did either side realize that ideological differences apart, both systems had created the same kind of Super Powers attended with a constant danger of nuclear annihilation of the world. Neither was interested in projecting its own socio-political system for its own sake, but only in order to extend their areas of influence. Both had failed in this; otherwise there could not have occurred a break, on the one side, between the two communist giants, and on the other, a total lack of understanding and appreciation of each other between the two largest democracies — the United States and India. The polarization in India came about, as one notices, between those political elements, who had been known to be anti-communist, congregating under the leadership of Jayaprakash Narayan, and those who were either pro-communist or did not consider communism much of a threat to India, remaining with Indira Gandhi.

A slight digression would further clarify the situation as it developed. Jayaprakash Narayan himself was a Marxist, not of the Bolshevik brand, but one who had his beliefs tempered by certain values holding high the freedom of the individual. This tempering came about during his contact with social democrats during his student days in the United States. Morarji Desai, the next most important leader, had never been enamoured of the communists and preferred to be a Gandhian. Among the socialists, the more important Lohia group was conditioned by its mentor's aversion to the communists, who had allowed Hitler to come to power in Germany at a time when they were the most powerful political group in that country. Hitler's fascism was the result of the wrong alliances the communists had made at that time. Lohia was then a student in Germany and came in contact with many European social democrats. Willy Brandt, former Chancellor of West Germany, also belongs to the same group, and that explains the contact these Indian socialists have maintained with the Socialist International. The B.L.D. leader Charan Singh and his socialist and Swatantra followers could never be expected to approve communistic policies in which the small farmer stood to lose his identity and independence. The Rashtriya Swayam Sevak Sangh was organized ostensibly to fight communists. Its own organization was very similar to the cell-based Communist Party before it decided to turn itself into a mass party and participate in elections. The R.S.S., however, continued its rigid formations and automatically became the militant cadre of the Jana Sangh. Culturally, the party derived inspiration from Indian ethos and could not, therefore, take on wholesale the graft of the idea of complete free enterprise with so much poverty prevailing in the country. Ultimately, it had to purge itself of the advocates of extreme rightism like Balraj Madhok and his followers. Even before the Jana

Sangh merged in the Janata Party under Jayaprakash's inspiration, its leaders, particularly Atal Behari Vajpayee and L. K. Advani, had started talking of an egalitarian society and the necessary socio-economic change needed to achieve that end without getting attached to any dogma. Similarly, people who had come from the Congress to accept JP's leadership, such as Chandra Shekhar, were also the ones who had all along been challenging the pro-communist radicals in that party. Thus, one notices a definite character in the growth of the Janata Party as it gradually evolved.

The evolution of this party was inherent in the conditions that were prevailing in the country. The American political scientists had at one time talked of the Jana Sangh, with its militant cadres provided by the R.S.S., as the best organization to back against the pro-Moscow Congress. But, subsequently, they realized that it was far too nationalistic to be an instrument in the hands of a foreign power. Ultimately, the only people who could be manipulated were those belonging to some socio-religious organizations which enjoyed a vicarious appeal abroad. It was also felt that the predominantly Hindu India was too favourably disposed towards such religious organizations to be too concerned about their activities. But the ban imposed on Anand Marg and the suspicion with which it was viewed even earlier was proof enough of how wrong they had been. It is, of course, well known that many a foreign agent was using such an organization as a cover for his activities. It is possible that such organizations were utilized for spreading a certain discontent against the established Government. There might have been cases of corruption at high places, but it was rather the widespread talk of corruption, as well as of the activities of certain unscrupulous businessmen in conjunction with foreign cartels, that had, to a large extent, undermined the moral sense of the people. It was during this period that smuggling and foreign exchange crimes reached their peak in the country.

It is also during these years that a vociferous campaign was started among the intellectuals against the undermining of certain values very essential for the proper functioning of a democracy. It is, no doubt, true that a conflict had developed between the political Executive and the Judiciary on certain issues of socio-economic change. But the conflict need not have assumed the proportions that it did, had not that conflict become part of a calculated public campaign against the established Government. One need not go to the extent of assuming that it was done in a calculated manner by a definite set of individuals, but it is possible to believe that at some crucial points certain catalytic moves could well have been made to make it into a widespread mass movement against the ruling party, forcing the latter step-by-step to make wrong counter-moves in the process.

It is also very true that during those fateful years, engulfed in economic difficulties, the number of agitations, bandhs, strikes and other campaigns had proliferated. There was acute industrial unrest following the suppression of the Railway strike, which may be said to mark the beginning of a rash of industrial strikes all over the country. The students, too, were on the war path. Every university campus was disturbed. In Lucknow there was an unholy alliance between the students and the Pradesh Armed Constabulary; in Gujarat the students had forced a Government to resign and had got the State Assembly dissolved; and in Bihar they had rallied round Jayaprakash Narayan in a movement to throw out the established Government through various means, including a no-tax campaign. They were also to establish a rival system of government right from the village level upwards.

And finally, the whole campaign climaxed in the adverse judgement in the election petition against the Prime Minister. Meanwhile, the Opposition parties had made the functioning of the elected Parliament and State Assemblies almost impossible. Whether it all happened by accident or there was a diabolical design behind it, is difficult to say. What is certain is that there was a surprising similarity in the events as they shaped in India and the steps outlined in the theory, referred to above, of subversion as a substitute for force as an instrument for attaining foreign policy objectives. The theory had been evolved about the same time in the western intellectual circles. Perhaps, there was no connection between the two. But one cannot suppress the suspicion that India could possibly have been the proving ground for a new strategy of the western intelligence agencies acting, perhaps, as catalysts at the appropriate time and in appropriate circles. The whole atmosphere, as it had built up prior to the imposition of National Emergency on June 26, 1975, appeared as if either side were determined to destroy democracy. The tactics that the Opposition had adopted in Parliament and in some of the State Assemblies were hardly conducive to people's continuing faith in those institutions. Similarly, the way Government reacted to the current political, legal and moral challenges through ruthless administrative action was hardly a proper way for a democratic government to meet those challenges. Both sides, it appeared, were bent upon destroying each other and their credibility among the people.

There is another aspect of the international ramifications of this fantastic drama in which a hitherto very successful Prime Minister of this great country was completely destroyed. The Russians, who knew the game of subversion far better than the West which has taken to it more recently, realized that the day Indira was unseated by the Allahabad High Court judgment, the game was up for her. It was only a matter of time before she would have to bow out, gracefully or otherwise. Along with this realization came the need to search for a successor who would be as friendly as Indira and the previous two Prime Ministers had been to the Soviet Union. They also knew that the best bet for them was a democratic system functioning as soon as possible. At that moment the Russians could not have imagined that the Congress itself would be thrown out of power. In their scheme of things, values like morality do not play much part in politics. In their search for a successor to Indira, they first hit upon the West Bengal Chief Minister, Siddhartha Shankar Ray, but soon rejected him, because he had still to build a strong enough political base for himself. Their next choice fell on the dynamic and able Chief Minister of Uttar Pradesh, H. N. Bahuguna, who had established himself as the man of the organization. Here was an individual who could rise to the highest seat of power in the country, provided the Congress continued to be in a majority at the Centre. Their own assessment made through their political officers was that even if elections were held right then, the Congress would be returned to power with a slightly lesser majority.

Realizing that the Indian politics was passing through a crucial phase, the Russians went about in a very calculated manner extending their support to their chosen successor to Indira. It was soon after the Emergency that a meeting of the Indo-Soviet Cultural Organization was called at Lucknow and the Chief Minister H. N. Bahuguna was invited to it. Also present on the occasion was the Russian Ambassador to India in Lucknow, specially for the purpose. During the speeches made on the occasion, it was made quite clear that the Russians had great future in mind for the Chief Minister of the most populous state in the country. In his reply Bahuguna, too, expressed sentiments which could be easily misinterpreted, as in fact they were, in circles close to the Prime Minister. As it was, the Prime Minister was not particularly enamoured of the U.P. Chief Minister. She had also received reports that Mrs. Bahuguna, a Congress leader of Allahabad in her own right, had been talking ill of the Prime Minister quite openly in public. In those days any criticism of the Emergency, or of the Prime Minister herself or of her son, was taken very seriously. With all such reports reaching Delhi through spies the days of H. N. Bahuguna were bound to be numbered. Soon enough he was forced to step down, although he enjoyed a majority not only in the legislature party, but also in Pradesh Congress Committee. It was Emergency time and he could do nothing but obey. He made room for a nominee of Sanjay Gandhi as the next Chief Minister, withdrawing himself to his home town of Allahabad. It was about the time the Prime Minister had come out with her twenty-point programme. Bahuguna wanted to keep himself alive in politics. So, he took up the task of propagating this programme in the villages of U.P. with an enthusiasm which made him a far more popular leader among the people than he had ever been. But he was careful enough to do anything to attract the attention of the ruthless caucus that had grown around the Prime Minister. His visits to Delhi used to be short, surreptitious and meant to have a quick and secret meeting with Jagjivan Ram, with whom he had become very close ever since he had served under him as the General Secretary of the Congress. Otherwise, for all practical purposes, Bahuguna's stance was one of total loyalty to Indira and her twenty-point programme. It was during these clandestine meetings with Jagjivan Ram that the plan was hatched to quit Indira's Congress at the appropriate time to form an alternative Congress organization.

The Russians, while keeping up the facade of a very cordial relationship with the Prime Minister, continued to extend their support to Bahuguna. At one time after the death of D. P. Dhar, his name was floated as a possible Ambassador to their country. But that was only a diversionary move. They still had hopes of this man somehow coming back to power with a bang. It should not, therefore, surprise anybody to notice a kind of dichotomy that developed in the Communist Party of India when elections were called in March 1977, and Jagjivan Ram, H. N. Bahuguna, Nandini Satpathy and K. R. Ganesh came out of the Congress to fight under the banner of their new Congress for Democracy. The latter two had been at one time cardholding communists until they joined the Congress around 1962. The C.P.I. continued its support to the Congress in certain areas, but also announced support for the Congress for Democracy in areas where the C.F.D. leaders were supposed to be strong, like in parts of Uttar Pradesh, Bihar and Orissa. However, it now looks that the calculations of the C.F.D. leaders, the Russians and the C.P.I. went wrong. All of them had expected the Congress to get many more seats than the 153 it actually got. The minimum anyone gave it at that time was anywhere between 220 and 250. If that had happened, Jagjivan Ram and Bahuguna, with their 30 to 35 members, would have been in the ideal situation for bargaining with the Congress. It was common talk on the eve of the elections that in such an eventuality, their price to come back to the Congress would be to ask Indira to step down from the Prime Ministership and to have a fresh election for the new leader. This never came to pass. The Janata's 'hurricane' swept the Congress of the entire northern Hindi belt. If Jagjivan Ram with his C.F.D. had not come out, perhaps the Congress might have saved some seats in this area, but it would have been the end of Jagjivan Ram and Bahuguna as well. As the election results came out, their joining the Janata Party became inevitable for their own political survival.

The Russians still had not given up. They had too high a stake in keeping India as a friendly country. It is, therefore, no surprise that the first important foreign dignitary to visit Delhi, after the installation of the new Janata Party Government in Delhi, was the Foreign Minister of the Soviet Union, Andrei Gromyko, who not only got satisfactory assurances on the continuance of the Indo-Soviet Friendship Treaty, but signed many more agreements with India's new Foreign Minister, Atal Behari Vajpayee. The latter was at one time the most effective and vociferous critic of Government's policy of close proximity to the Soviet Union. As has been already said above, the Russians have developed a far better technique and style of dealing with the sensitive democratic leaders of countries of the Third World than have the Americans. After Gromyko's visit it seemed as if there had hardly been any change in India's Government as far as the U.S.S.R. was concerned.

What about the Americans and the other western powers? It has long been noticed in India that outside their country the Americans prefer to deal with military regimes or despotic leaders, because the deal is pushed through only a handful of individuals and not through layers and layers of committees and individuals at various levels, as in a democracy. For a long time it was the bane of Indo-American relations that things did not move because the democratic process was far too slow. What the Americans could achieve in Islamabad in days, took months together and a lot of convincing in New Delhi. Many a multi-national found it too expensive to grease the palms at so many levels and preferred to make the payoff for any contract or concession at just one point. Democracy, according to them, was a luxury that a poor country like India could ill afford. Besides, they had found over the years that the system had built-in checks and balances against the possibility of the top one or two persons falling in their pockets as had happened in some of the other underdeveloped countries in Africa and Latin America. Indians insisted on equality of treatment, as behoves democrats irrespective of their qualifications and wealth, even in international forums. They could not be pressurized or corrupted easily. When in the wake of the Emergency, an authoritarian rule developed round one individual in New Delhi, many in Washington, who had despaired of having good relations with India, sat up to take stock of the new situation. On the one hand, Indira could be beaten in public for crushing all civil liberties and destroying democracy, and on the other, she could be pressurized in private to deal with them in the way they wanted. They now found the circumstances similar to those that had made them so successful in some other countries.

It is not just by accident that soon after the imposition of Emergency, there was a distinct pragmatic change in the economic policies of the Indian Government. Washington praised India for its wonderful performance in the economic front. With inflation reaching a negative rate, the granaries bulging with a buffer stock of 18 million tonnes, the western multi-nationals started showing a great interest in extending investments in that country. It was also during this time, that certain agencies were given to Sanjay's Maruti Private Limited by some foreign manufacturers of small aircraft and rumours had it that a big payoff had been made in the wake of the deals for the Airbus for Indian Airlines. Perhaps, it was thought that the dynastic rule, that was projected during those days, would not allow a return of the type of democracy that had existed prior to the Emergency. Noticed also was the amount of fear, not so much of authority, as of a handful of people in New Delhi around the seat of power. It was a classic example of a coup having been effected by a Junta without any bloodshed or the use of the armed forces. In such a situation, it was suicidal to order an election, without having first made sure that it could be rigged in favour of those who had thus usurped power.

According to the theory of subversion, perfected in the West, the last phase should have been overthrow of the legally established government. But the chances of such an overthrow had disappeared with the clamping of the Emergency, the muzzling of the press and the relentless hounding of persons who had either gone underground or were indulging in clandestine activities prejudicial to the people in power and authority. It was a strange sight in India in those days to see the democratically elected individuals behaving like little czars, threatening law-abiding citizens with immediate arrest, for not conforming with alacrity. This was the style of functioning in some of the underdeveloped countries, which the Americans understood and appreciated. In a way, prior to the Emergency the opposition movement, which they had supported, had achieved their purpose. They knew that once the respected leaders who were put in jail were released, they would once again demand a return of the democratic process and then the system would again become immune to outside manipulation, whatever be the ideological colour of the new government.

It came as a big surprise to them, when not only did Indira order release of all the Opposition leaders kept in jail, but also ordered an election within two months. Her decision to hold the elections in March 1977, was announced on January 18. Everyone, including herself and her party, thought that the Opposition would not have enough time to organize itself to fight the elections. But their common incarceration in jail had given the Opposition leaders enough time to do some heart searching and to find ways of coming together as a true and viable alternative to the Congress. The mood of the people, particularly in the north, was for once not only against the Congress but against Indira herself. The result was a massive vote against the Congress and in favour of the Janata Party. As soon as the Janata Government was established in New Delhi, it was clear that no outside interference would be tolerated in India's internal affairs, and that is guarantee enough against any operation, 'overt' or 'covert', of foreign intelligence agencies in the country. Espionage has become part and parcel of international politics. It is another level, the clandestine one, at which international politics is played. India is now mature enough to take it in her stride.

CHAPTER XI

END OF AN ERA
(June 1975 to March 1977)

THE day internal emergency was proclaimed on June 26, 1975, the Nehru era ended in Indian politics. All that had been made dear to Indians by that great man was finished at one stroke by his own daughter who, till then, had herself been a great Prime Minister of India. As is now well known, the President, Fakhruddin Ali Ahmed, was made to sign the Presidential proclamation on the night of June 25, and the contingency plans, that had been prepared by the Chiefs of the Intelligence Bureau and the Central Bureau of Investigation, were put into operation even before Indira's colleagues in the Cabinet knew anything about them. Before it was dawn, almost all the leaders of the Opposition, including Jayaprakash Narayan, Morarji Desai, Atal Behari Vajpayee and even a Congress Working Committee member, Chandra Shekhar, a former Minister of State, Mohan Dharia, and the Secretary of the Congress Parliamentary Party, Ram Dhan, were rounded up. The roundup continued all over the country till much later. Strict censorship had been imposed on the newspapers and the mass media. The first reports of the arrests of the opposition leaders had already landed in newspaper offices. To prevent special editions being brought out, in Delhi particularly, power supply to most newspaper offices was cut off. By about midday, instructions had been flashed to newspapers all over the country not to publish the names of those arrested. But press censorship of this type was something new to the country. Some papers, therefore, ignored the instructions and went ahead printing as many names of the arrested leaders as were known. They were to find soon that a stricter watch was being kept on them by the censorship machinery.

A meeting of the Union Cabinet was called at the Prime Minister's house at six early in the morning of June 26. It was in a grim atmosphere that Indira announced what had already been done. Most of her senior colleagues were not only taken by surprise but seemed too stunned to say anything. The stark reality that stared them in the face was that any dissent at that moment meant their certain dismissal and arrest as well, without the people getting to know about it till it was already too late. Perhaps, one or two of them had been warned in advance by the President, who had signed the proclamation, of the mood in the coterie surrounding the Prime Minister. A mild expression of doubt about the efficacy of such drastic action by Swaran Singh was brushed aside by the Defence Minister, Bansi Lal, with the assertion that there was no other way to deal with people like Jayaprakash Narayan who had openly called upon the armed services and the police not to carry out orders that they considered unlawful. This call was made out to be an open incitement to revolt among the defence and security services that could lead to a civil war in the country. It was considered a serious threat to the security of the country as a whole and, therefore, it was felt that all those Opposition leaders, who had subscribed to JP's view, should be detained under the Defence of India Rules or under the hated Maintenance of Internal Security Act. It was also argued that nobody could be detained under the D.I.R. or the MISA without the proclamation of an internal emergency and the whole operation had to be carried out in strict secrecy and with utmost speed. It was not found possible, therefore, to consult the Cabinet in advance. A very lame explanation indeed and truly indicative of Indira's distrust of her senior colleagues.

As days passed, the ruthlessness of the administration became blatantly obvious. Certain handpicked officials, particularly in Delhi, acquired undue importance and consequent arrogance. For instance, a mere Deputy Inspector General of Police acquired such importance and powers as to become the most feared person in those days. The Inspector General was the head of the police force only in name. Fear stalked the streets of Delhi. One wondered whether it was really Indira who had ordered all this; was she not herself, perhaps, a prisoner in the hands of a handful of people around her, who had usurped effective power. They had now started openly ordering officials to carry out their dictat, although they had no political legitimacy or legal sanction behind them. The most feared among the caucus was Sanjay, the over-ambitious son of the Prime Minister. Next in importance came the Defence Minister Bansi Lal, who was already known for his unorthodox and ruthless manners in dealing with bureaucrats and officials. He had annoyed the three Service Chiefs, but cared little for their resentment or feelings. He was seldom bothered about advice which did not form part of his overall design to help Sanjay to acquire absolute power in the name of his mother. It is not yet clear whether Sanjay dominated Bansi Lal or the other way round. The role of Mohammed Yunus, who had been appointed Special Envoy of the Prime Minister — a job carrying no particular responsibility — after his retirement as Secretary in the Commerce Ministry, was also not very clear, except that he was one of the most trusted friends of the family of the Prime Minister.

Anyone who declined to take orders from this select set — Sanjay, Bansi Lal, Mohammed Yunus and even R. K. Dhavan, personal private secretary to the Prime Minister — had to go unceremoniously. Inder Gujral, perhaps one of the ablest Information and Broadcasting Ministers of this country, was the first casualty; because his instructions to All India Radio and Delhi Television conflicted with those that were given orally on telephone by no other than Sanjay himself. The very next day Sanjay's threat, expressed in front of some close friends that Gujral must go, found immediate expression. One wonders how he escaped outright dismissal and was allowed to lie low as Minister of State in the Planning Commission until he was found good enough by the Prime Minister to represent India as her Ambassador in the Soviet Union as D. P. Dhar's successor. The person to replace Gujral in the Information and Broadcasting Ministry was Vidya Charan Shukla, who immediately projected a picture of being more loyal to the powers that were than even those powers themselves. He was provided the services of two senior police officers, who had served in the Intelligence Bureau as Additional and Joint Secretaries to carry out, as put in those days, a cleaning operation in the mass media, particularly the Press. Senior Editors and correspondents were insulted at the slightest pretext and all the privileges enjoyed by correspondents accredited to the Government of India were summarily withdrawn. Instructions were issued from the top to officers of the Press Information Bureau to make sure that a particular publication stopped appearing immediately, because the Minister or his police officers did not like the face of its proprietor or editor.

Security men were placed outside the residence of senior Ministers, such as Jagjivan Ram, Y. B. Chavan and even Swaran Singh, to note down the car numbers of all who visited them. The first few months were really the crucial ones, when the image of the Government had to be refurbished with stories and features planted in newspapers after prior clearance not so much by professional people in the Press Information Bureau — which could be understandable in special circumstances — but by people who had no idea whatsoever of the functioning of a newspaper or of a news organization. The author himself had the disconcerting experience of being advised, by somebody close to the Prime Minister's house in those days, to avoid meeting either Chavan or Jagjivan Ram. It is still a mystery how the informant had come to know that the author, in his professional capacity, had asked for appointments with these Ministers just as he had asked for an appointment with the Prime Minister herself, during a short visit to Delhi. He was also told in no uncertain terms that since he had editorially advised Indira's resignation after the Allahabad High Court judgment on June 12, 1975, he had become a *persona non grata* with the new power elite and was no longer welcome. Similar was the experience of many other newspapermen, perhaps worse, whose writings had not been liked by Sanjay, Bansi Lal, Mohammed Yunus or V. C. Shukla *et al*. A stage came when these mighties had no time to see first hand what was being written and by whom. They depended entirely on the officers of Information and Broadcasting Ministry, to provide them a daily digest with an assessment of the various individuals in the profession at various centres. Pressures were also brought upon friendly proprietors to get rid of undesirable journalists. The most notorious was the case of George Verghese, the then Editor of the Hindustan Times. Not only had he to leave his job, but because he had dared to question the propriety of his dismissal in the Press Council, even that body had to be dissolved lest its judgement should turn out to be adverse. In due course, almost all newspapers acquired an identical flavour, particularly after the virtual takeover of the four news agencies, not by the Government as such, but by individuals wielding undue power. Truth was the first casualty, courage the second. Conformity became the easy and often the only way out for survival. Most, naturally, preferred to keep quiet, hoping for better times.

After her defeat, in an interview to a very senior and seasoned journalist like Prem Bhatia, Indira Gandhi complained of harassment by security people outside her house, who were taking down the car numbers of any visitor. She considered it in very bad taste. But when it was pointed out to her that the same thing had been done only a few furlongs away from her house at the residence of her former senior colleague Jagjivan Ram when he was still a member of her Cabinet, she expressed surprise and said that she had not known anything about it. Perhaps, some others in her house had ordered it in her name and kept her in the dark. But one can never imagine such a thing happening during Nehru's time, even if Indira, who was his housekeeper, had ordered it. The times had changed, the style had changed and the ambitions of people, who had never imagined to be anywhere near the seat of power, had skyrocketted.

Apart from the Information and Broadcasting Ministry, the Intelligence Services — particularly the Revenue Intelligence and Enforcement Directorate — and the Home Ministry were utilized specially to pressurize and blackmail people who refused to conform with alacrity. There were any number of raids carried out on the houses of such people, ostensibly for evasion of taxes or for involvement in black money operations, but actually for the purpose of harassment. Even relatives of Ministers were not spared, because they refused, as heads of business organizations, to pay underhand so-called donations for the party at the behest of powerful individuals like Sanjay and Bansi Lal. This was the common manner of dealing with recalcitrant people in Bombay. In Delhi, the sheer fear of being arrested for no reason whatsoever was enough to control anyone who showed any signs of revolt. The Lieutenant Governor, a retired I.C.S. officer, who had been appointed to that post a few months before the Emergency was imposed, was the main agent for transplanting and terrorizing people in the name of cleaning the capital. Actually, it was a young I.A.S. officer, Special Assistant to the Lt. Governor, who was the main power behind the local throne, because he happened to be a class fellow of Sanjay in his school days. Another person, who suddenly shot into prominence in the industrial circles of West Bengal, was a young entreprenuer, Kamalnath, also a school crony of the powerful son of the Prime Minister, and who became now the focal point of all fund raising operations for the power elite. Many a West Bengal Minister used to pay court to him at his residence in Calcutta. His exposure came about only after Sanjay had denounced the Communist Party of India and Indira had openly supported the new pragmatic approach. Some of the important leftist journals, like the *New Age* and *The Mainstream*, carried on a relentless exposure of Sanjay and his henchmen until pre-censorship was imposed on them. *The Mainstream* ceased publication as did so many other journals.

One wonders whether the Union Home Minister, Brahmananda Reddy, was aware of what was happening in his Ministry and the country at large and whether he was at all consulted on matters which should have been ordinarily his concern. Of course, during the Emergency he had taken a back seat to his far more important deputy, the Minister of State for Home Affairs, Om Mehta, who had direct access to the Prime Minister's house. Anything that had to be done through the intelligence services or the police was routed through Om Mehta. In due course, he became the main hatchet-man in spheres other than that of the mass media, where this function was being performed admirably by Shukla. It was Om Mehta's responsibility to get George Fernandes arrested. George had gone underground in Orissa, where he was visiting his in-laws when the Emergency was imposed. He carried on a relentless propaganda campaign against the ruthless and authoritarian methods of Indira Gandhi and her Government. His sources of information were excellent despite his being underground. The underground sheet, that he used to circulate in those days almost every week, used to be a fiery indictment of all that was inhuman in the regime those days. He managed to inform a set of intellectuals of the tortures of some of his colleagues in jails. This underground sheet naturally infuriated the Prime Minister very much, because they were a direct indictment of her own actions. Her clear orders were: George must be arrested anyhow. It was not only that he should be detained like other political leaders of the Opposition, but a campaign was started to denigrate the labour leader for his connections with certain organizations abroad, like the Socialist International, and stories were circulated about his having received funds from abroad to carry on his campaign of denigration against Indira personally. The police and the Intelligence Services were under constant pressure, directly from the Prime Minister's house, to find out the whereabouts of George Fernandes and to arrest him.

Meanwhile, George, in one of his underground letters, had called for a countrywide movement, like the one of the 1942, to disrupt train services, to carry on a satyagraha and to circulate from hand to hand all the news about arrests and torture of people in jails. The cyclostyled sheets used to reach almost all newspaper offices by mail and yet the police were unable to trace the origin of those letters. Sometimes they were posted from Gujarat, which had a Janata Front Government, at other times from Tamil Nadu, where the DMK Government had successfully defied some of the orders received from the Centre under the Emergency. Apart from these Governments of the Opposition, there were any number of people in the country, who risked their own lives — some like Snehalata Reddy, a well-known actress of Karnataka, actually paid with it — to help George continue functioning effectively underground.

There is no doubt that George Fernandes did plan a countrywide scare through explosions; but it appears that the strict instructions to the volunteers, indulging in the explosions of dynamite acquired for the purpose, were to make sure that there was no loss of human life and no major loss of national property. The idea was to create a scare in the minds of the people on the one hand, and to win as much propaganda advantage as possible on the other. In Bombay alone there took place a number of suspected explosions of this kind, but not a single life was lost, nor any major damage done to public property. Similarly, there occurred a large number of explosions and derailments in Karnataka, Maharashtra and Tamil Nadu, but not a single passenger train was ever affected. Mostly it was the goods traffic that was disrupted. One has to view the alleged conspiracy behind what came to be known as the dynamite case in this context. It is true that George Fernandes did mastermind a countrywide movement of this type. The police, when they got to know of it, built it up into a criminal case and arrested almost everyone, even remotely suspected of being connected with it. Under the regime at that time, it was made out as a criminal conspiracy against the legally established Government, in the same manner as the British had accused some of the terrorists of the twenties and thirties as traitors. But those very people, like George Fernandes today, finally became popular heroes, because they were fighting, as was George, for their country's freedom. Had Indira won the elections in March 1977, it is almost certain that George and his colleagues, who had been kept in chains during their detention, would have been tried as ordinary criminals. The electorate's verdict, against Indira and the Congress, was justified enough for the immediate release of George and all those accused with him, for, they had done nothing to harm the people or to destroy national property. Rather, they had courageously fought for freedom and democracy which were in dire peril in those dark days. It will not be out of place to mention here the torture of George's own brothers and some of his friends, to force him to surrender himself. This kind of third degree methods employed in dealing with political prisoners are the hallmark of an authoritarian regime. It is often said that Indira herself was not aware of what was happening in the country in her name and in the name of Emergency. But what about the letters that were sent to her directly by George's mother herself and by many others? Is it that those letters never reached her, or that Indira never cared to find out whether there was any truth in the allegations made in those letters to her against the local police? The author himself had the disconcerting experience of being told by a socialist friend of the torture undergone by a husband and his wife, both teachers of Bombay University. When he brought the allegation to the notice of the then Chief Minister, S. B. Chavan, the latter immediately offered to inquire about it and within twenty-four hours conveyed to the author that there had been no truth in the allegation. Soon after the fall of Indira's Government at the Centre, S. B. Chavan's Government in Maharashtra also fell. And then came out the real story of the tortures that the husband and wife had been put to during their detention for something they knew nothing about.

These are only a few instances of what had gone on all over the country, particularly in the Hindi belt, where the Chief Ministers tried to implement the directions from the Prime Minister's house with ruthlessness that was unimaginable. As a consequence, a very essential family planning programme turned into the hated issue on which Sanjay and his mother stood condemned in the eyes of the people. But, of course, long before this retribution was to come, the people in authority, in the Congress party and its Governments, had themselves to be emasculated for the promotion of absolute, but unconstitutional, power of one individual. Anyone daring to criticize even in private what was happening in the Prime Minister's house and around her was threatened with arrest and harassment. One such individual, who bore every such humiliation with tremendous stoicism, was no other than the once very powerful Principal Secretary of the same Prime Minister, P. N. Haksar. Belonging to the same community and clan as the Prime Minister, his wife apparently expressed her views about the goings on at No. 1 Safdarjung Road in a community gathering one day. From that day started the harassment of the family. The wife herself was threatened with arrest. A very senior and respected relative, engaged in business for years in New Delhi and held in very high esteem in the Kashmiri community, was paraded along Parliament Street of New Delhi under arrest on some flimsy charge. That was not all. The house built in New Delhi by Haksar on his retirement was raided a number of times by

Revenue Intelligence people seeking to involve him somehow or other in any activity that could be made to look not strictly legitimate. All this went on while Haksar was still the Deputy Chairman of the Planning Commission. Why did he not quit at that time and why had he, in the first place, agreed to rejoin the Government of Indira Gandhi after once having been disillusioned with the way of functioning of the people around her are questions whose answers can at best be surmised. For, no one, least of all Haksar himself, would say anything. So far as the second question is concerned, many people had noticed a quality in Indira of becoming most charming and convincing when she wanted something done. Apparently, her request of her former Principal Secretary to help her with the economic planning, which had been going haywire, was couched in words and manner that made even a seasoned bureaucrat like Haksar to perhaps believe that she was turning a new leaf. The answer to the first question is all too simple and needs no corroboration. Anyone of importance creating a public scandal by resigning in those terror-stricken days of the Emergency would have invited the most ruthless reprisal from the caucus. Haksar had already been humiliated enough and he could well imagine what would be in store for him if he were to resign on that issue. Besides, he might have argued that remaining in his post he might still be able to prevent total damage to the administrative machinery because of his influence and standing with the bureaucracy and thereby serve the national interest at large.

Perhaps, similar considerations had kept many a senior Minister, such as Jagjivan Ram, T. A. Pai, and even Subramaniam, at his post. They had watched the unceremonious dismissal of their senior colleague, Sardar Swaran Singh, for his mild dissent expressed at the time Emergency was imposed. In T. A. Pai's own words 'Sanjay had access to all Government files without the responsibility that was imposed on Ministers by the oath of office and secrecy'. Pai, who was one of the abler Ministers in Indira Gandhi's Cabinet, made these disclosures at the A.I.C.C. Session held in May 1977 to discuss the debacle suffered by the Congress in the Lok Sabha election earlier in March. Pai went on to allege that Sanjay used to decide on promotions and appointments and even dictate to a Chief Minister on his Cabinet appointments. Honest officials' houses were raided and they were terrorized in various other ways. Many officials were brought to paying court to Sanjay for promotions. The ones who remained unobliging and honest paid a heavy penalty. Everybody sought to escape unpalatable responsibility by saying that instructions had come from 'above' or from the 'palace'.

Pai's description of the conditions prevailing in New Delhi those days reminds one of the atmosphere of intrigue and corruption that used to prevail in the Mughal Courts in Delhi just before or about the time of succession battle. How men and women in high places used to behave in the most low and atrocious manner in order to place somebody they wanted on the throne! Even ruling kings were put behind bars and brothers and sisters murdered in cold blood to achieve that single aim — to acquire absolute power. As Pai described it in his speech at the A.I.C.C., the atmosphere in and around No. 1 Safdarjung Road in those fateful days was very similar.

Pai further divulged that Ministers and officials who refused to meet Sanjay were subjected to harassment. The caucus, that had so misbehaved during the Emergency to please one person, had, according to him, 'either the control of the Prime Minister or claimed such control; the Prime Minister was helpless while efforts were on to make even her a nonentity'. The administration was geared to fulfil the personal ambitions of a few individuals in the Centre and the states. An attempt was made to plant a reliable person — or to be more accurate a spy — in every important office. Nobody wanted the truth. Intelligence reports were tailored to suit the whims and fancy of the wielders of power. Nonconforming Chief Ministers were toppled or sought to be toppled, and the Congress organization became the handmaiden of some selected people in positions of power and influence.

T. A. Pai, a well-known banker and businessman before he was inducted into the Union Cabinet by Indira herself, is not prone to exaggeration. In fact, as a true businessman, he should rather understate a case. He was one of the Ministers who was himself harassed in those days. If he had all this to say about those dark days of Emergency, there were others who had far worse stories to tell, but kept mum for fear of reprisal. Pai related a common joke current in those days that 'if a peon accepted money, it was called bakshish; if a clerk took it, it was mamool; if an officer took it, it became bribe; and if a Minister took it, it was called party funds'.

In contrast with the disclosures made by Pai, Indira's own statements, made at the time of the proclamation of the Emergency, read like half truths. For instance, broadcasting to the nation on the day the Emergency was proclaimed she said, 'The forces of disintegration are in full play and communal passions are being aroused, threatening our unity. There has been a deliberate political attempt to denigrate the office of the Prime Minister, which is neither in the interests of democracy nor of the nation.' She further warned the people that the 'actions of a few are endangering the rights of the vast majority': At the same time, she assured the nation in no uncertain terms that 'the new emergency proclamation will in no way affect the rights of law abiding citizens'. In retrospect, these assurances seemed to have been given without any serious thought of the natural consequences that were bound to follow her decision to meet a purely political and moral challenge through ruthless administrative action.

Speaking again on June 27, Indira made a public allegation that Jayaprakash Narayan's call for 'total revolution' seemed to be receiving encouragement from 'outside the country'. Whether that was so or not, despite the hue and cry raised by Amnesty International and other such organizations, she had already lost credibility with the people who stopped taking her statements or those made on behalf of her Government seriously. The same day she made another statement that 'the purpose of the Press censorship is to restore a climate of trust'. What happened was absolutely the opposite. Nobody believed in those troubled days what was printed in the newspapers. Even those among the newspapermen, who had enjoyed a reputation for authenticity and courage, were looked down upon either as propagandists of the Government, or, worse still, as cowards, because they lacked the courage to expose its nefarious activities. A whole set of sycophants in the profession started speaking in the name of the majority of the editors and evolved a code of conduct, which was nothing else but what the policemen sitting in the Information and Broadcasting Ministry wanted them to follow. It was the worst kind of self-correction to which no self-respecting journalist could voluntarily subscribe.

Talking informally to newspapermen once about the developments in the wake of the Watergate scandal in the United States, Indira had remarked that all that had followed was the result of the lies spoken by the U.S. Head of the State, President Richard Nixon. But in her own case, half-truths had become her undoing, because, they are even more dangerous than downright lies. At least one knows why a lie had been told. But one can never make out, until it is too late, the real purpose behind half-truths. Indira's style of functioning in the last two years of her rule had been vitiated by such half-truths uttered by people who had no compunction whatsoever in exploiting her name or position. Take, for instance, the fanfare with which her twenty-point economic programme was launched only to be completely overshadowed by a rather simplistic five-point programme in the name of her overly ambitious son. The Chief Ministers were required to ensure, not so much the implementation of her economic programme, which at least had some very radical points in it aimed at transforming the socio-economic conditions in the countryside, but rather the implementation of the five-points enunciated by Sanjay. The whole programme had been made subservient to one aim — to make the young man the *de facto* leader of the country without any constitutional sanction.

One has to view, in this context, the subsequent farcical debate that was started among like-minded people and parties about the future shape that should be given to India's democracy. The whole idea behind this exercise was to build up a matching movement to counter the movement, called 'Citizens for Democracy', that had already been launched against the allegedly arbitrary and uncalled for tinkering with the Constitution with the sole purpose of consolidating power in one person. Various ideas were floated, such as direct election of the Prime Minister or even wholesale grafting of the American system so as to make the chief executive of the country immune from the day-to-day attacks in Parliament. It was also meant to give a kind of wide acceptability, among the so-called intellectuals on their side, to the comprehensive 42nd Constitution Amendment Bill aimed at drastically reducing the powers of the Judiciary. It was all meant to establish the supremacy of the chief political Executive who was none other than the Prime Minister herself.

During this public debate, organized at considerable expense, it suddenly dawned on the organizers that the consensus, as they put it, was not developing the way that had visualized. One thing emerged very clearly — the faith of the majority in the parliamentary system of democracy as the best suited to India. There was also no consensus on the proposed direct elections of the chief executive. Finally, even on the question of judicial review there were sharp differences. The debates ended as abruptly as they had begun. More reliance was now placed on the blacking out of the other point of view, which was being consistently plugged through small meetings addressed by eminent jurists like M. C. Chagla.

While preparations were on to get the captive Parliament, as it was called then, to pass the proposed constitutional amendments, the caucus around the Prime Minister felt that even those amendments, drastic as they were, would not ensure perpetuation of their own power. Sometime or other, they would have to face elections and, in a vast country like India, they could not be rigged wholesale. It was against this background that a sudden move was made in three Pradesh Congress Committees to call for a new Constituent Assembly to frame an entirely new Constitution. The idea was to convert the existing Parliament itself into the proposed Constituent Assembly and then let it go on leisurely with its task for the next five to six years. Meanwhile, the caucus was to entrench itself in power, and at an appropriate time even ask Indira to step down in favour of her son. How this plan had been worked out, in such meticulous detail, is difficult to say. But the moment the move for the Constituent Assembly ran into heavy weather with some senior leaders in the party itself, it was given up as hurriedly as it had been cooked up.

All this will not, however, wash away the achievements that India did make during the eleven years of Indira Gandhi's rule. One must never forget that it was during her time that India established her position as a middle power in her own right in the comity of nations. Indians who had had the opportunity to travel abroad soon after the country suffered its debacle against the Chinese, perhaps, know how Indians were looked down upon. Often they were faced with embarrassing questions such as whether they had enough foreign exchange or not. These enquiries were most often made only to hurt the self-respect of an Indian. India was usually described abroad as a poor country of hungry millions, and could ill afford the luxury of an expensive democratic system. That is why, it was patronizingly stated in those days that India was a soft state, where every one wanted to be in power, but none could rule with a firm hand. It was only under Indira Gandhi that this view of India the world over underwent a change. After the fantastic victory against Pakistan, resulting in the creation of an independent sovereign Bangladesh, an Indian could go anywhere in the world with his head held high, having taken part in ensuring the success of one of the biggest liberation struggles in history. This was in itself a great achievement after two decades of patronage by donors who virtually thought of Indians as persistent beggars, despite the fact that India was one of the few countries which never defaulted on its repayments.

It was again during Indira's regime that Indian scientists and technologists showed to the world what they were capable of, whether it was in the sphere of nuclear technology, space technology, or the applied technology of modern industry. Within a decade, India had transformed herself from a poor and developing country into a middle level developed country. Foreigners were always taken aback by the wide spectrum of technology that India possessed. On the one extreme there was still the bullock-cart criss-crossing the muddy village roads; on the other, the country was now capable of producing supersonic jets. This was no mean achievement for a country which had been free for only thirty years and had, at the time of independence, hardly half a steel mill and a few textile mills to boast of. India had now become a modern industrialized nation. In the final analysis, Indira had given direction, during the eleven years she ruled, that produced in the nation a maturity and self-confidence which comes only with hard work and consequent achievements.

Keeping these great achievements of Indira in mind, one cannot escape the conclusion that at some point of time she allowed her own judgement on political and moral issues to be clouded by the judgement of some ambitious people around her. Who were these people and what was their hold on her are questions which will continue to be debated for years. Among the few who were in the forefront, the most important was her own son, Sanjay, a ruthless and ambitious young man prone to strong-arm bullying tactics, which are, perhaps, common to many successful politicians, except that he did not have the vision and graciousness which comes only from a deep understanding of the historical forces, which his grandfather had. Perhaps, there was a lacuna in Sanjay's education; and the blame for this must go to the surviving parent who should have ensured better and longer grooming before projecting him as the future leader of this ancient land.

The second person in the caucus who apparently exercised considerable influence and power, while it lasted, was the newly appointed Defence Minister Bansi Lal. He had made more enemies during his spell as Chief Minister of Haryana since 1968 than any other Chief Minister in the country since Independence. But he cared little for what people thought of him so long as he got his way, irrespective of the methods he had to use to attain his ends. For him, there was nothing like the Gandhian philosophy, on which Congressmen should have been nurtured, that means are as important as the end and if wrong means are adopted, the end invariable gets vitiated. Recently a reporter in a national daily described the functioning of this man very aptly when he said that Bansi Lal provided 'respectability to the politics of treachery, opportunism and intrigue'.

The third person that stood out most prominently in the Prime Minister's house those days was her faceless personal private secretary, whose name alone sometimes used to make Congress members of Parliament sit up. He was no other than R. K. Dhavan, a nephew of Yashpal Kapoor. Dhavan was a feared man in the black days in New Delhi. Unless he wanted, nobody could have access to the Prime Minister. He could speak in her name to any Minister to get things done, specially the ones that Sanjay wanted done. It was no secret that even Chief Ministers had to cool their heels in Delhi for days together, because Dhavan had not thought it proper for them to meet Indira. Sometimes, the Chief Ministers had to return to their capitals without meeting the Prime Minister.

The fourth person in the caucus was Yashpal Kapoor who had assumed considerable political importance ever since he was brought into the Rajya Sabha from Uttar Pradesh. Kapoor, originally from the Frontier Province, started life as a clerk and typist in the secretariat attached to Prime Minister Jawaharlal Nehru. His services were loaned to Indira Gandhi, as her personal private secretary, when she became the official hostess in the Prime Minister's house. She had a number of things to attend to and Kapoor helped her out as her personal assistant. Gradually, he won her confidence and, by the time she succeeded Lal Bahadur Shastri as the Prime Minister, Kapoor had officially taken over as her personal private secretary. In due course, Indira started giving him important political chores, which required delicate handling. Soon he was promoted as officer on special duty in the Prime Minister's Secretariat, while Dhavan took over his previous job. It was in this capacity that Kapoor started acting as her Chief Election Agent at Rae Bareli in 1971. There was, perhaps, a time lag in his being relieved of his official post and his activities as her election agent — a purely technical matter, but which became one of the two grounds on which the election petition against her was upheld by Justice Jag Mohan Sinha of the Allahabad High Court on June 12, 1975. This was the most fateful day in the life of Indira Gandhi; it marked the beginning of her downward slip.

The other two names, often mentioned as members of the caucus, are those of the then Minister of State for Information and Broadcasting, Vidya Charan Shukla, and Minister of State for Home Affairs, Om Mehta. The fact is that neither was admitted to the inner conclaves of the caucus. They were only on the periphery and used as hatchet-men to perform the more ruthless and undignified tasks. Perhaps, Mohammed Yunus, Special Envoy to the Prime Minister, did enjoy an entry to the caucus because of his proximity to Sanjay. But his main task was to oversee the functioning of the reorganized news agency, Samachar. One could discern an element of total and unselfish loyalty in Yunus for Nehru's family. His admiration for Nehru was unalloyed, and his attachment to Sanjay bordered on sentimentality, probably because his own son and Sanjay had grown up together. He could see no faults in the young man.

This formed the ring of powerful people around Indira. She was thus completely isolated from the rest of her political colleagues and even the world. She had lost her feel for the people, partly also because all her meetings, including the ones outside her house, had become increasingly stage-managed and the feedback she got was only what this caucus wanted her to have. The entire mass media had been effectively controlled. The newspapers perforce published the same kind of news and the same kind of comments, or no comments at all. If she listened to All India Radio or Delhi Television, she got the same kind of information. Outside Radio stations, such as the B.B.C., had become taboo for nursing an innate hostility to her personally. She had become at last the victim of her own propaganda, which inevitably happens to most authoritarian rulers. There had been statements by Indira after her displacement from power saying that she was totally unaware of some of the excesses perpetrated during the Emergency. These statements make her doubly condemned. Either she was a party to all that went on during those nineteen months and must face the consequences, or she had become thoroughly incompetent as the Prime Minister, which was worse.

Despite all this, one must give Indira the benefit of doubt for having called the elections when she did; because, if the elections had not been held, the peaceful revolution in India's politics could never have taken place. Even if her decision was motivated by a desire to exploit the possible unpreparedness of the Opposition and the paucity of time at their disposal, it must be said to her credit that, at some moment of introspection, the spirit of Nehru in her must have reminded her that people alone could give her the legitimacy which she required most at that time. She talked of people's power and fought the election, as she had done in the past, single-handed on the one slogan of her own survival.

After the din and dust of the electioneering had settled down, the country waited expectantly for the results — the most dramatic in the six elections that have been held since Independence. As the counting progressed late into the night on March 20, the country waited with bated breath about the future of Indira. The charismatic leader of six years ago, started trailing behind her rival, Raj Narain, within the first few hours of counting. At Prime Minister's house nobody dared to tell her the ominous news. All India Radio kept repeating that she was trailing behind by only 12,000 votes. By midnight, however, the B.B.C. had announced to the world that India's powerful third Prime Minister, Indira Gandhi, had lost in her own constituency of Rae Bareli to the same individual who had successfully challenged her election in 1971 in the Allahabad High Court. It was now immaterial that that election had been upheld by the Supreme Court after Parliament had amended the electoral law with retrospective effect to remove all those grounds on which her previous election had been set aside by the High Court. It was sometime in the early hours of March 21 that Indira was confronted with the fateful news, that the people had not only rejected her son, but also herself and every single candidate of her party in her own home state of Uttar Pradesh. She heard the news without the slightest trace of emotion on her face and then retired for what was left of the night. That was the end of India's third Prime Minister, Indira Gandhi.

DATE DUE

OCT 1992